Latimer Briefing 17

True Devotion

In Search of
Authentic Spirituality

by Allan Chapple

The Latimer Trust

True Devotion: In search of Authentic Spirituality © Allan Chapple 2014

ISBN 978-1-906327-27-9

Cover photo: traces de pas dans la neige © Patrice BOUCHER - Fotolia

Published by the Latimer Trust November 2014

The Latimer Trust (formerly Latimer House, Oxford) is a conservative Evangelical research organisation within the Church of England, whose main aim is to promote the history and theology of Anglicanism as understood by those in the Reformed tradition. Interested readers are welcome to consult its website for further details of its many activities.

The Latimer Trust
London N14 4PS UK
Registered Charity: 1084337
Company Number: 4104465
Web: www.latimertrust.org
E-mail: administrator@latimertrust.org

CONTENTS

You can't produce a book without accumulating some debts, and I want to acknowledge mine.

I want to thank my friends Simon Bibby and Don West, who read the book and encouraged me to get it published.

It has been good to work with Margaret Hobbs again. Her careful editorial work has made it a better book. She also gave very helpful feedback about the contents which enabled me to make some changes that were needed.

Without all of Allison's service and sacrifices, I wouldn't be in a position to write books—and while I write about it, she practises true devotion.

My greatest debt is unpayable, to a Saviour whose grace is more amazing now than ever. In the face of years of half-hearted devotion and serial unfaithfulness, he has held me fast and continued to lavish love upon me and to prepare me for an eternity of glory and grace. It is an immense privilege to know him and to serve him. Whatever else it does, I hope reading this book will cause you to be more truly devoted to this God of all grace.

I.   Introduction

In his exposition of Ephesians 3:14-19, John Calvin refers to people who 'hope to be abundantly welcome to God.' I am assuming that you and I share this hope – which means that Calvin has our attention as he goes on to ask what justifies it:

> Who has promised them that God will accept their devotion and all that they offer him? ... all our prayers and supplications will never be worth anything, but prove utterly unprofitable and vain, if they are not conformable to God's Word. From that Word we must take our rule.[1]

That is what this book is about: how God's Word shapes and rules our devotion to him.

1.1.   *Our focus*

What is the best way of talking about this? 'Spirituality' is what many people call it, but this is not the ideal word. It can mean a great many things, some of them very far removed from anything the Bible teaches. 'Piety' is another possibility, but this is sometimes used in a rather negative way. My preference is 'devotion'. When we speak of a couple being 'devoted' to each other, we mean that their relationship is strong, loyal, and loving– which is how we should relate to God.

In this book we will use all three words. In each case we will be talking about how we relate to God, that is, how we express and exercise personal relationship with him. Our aim is to examine what the Bible teaches about knowing God and living with him. I have called the book *True Devotion* for two reasons. We must be truly devoted to God: our relationship with him must be real and deep. And we must be devoted to him truly: our devotion must be grounded in and governed by the truth, by the teaching of the Bible.

There is a danger here. Our focus might give the impression that the vertical dimension of our relationship with God is the only one that matters. So it is important to acknowledge at the outset that true

---

[1]   John Calvin [1509-1564], *Sermons on the Epistle to the Ephesians* (Edinburgh: Banner of Truth, 1973 [1562]), p 286.

devotion is bigger than what we are looking at here – there is obviously more to authentic Christian living than prayer, for example. True knowledge of God is lived out in our fellowship with God's people and our service in the world: it has a horizontal axis as well as a vertical one.[2] There are two great commandments, not just one.[3] And while I must know God *for* myself, I do not know God *by* myself: true knowledge of God is personal but not individual. While this horizontal dimension is very important, we are not dealing with it in this book. Instead, in order to understand it as clearly as possible, we will confine our discussion to the vertical axis: to how we live with God.

Why have I chosen to write about this subject? Most certainly not because I am a guru or spiritual master! Nothing could be further from the truth. It would be more accurate to say that you are reading the words of a spiritual pygmy. But the 'greatest commandment' has caused me to learn as much as I can about true devotion. This command makes it clear that the highest responsibility of every human being is to love God wholeheartedly. This is the most important issue I face: do I know and love the God who made me and before whom I will stand on Judgment Day? And because personal knowledge of God is the root upon which all the fruits of Christian character, Christian discipleship, and Christian ministry depend, we should all return to this theme as often as we can. As I have done so over the years, I have benefited greatly from the writings of people who have understood the Bible very well and opened its treasures with great clarity and insight. I want to pass on what I have learned from them so that you can be encouraged and enriched as I have been.

1.2.   A fascination with 'spirituality'

There is another reason for this book – and this has to do with the setting in which we live. As a brief visit to any bookshop demonstrates, our society is fascinated with 'spirituality' – something that has been true for at least the last few decades.[4] We cannot afford to ignore such a

---

[2]   See, for example, Jeremiah 22:15-16; James 1:27; 1 John 2:3-10; 4:7-8, 19-21.

[3]   See Mark 12:28-31.

[4]   See the helpful survey by Michael Raiter: *Stirrings of the Soul: Evangelicals and the New Spirituality* (Sydney: Matthias Media, 2003). The picture has not changed to any great extent in the years since this book appeared.

major feature of our cultural setting, if for no other reason than the fact that what we see in the secular bookshops is mirrored in the Christian ones. Like their secular counterparts, the 'spirituality' section in Christian bookshops is both much larger and more diverse than it was a decade or two ago. And when we search through this material, what do we find?

Perhaps the first thing we will notice is the fact that a richer, deeper spirituality is said to be found in some very surprising places. Two examples must suffice, both published in 2005. The Reverend Nancy Roth's book, *Spiritual Exercises: Joining Body and Spirit in Prayer* aims to help us decide which of the following to incorporate into our prayer-lives: Pilates, Tai Chi, yoga, dance, strength training, aerobic exercise, breathing and posture, and massage.[5] I have to confess that, try as I might, I simply cannot get my head around the concept of massage prayer! But it is hard to beat the offering from SkyLight Paths Publishing entitled, *The Knitting Way: A Guide to Spiritual Self-Discovery*. This unlikely guide to spiritual growth has chapters devoted to *Knitting into Awareness*; *Science, Mystery and Knitting*; *Spiritual Space: Your Knitting as an Opening and a Sanctuary*; and *Bearing Witness: Following Your Own Knitting to Find Your Story*.

The smorgasbord of views and practices on offer is so great that it is easy to feel overwhelmed. We can quickly become uncertain about whether we will be able to sort the wheat from the chaff – or, indeed, whether there is any chaff here. Are there just many varieties of devotional wheat? This uncertainty is compounded when we discover in this section of the bookshop works by Evangelical writers – including some by theologians[6] – that in one way or another make the following five points.

First, they say that because Evangelicalism values orthodoxy so highly it is heavily reliant on the mind and deeply wary of the emotions. So, sooner or later, these writers came to realize that their inner life was dry and barren. We find an example in Bruce Demarest, who tells how

---

[5] Nancy Roth, *Spiritual Exercises: Joining Body and Spirit in Prayer* (New York: Seabury, 2005).

[6] Good examples are Bruce Demarest, *Satisfy Your Soul: Restoring the Heart of Christian Spirituality* (Colorado Springs: NavPress, 1999), and David K. Gillett, *Trust and Obey: Explorations in Evangelical Spirituality* (London: Darton, Longman & Todd, 1993). For convenience I have taken the following quotations from these two books. Readers who are familiar with the literature will not find it difficult to locate similar passages in other books.

he discovered that his Christian life had been thoroughly defective, because he had 'substituted knowledge of the Bible for knowing how to interact with God Himself ...'[7]

Secondly, they discovered that what they needed to bring them into a deeper, richer fellowship with God was not to be found in their Evangelical roots, but in the spiritual resources of the wider Church, and especially in a range of Catholic traditions and practices that belong to what is sometimes called the 'mystical way'. So Demarest testifies,

> I found it exhilarating to enter into the Christ-centered experiences of church fathers, desert mothers, ancient martyrs, scholastics, and responsible Christian mystics through the centuries... Discovering these perspectives and practices of an older Christian spirituality has led me into the most transforming time of my four decades as a Christian.[8]

Thirdly, having adopted an eclectic approach in their own piety,[9] they welcome the increasing trend they see amongst those Evangelicals for whom:

---

[7] The words are Demarest's, and he goes on to say:
'My evangelical culture and training led me to this belief: Personal experience is an untrustworthy pillar for Christian faith and life. Therefore you should relegate ... matters of the heart to an inferior place. This approach to Christianity had formed the path of my life and career. I felt no reason to alter anything until, in the late 1980s, an unexpected encounter opened my eyes ... It was the first time in a long while that I had experienced the sense of actual growth in the inner man. And I had to admit that although some of the approaches were new to me, spiritual truth was being presented that was satisfying and transforming. What was it in me that was coming to life, or at least opening up in new ways? ... What I was discovering was the *intuitive* way of engaging God; that is, learning how to open my *heart* as well as my *head* to truth... *Knowing from the heart*, in a daily, growing relationship, was my problem. When it came to relating to God with my inner being, trusting Him, letting His Spirit search my heart, allowing Him to clear a path in my spirit so He could change me from the inside out, in all honesty, this was foreign territory.' (*Satisfy Your Soul*, pp 25f, 27 [his italics]).

[8] Demarest, *Satisfy Your Soul*, pp 34-35.

[9] The following example is representative:
'Since my conversion ... I have been nurtured for many years within a definite evangelical tradition... Along the way I ... moved from a staunchly anti-charismatic position ... to a personal commitment and involvement [sc., in the charismatic movement]. Then came ... an ongoing commitment to explore more widely than my evangelical formation had encouraged, and that has led me since into an ever-deepening study of, and sharing in, the spiritual tradition of the Church, East and West.' (Gillett, *Trust and Obey*, pp vii-viii).

contemplation, picture, symbol, sacrament, colour, dance, drama, and the like, have become part of the widened horizons of their spirituality ...[10]

Fourthly, one of their principal aims in testifying to the newfound vitality in their Christian life is to reinforce this trend. They are advocating a greater openness on the part of their fellow-Evangelicals to other spiritual traditions, because the result will be a much richer spirituality for all. So David Gillet maintains that when Evangelicalism

> lets down the barricades and begins to explore the diverse traditions within the Church it can discover wealth where once it saw only dross ...[11]

Demarest speaks about a six-week retreat in a Catholic monastery that he says was 'one of the brightest defining moments in my spiritual life...' The main reason this retreat had such a profound impact on him was that it meant immersing himself

> in spiritual traditions, views, practices, and insights as ancient and true as the church. It was an encounter with God, shaped and formed by spirituality with great treasures to offer us all... it was truly a treasure to *connect with the classic understandings of Christian spirituality –especially through the spiritual masters* ...[12]

Fifthly, the flipside of this call for openness is found in expressions of regret about what is seen as an unhelpful legacy of the Reformation. The Reformers are regarded as having thrown out the baby with the bathwater, with the result that, until recently, Protestants were unaware of the powerful sources of deeper spirituality to be found in the longstanding traditions of Catholic piety. Demarest puts his experience this way:

> Previously I would have felt out of place at a Benedictine abbey. To me, the Protestant Reformers ... separated from the Roman church over critical matters ... And like most other evangelicals, I had rejected the idea of receiving *any* spiritual instruction from the ancient church. But having gotten to know many wonderful, vibrant Christians in the Catholic renewal movement, I'd come to realize we had made an error. The Reformers and we their evangelical

---

[10]   Gillett, *Trust and Obey*, p 184.

[11]   Gillett, *Trust and Obey*, p 182.

[12]   Demarest, *Satisfy Your Soul*, pp 31, 34 (his italics).

descendants, acting in reaction to medieval Rome, threw out a great deal of spiritual wisdom, insight, and important practices ... God was leading me to honor what was true in my own tradition while welcoming back authentic Christian insights and practices from the older tradition...[13]

What are we to make of such testimonies and claims? What is the right spirit in which to investigate this important area of Christian living? In advocating a new way forward, these writers are also calling for openness on our part, a willingness to find authentic spirituality in unexpected places. I have no problem with this – providing that the openness we display is properly critical. By 'critical' I am referring to the stance the Bible tells us to adopt: 'test everything; hold fast to what is good; abstain from every form of evil'.[14] How are we to do this? How does 'critical openness' work?

1.3.   *'Critical openness'*

First of all, it means avoiding two common extremes. In the name of Christian truth, the first extreme is unwilling to be open. It is very reluctant to ask new questions, to consider new answers, or to explore new territory. It is, in effect, a suspicious conservatism that is closed to anything that doesn't come packaged with the right brand-name. It is hard to see how this honours the Lord of truth or his word of truth. As Augustine wisely observed,

> A person who is a good and a true Christian should realize that truth belongs to his Lord, wherever it is found ...[15]

There is nothing to be gained – and much that could be lost – by those who do not hold such a view.

In the name of Christian love, the second extreme is unwilling to be critical. It is reluctant to exercise discernment, to distinguish between what is true and what is false, between what can be embraced and what should be avoided. As a result, it can end up as a naïve credulity that is easily swayed, 'blown here and there by every wind of teaching'.[16] It is

---

[13]   Demarest, *Satisfy Your Soul*, p.29 (his italics).

[14]   1 Thessalonians 5:21-22 NRSV; cf. Matthew 7:6, 15-20; 1 John 4:1.

[15]   Augustine [354-430], *On Christian Teaching* (Oxford: OUP, 1997 [ca.426]), p 47.

[16]   Ephesians 4:14.

true that there is no straining out of gnats here[17] – but sadly, there is too much swallowing of camels! In the end, this approach, too, represents a failure to honour the Lord of truth and his word of truth.

So we need to steer away from both a stance that is critical but closed and one that is open but undiscerning. In contrast to these extremes, critical openness is genuinely open but properly critical. In the first place, this means an openness that is both discerning and anchored. It must be discerning because, as we have just seen, Scripture requires us to test everything. This openness must also be anchored because Scripture gives us non-negotiables without which we cease to be Christian. What this means in practice is that we must stay rooted in the Bible:

> The word of God, which is our rule, must ... be the only test and touchstone to try and discover errors ...[18]

Yet while critical, our stance must also be open, because our grasp of what the Bible teaches is neither complete nor infallible. We always have much to learn – and to unlearn!

Perhaps the most famous expression of this critical openness comes in the sermon preached by John Robinson to the 'pilgrims' who sailed for Virginia in the *Mayflower*:

> I am verily persuaded the Lord has more truth yet to break forth out of his holy Word ... I beseech you ... that you be ready to receive whatever truth shall be made known to you from the written Word of God.[19]

The crucial phrases, of course, are 'out of his holy Word' and 'from the written Word of God': this is the anchor that keeps us from drifting off course and ending up shipwrecked; this is what enables us to be discerning, the yardstick by which we weigh and assess everything. A spirituality that is not grounded in the Bible, given shape and substance by the Bible, and constantly renewed by the Bible is no way forward for the people of God. So our over-riding concern in this book is to discover

---

[17] Matthew 23:24.
[18] John Flavel [1628-1691], *The Works of John Flavel*, six volumes (Edinburgh: Banner of Truth, 1968), vol 3: p 426.
[19] John Robinson [1575-1625], quoted in Meic Pearse, *The Great Restoration: The Religious Radicals of the 16th and 17th Centuries* (Carlisle: Paternoster, 1998), p 277.

what the Bible teaches us about 'true devotion'.[20] Above everything else, we want to be true to the Bible, for unless we are, we cannot be true to the Lord. So throughout the book you will find many footnotes listing passages in the Bible that speak about the point we are considering. You will find it helpful to look them up, so that you can check whether the Bible does teach what I am claiming. Calvin puts the point we are making this way:

> we ought to be admonished not to follow our fancies when it is a matter of honouring God, but to please His will in everything and by everything. So then, let us not conjure up any devotion according to what seems good to us, but let us be satisfied to do what God orders us to do and what He approves... if we wish to have a zeal which God approves, we must be ruled by true knowledge and be taught by His Word.[21]

1.4. Evangelical and Reformed

This quotation highlights another feature of this book – the fact that it is written from an Evangelical and Reformed perspective. Why do we take this approach? Because I believe that this is where the quest to be consistently and thoroughly biblical leads us. So, while seeking to display openness in the ways that we should, we will give particular attention to the views of the Reformers, the Puritans, and Evangelical leaders. In round figures, this means visiting the 16th, 17th, and 18th centuries. We will quote these writers a great deal. This does not mean that they have the same authority as the Bible. Their views must be tested and weighed by what the Bible teaches, just like everybody else. The reason I have turned to them often is that they have a great deal to teach us here. In addition, their views about true devotion have not always been given a satisfactory hearing. Because not everyone will be familiar with all of the people whose views we will consider, I have given their dates the first time they are mentioned. (This applies to all except those authors who have lived from around the mid-20th century

---

[20] A wonderfully rich and insightful treatment of this subject is to be found in Peter Adam, *Hearing God's Words: Exploring Biblical Spirituality*, New Studies in Biblical Theology 16 (Leicester: Apollos/Downers Grove: InterVarsity, 2004). Our investigation takes a different but complementary approach to his.

[21] John Calvin, *The Deity of Christ and Other Sermons* (Audubon, NJ: Old Paths, 1997), pp 124, 127.

onwards.) This will show whereabouts each one fits in the unfolding story of Christian thinking.

The first section of the book spells out the principal characteristics of an authentic spirituality, one that is true to the Bible. The second section contrasts this spirituality with one that is increasingly promoted in the Evangelical community – that of 'the mystical way'. The third and final section makes some suggestions about the right way forward into deeper devotion to our great and gracious God.

PART I: THE SPIRITUALITY OF THE GOSPEL

If we are to be faithful and consistent as Christians, the gospel must be at the centre of our lives. Yet this isn't always true of us. One reason for this can be stated as follows. It is obvious that the gospel is our starting-point, the key to our salvation. It is by believing the gospel that we know God and have a place in his great salvation.[1] It is the gospel that brings us to new birth, launching us into a new life.[2] But this is where we can make a simple but serious mistake. It is possible to treat the gospel as the rocket that gets us launched – and once that has happened, it simply falls away, its job done. So the further we go in the Christian life, the further we leave the gospel behind: it becomes less important the longer we live as Christians.

The New Testament sees things very differently. For one thing, to abandon the gospel is to sever our connection with the Lord Jesus and the Spirit, to walk away from God and his grace.[3] And the gospel is to be the measure of our way of life – our calling is to live in a way that is true to the gospel and worthy of the gospel.[4] More than that, we should be ready to forego any rights, accept any hardship, and make any sacrifice in order to ensure the triumph of the gospel.[5] In fact, the gospel and its mission is so precious and important that we should be prepared to lose our lives for it.[6] So the gospel is not to be a faded memory from the increasingly distant time when we began the Christian journey. It must remain at the centre, shaping our motives and ambitions, determining our priorities and values – and fuelling our passions:

> is there anything which Christians can find in heaven or earth so worthy to be the objects of their admiration and love, their earnest and longing desires, their hope, and their rejoicing, and their fervent zeal, as those things that are held forth to us in the gospel of

---

[1]   Acts 15:7-11; Romans 1:16; 10:8-10; 1 Corinthians 1:17-18; 15:2; Ephesians 1:13; Colossians 1:21-23; 2 Timothy 2:8-10; James 1:21; 1 Peter 1:10-12.

[2]   John 3:3-15; James 1:18; 1 Peter 1:23-25.

[3]   2 Corinthians 11:2-4; Galatians 1:6.

[4]   Galatians 2:14; Philippians 1:27; Titus 2:5.

[5]   Mark 10:29; Acts 20:24; 1 Corinthians 9:12, 18-23; 1 Thessalonians 2:2; 2 Timothy 1:8; 2:8-9; Philemon 13.

[6]   Mark 8:35; Revelation 6:9; 20:4.

Jesus Christ?[7]

So the gospel is foundational for the whole of our life as Christians – including our spirituality. The gospel lies at the heart of true devotion:

> there is no intercourse with Christ save for those who have perceived the right understanding of Christ from the word of the gospel.[8]

We see this, for example, when Paul expresses his concern that the Corinthians might 'somehow be led astray from [their] sincere and pure devotion to Christ'. How could this be? It would happen if they accepted a different gospel.[9] Paul's point is clear: it is only by holding fast to the gospel that they would maintain their devotion to Christ. That is because there is no genuine spiritual life, no growth in godliness, without the gospel. And all claims about life with God must be tested by the gospel.[10] To be true, our devotion must be a spirituality of the gospel. That is what this first section of the book is about. We begin by establishing what the gospel is (Chapter 2). We then consider three major perspectives this gives us on life with God: that it is responsive (Chapter 3), paradoxical (Chapter 4), and relational (Chapter 5).

---

[7] Jonathan Edwards [1703-1758], *The Religious Affections* (Edinburgh: Banner of Truth, 1961 [1746]), p 52.

[8] John Calvin, *Institutes of the Christian Religion*, two volumes (Library of Christian Classics; London: SCM, 1961 [1559]), III.vi.4 (1: p 687).

[9] 2 Corinthians 11:3-4.

[10] See 1 John 1:1-3, 5-7; 2:22-24; 4:1-3, 7-10, 14-16; 5:6-13.

2.   Beginning with the Gospel

We are beginning with the gospel because that is what God does. It is
with the gospel that he breaks into the sinner's life with saving power,
bringing us to new birth and raising us to new life. This is so
momentous that Paul likens it to a new creation.

> The god of this age has blinded the minds of unbelievers, so that
> they cannot see the light of the gospel that displays the glory of
> Christ, who is the image of God. For what we preach is not
> ourselves, but Jesus Christ as Lord, and ourselves as your servants
> for Jesus' sake. For God, who said, 'Let light shine out of darkness,'
> made his light shine in our hearts to give the light of the knowledge
> of God's glory displayed in the face of Christ.[1]

God began his work of creation by speaking his word: 'Let there be
light'.[2] Through the power of his word, where once there was only
darkness, light now shone. In much the same way, the gospel brings
light where once there was only darkness – in the blinded minds and
darkened hearts of unbelievers. When the gospel is proclaimed, the
glory of Christ is displayed – his glory as the risen, reigning Lord of all.
And because he is the image of God, his glory reveals God's glory. In
the gospel, the proclamation of Jesus Christ as Lord, we see his face;
and in his face, we see God's glory. Here Paul is contrasting what the
gospel does with what God did when he revealed himself to Moses.[3]
Then, the revelation of God's glory to Moses meant only a glimpse of
his back, for he was told that God's face must not be seen.[4] But now,
through the gospel, all believers see his glory front-on, in the face of his
Son. So the ministry of the gospel far outshines the ministry of Moses.[5]
And through the gospel the prayer of Asaph is answered: 'make your
face shine on us, that we may be saved'.[6] The point Paul makes so
dramatically in this passage is found throughout the New Testament:

---

[1]   2 Corinthians 4:4-6.
[2]   Genesis 1:3.
[3]   2 Corinthians 3:7-13; cf. Exodus 33:18-34:7; 34:29-35.
[4]   Exodus 33:23.
[5]   2 Corinthians 3:7-11.
[6]   Psalm 80:3, 7, 19.

God makes himself known by the gospel. It is through the gospel that we meet the Saviour and enter his salvation.

We see this in the chain of questions Paul constructs in Romans 10:13-17. He begins by quoting Joel 2:32, which tells us that we are saved by calling on the name of the Lord. He then asks his questions:

> How ... can they call on the one they have not believed in? And how can they believe in the one of whom they have not heard? And how can they hear without someone preaching to them? And how can anyone preach unless they are sent?

His conclusion is that faith comes from hearing the gospel message. So it is the gospel that brings salvation – salvation comes through faith in Christ, and faith in Christ comes through hearing the gospel. We see this again in 1 Corinthians 15. How did the Corinthians come to participate in God's salvation? By receiving the gospel which Paul proclaimed to them (15:1-2, 11). And what about the Galatians? They began new life by believing the gospel they heard from Paul, the gospel which presented Jesus Christ crucified.[7] The same is true of the Ephesians, who were included in Christ when they heard and believed the gospel of salvation.[8] And so with the Colossians: they received Jesus Christ as Lord by hearing, understanding, and responding to the gospel, the word of truth about the grace of God.[9] The point is clear: new life in Christ begins with the gospel. We enter God's salvation by faith – the faith that responds to Christ and his gospel.

The New Testament does not leave the gospel there, at the beginning of our new life in Christ. We have made the point this way: the gospel is not like the rocket which launches a satellite into orbit – and once it has done its job, it falls away, leaving the satellite to travel on without it. So the gospel does not get us launched, only to be left further and further behind as we go on as Christians. According to the New Testament, the gospel is not only the key to the beginning of the Christian life; it is the basis for the whole of the Christian life. Consider what Paul tells the Colossians, for example:

> just as you received Christ Jesus as Lord, continue to live your lives

---

[7]   Galatians 3:1-2.
[8]   Ephesians 1:13.
[9]   Colossians 1:5-6; 2:6.

in him, rooted and built up in him, strengthened in the faith as you were taught ...[10]

How are these believers to grow and make progress in the Christian life? The answer is very simple: they are to continue as they have begun. They will grow not by moving on from Christ and the gospel but by moving deeper into Christ and the gospel. That is the point Paul makes by using two word-pictures, drawn respectively from the garden ('rooted') and the building-site ('built up'). A plant grows not by moving elsewhere but by spreading its roots deeper into the soil in which it has been planted. A building grows not by moving outwards from its foundation but by rising up from the foundation. So the Colossians will grow, not by moving away but by staying put. They began by receiving Jesus as Lord – and they did this by responding to the gospel, God's word of truth about God's work of grace (1:5-6). They are to continue living in Jesus as Lord – and this means growing stronger in the faith that they were taught by Epaphras at the beginning (1:7; 2:7).

Paul makes the same point when he tells the Corinthians that they are saved by the gospel only if they keep holding firmly to it.[11] And Hebrews makes this point by telling its readers that they share in Christ by holding their original conviction firm to the end.[12] John tells his readers that they remain in the Son and the Father only if what they heard from the beginning – the gospel – remains in them.[13] What such passages make clear is that Christian life is based on the gospel, not just at the beginning but all the way along. (This is such an important point that we will return to it at the conclusion of this chapter.)

In view of the crucial and continuing role that the New Testament gives to the gospel, we have said that authentic spirituality must be *a spirituality of the gospel*. It will be based on the gospel, shaped by the gospel, and renewed by the gospel. The gospel is to be its foundation, its governor, and its dynamic. This means that no conviction or practice can be regarded as authentically Christian, no matter how powerful or blissful it is, if it does not conform to the gospel. The gospel is in fact a powerful source of true devotion. If this is so, we need a clear understanding of what the gospel is. But before we investigate what the

---

10   Colossians 2:6-7.
11   1 Corinthians 15:2.
12   Hebrews 3:14.
13   1 John 2:24.

New Testament has to teach us here, we must deal with a widespread misunderstanding. This is the mistaken view that the word 'gospel' means 'good news'. This claim is based on the fact that the Greek word for 'gospel' is made up of the words for 'good' and 'news'.

2.1.   'Gospel' means 'good news'?

So what is the problem here? What is wrong with this explanation? The answer will become clear if we switch our attention for a moment to the word 'butterfly'. This too is a compound word, made up of two other words. So why doesn't 'butterfly' mean 'airborne dairy produce'? The principle at work here is this: where a word comes from tells you something about its history – but it might not tell you anything about its meaning. That is because it is use that determines meaning: a word means what it is used to mean. And there are some obvious places where the word 'gospel' does not mean 'good news'. Would the people who heard what John the Baptizer said in Luke 3:17 think that they were hearing good news (3:18)? Surely they would be quaking in their sandals! Or was the angel who made the announcement in Revelation 14:7 proclaiming good news? No, 'gospel' doesn't mean 'good news'. Rather, it means 'great news', 'momentous news', news of the greatest possible importance. Whether it is good or not depends on who is hearing it and on how they are related to the one it is telling us about. So when Jesus began his public ministry by announcing, 'Time's up! God is taking over!',[14] can you see why not everyone would have welcomed this news? It is wonderful news if you trust God's promises and love God's purposes – but very threatening and unsettling news if you do not.

Why make such a fuss about this? Does it really matter if we translate 'gospel' as 'good news'? After all, aren't there plenty of passages where this meaning fits very well? The main problem here is not that 'gospel' never means 'good news', but that it is far too easy to move from 'the gospel is good news' to 'good news is the gospel'. That is, if we begin by defining the gospel as good news, it is all too easy to treat as gospel any news that we welcome and approve. And there is the problem – news that we find appealing is going to be news that suits us, not news that confronts and challenges us. The great danger in all of

---

[14]   Mark 1:15.

this is that we can end up domesticating the gospel, so that it supports our agenda rather than serving God's purpose.

This makes it even more pressing that we establish what the gospel is. So, what is a 'spirituality of the gospel' actually about? What does the New Testament mean by 'the gospel'? It is so important that we get this right that we will use two complementary ways of discovering the answer.

2.2. 'The Gospel': some key passages

The first involves examining passages which specify the content of the gospel. As there are many such passages, we will concentrate on just three that state the gospel succinctly.[15]

2.2.1. Mark 1:14-15

> Now after John was arrested, Jesus came into Galilee, proclaiming the gospel of God, and saying, 'The time is fulfilled, and the kingdom of God is at hand; repent and believe in the gospel.' (ESV)

This passage makes the following points. First, the herald who proclaims the gospel is Jesus. He carries out his ministry as an evangelist.

Secondly, his gospel is 'the gospel of God'. What does 'of' mean here? It probably points us in two directions: the gospel is momentous news *from* God, and it is momentous news *about* God.

Thirdly, this news is about the fulfilment of God's promises and purposes. 'The time is fulfilled' means that waiting is now at an end: promise-time is over and fulfilment-time has come. What the prophets have foreseen and foretold is now here: God is taking action to do what he said he would do.

Fourthly, what God is doing at this decisive moment is establishing his promised kingdom. This promise lies at the heart of the prophets' message about the coming new age. When the great day came for God to save the world, putting everything right and making everything new, he was going to set up his own eternal kingdom.[16] Jesus is announcing that this long-awaited day has now come.

---

[15] Other passages include various proclamations of the gospel recorded in the book of Acts.

[16] Note especially Daniel 2:19-45; 7:1-27.

Fifthly, this news about God and his saving work requires a response. Those who hear the gospel are to 'repent and believe'. In this context, repenting means turning away from rebellious independence and turning to God. Believing the gospel means accepting that what Jesus has declared is true. This means trusting that in accordance with his promises, God is bringing in his great salvation – a salvation that includes in its scope all who turn and trust. It also means accepting the rule of God as King.

Sixthly, all of this has to be read in light of the first verse of this Gospel, in which Mark tells us that he is writing the 'gospel of Jesus Christ' (1:1). This means that what we have just learned about the gospel from verses 14 and 15 must be related to the Lord Jesus. We find out how Mark wants us to do this by reading the rest of his Gospel. As we do so, it becomes clear that it is because of Jesus that fulfilment-time has arrived; it is in and through him that God is beginning his long-awaited reign and establishing his salvation.[17] So Jesus is the promised King, the Messiah.[18] Accepting the kingly rule of God thus means living under the rule of King Jesus.

2.2.2. Romans 1:1-5

> Paul, a servant of Christ Jesus, called to be an apostle, set apart for the gospel of God, which he promised beforehand through his prophets in the holy Scriptures concerning his Son, who was descended from David according to the flesh, and was declared to be the Son of God in power according to the Spirit of holiness by his resurrection from the dead, Jesus Christ our Lord, through whom we have received grace and apostleship to bring about the obedience of faith for the sake of his name among all the nations ... (ESV)

This gives us seven points we must note. The first is that Paul is the evangelist, the herald who proclaims the gospel. He is 'set apart for the gospel' (v.1), having received an apostolic commission to take the gospel to the Gentile world (v.5).

Secondly, like Mark 1:14, this passage indicates that the gospel is 'of God' (v.1) – momentous news from God and about God.

---

17 Mark 2:5-10; 4:41; 5:18-20; 7:37; 10:42-45; 14:24, 49.
18 Mark 8:29; 14:61-62; 15:26, 32.

And, thirdly, the gospel concerns the fulfilment of what God promised through the prophets (v.2). The gospel is 'according to the Scriptures': the future that was announced in advance by the prophets is now announced in the gospel. Again, promise-time is over and fulfilment-time has come. God's words to Israel and his work in Israel have now reached their intended climax – the person and work of the Lord Jesus. This means that the Scriptures must be read in light of the gospel: 'The Gospel is the interpretation of the prophets'.[19]

Fourthly, the subject of the gospel is God's Son, Jesus Christ our Lord (vv.3-4). The proclaimer[20] is now the proclaimed: the gospel of God is the gospel of Christ. It is because of who Jesus is and what he has done that the focus of the gospel has changed, that the proclaimer of the gospel has become the subject of the gospel, the evangelist has become the evangel. This becomes clear as we consider the next two points that Paul makes here.

Fifthly, the gospel concerns the fact that Jesus is the promised Messiah, the long-awaited King descended from David (v.3).

Sixthly, the gospel is about his resurrection from the dead and his exaltation as Son of God and Lord of all (v.4). The focus of the gospel is thus the supremacy of Jesus as Messiah, Lord, and Son of God.

The seventh and final point is that the gospel requires a response: what Paul calls 'the obedience of faith' (v.5). This means yielding to Jesus as Messiah and Lord, accepting his rightful rule over our lives ('obedience'). It also means trusting the promise of salvation held out in the gospel ('faith') – something that becomes clear in Romans 1:16-18:

> For I am not ashamed of the gospel, because it is the power of God that brings salvation to everyone who believes: first to the Jew, then to the Gentile. For in the gospel the righteousness of God is revealed – a righteousness that is by faith from first to last, just as it is written: 'The righteous will live by faith.' The wrath of God is being revealed from heaven against all the godlessness and wickedness of people ...

---

[19] Philip Melanchthon [1497-1560], *Loci Praecipui Theologici 1559*, translated by J.A.O. Preus, 2nd English edition (St Louis: Concordia, 2011), p 336.

[20] Mark 1:14-15.

Here we discover that the gospel of Christ is the gospel of salvation. It is the dynamic agent by which God brings people into his salvation (v.16).

These verses make three points about this salvation.

First, it is entered only by faith. This is true for both Jews and Gentiles (v.16). A believing response to the gospel is the only point-of-entry into God's salvation for any human being, irrespective of their background.

Secondly, at its heart lies the fact that God saves people by putting them right with himself (v.17). That we are not right with God is made clear in verse 18. We do not respond rightly to God's word and worth – and our rejection of God deserves and receives God's rejection.

Thirdly, this salvation delivers believers from God's wrath (v.18), the judgment of condemnation and exclusion that he will impose on the last day. And just as his wrath is already having an impact on sinful people, so too God's work of righting people – forgiving our sins and making us his own – happens now, and not just on the last day.

2.2.3. 1 Corinthians 15:1-5

Now, brothers and sisters, I want to remind you of the gospel I preached to you, which you received and on which you have taken your stand. By this gospel you are saved, if you hold firmly to the word I preached to you. Otherwise, you have believed in vain. For what I received I passed on to you as of first importance: that Christ died for our sins according to the Scriptures, that he was buried, that he was raised on the third day according to the Scriptures, and that he appeared to Cephas, and then to the Twelve.

Here again, Paul is the evangelist. However, he is not the only one: the other apostles too are evangelists, proclaiming the same message he does (15:9-11).

The second thing we learn here is that this apostolic gospel is the gospel of Christ. He is the subject of all four of the 'that'-clauses that summarize the gospel: 'Christ died ... was buried ... was raised ... and ... appeared ...' (vv.3-5). Clearly, the gospel is all about Jesus Christ.

Thirdly, the gospel centres on his death and resurrection. This is clear from the way the first and third clauses are much longer than the second and fourth: in accordance with the Scriptures, Jesus died for our sins and was raised on the third day. So the gospel is not just about who Jesus is; it focuses on what he has done by dying and being raised. The gospel we proclaim is about Christ crucified and Christ glorified.

Fourthly, these gospel-events are real events. The gospel has a clear historical core – it is not about abstract ideas or theoretical constructs; it is about what has actually taken place. So the second clause – 'that he was buried' – is meant to confirm the factuality of the first one: he was buried because he had died. (It also serves to indicate the bodily character of the resurrection, which reversed Jesus' burial as well as his death: the empty tomb is implied by verse 4.) Likewise, the fourth clause – 'that he appeared' – underlines the reality of the resurrection: the once-dead Jesus was known to be alive in a new way because he met many of those who had known him before his death.

Fifthly, the gospel-events have a definite meaning: they have occurred 'according to the Scriptures' (vv.3, 4). This tells us two things about these events. The first is that they fulfil the promises and purposes of God. The death of Jesus was not a tragic mishap; it was in accordance with God's plan and purpose, declared beforehand in the Scriptures. And the same is true of the resurrection: this was not a random miracle; it took place to accomplish God's revealed purpose. Jesus' death and resurrection bring God's prior words and works to their intended climax. The second thing we learn from 'according to the Scriptures' is that the Old Testament ('the Scriptures' being referred to here) is the interpretive key which unlocks the meaning of Jesus' death and resurrection. What God has said to Israel and what God has done in Israel forms the background for understanding the significance of the cross and the resurrection. That is why we find Paul and the other New Testament writers consistently using Old Testament ideas and events to explain what Jesus' death and resurrection have accomplished.

Sixthly, this gospel is the gospel of salvation. Jesus died 'for our sins' (v.3). His death had a purpose – he died to deal with our sins; to save us from all that they involve. And because his death was followed by his resurrection, we have been rescued from our sins and the judgment they deserve (note 15:17).

And finally, the gospel is to be 'received' (v.1). Paul is referring to the fact that the Corinthians had believed the gospel (15:11). In particular, they believed the promise of the gospel, that Jesus' death and resurrection will deliver them from their sins (15:3, 17).

Our study of these three passages leads us to two conclusions in particular. The first is that the New Testament doesn't have one and only one way of stating the gospel. Each of the passages we have analysed is quite different from the others. If we had the space to investigate other parts of the New Testament as well, this conclusion would be strongly reinforced. There is great diversity in the way it presents the gospel.[21] But this doesn't mean that the New Testament knows several different gospels.[22] We have seen that all three passages revolve around the same fundamental events and themes. With these passages as our guide, the only conclusion we can reach is that the gospel has a quite definite character and content. We will return to the question of what that is once we have considered the second way in which the New Testament tells us what the gospel is.

2.3. 'The Gospel': some key expressions

Instead of analysing particular passages, this involves noting what the New Testament calls the gospel. The obvious place to begin is with the fact that it is often called 'the gospel of God'.[23] Even more often, it is called 'the word of God'.[24] As we have already noted, this is most likely to be telling us that the gospel comes from God and also that it is about God. The gospel is God's news, the word of God about the work of God. As a message that comes from God, the gospel is also called 'the word of truth'.[25] As a message about God, the gospel is 'the gospel of the grace of God',[26] the 'word of his grace'.[27] The gospel is thus God's truth about God's grace. It is also 'the gospel of the glory of God',[28] the word of God about the worth of God.

---

[21]   Note, for example, the three quite different proclamations of the gospel by Peter: Acts 2:14-40; 3:12-26; 10:34-43.

[22]   What the New Testament recognizes is that there is only one authentic gospel, the apostolic one (1 Corinthians 15:9-11)– but that there are various ways in which this gospel was being perverted: see, for example, 2 Corinthians 11:2-4; Galatians 1:6-9; 1 John 4:1-6; Jude 3-4.

[23]   Mark 1:14; Romans 1:1; 15:16; 2 Corinthians 11:7; 1 Thessalonians 2:2, 8-9; 1 Peter 4:17.

[24]   Acts 4:31; 6:2, 7; 8:14; 11:1; 12:24; 13:5, 7, 46; 17:13; 18:11; 2 Corinthians 2:17; 4:2; Colossians 1:25; 1 Thessalonians 2:13; 2 Timothy 2:9; Titus 2:5; Hebrews 13:7; 1 Peter 1:23; Revelation 1:2, 9; 6:9; 20:4; cf. Acts 8:25; 13:44, 48, 49; 15:35, 36; 16:32; 19:10; 1 Thessalonians 1:8; 2 Thessalonians 3:1.

[25]   Ephesians 1:13; Colossians 1:5; 2 Timothy 2:15; James 1:18.

[26]   Acts 20:24.

[27]   Acts 14:3; 20:32; cf. Acts 13:43; Galatians 1:6; Colossians 1:6.

[28]   1 Timothy 1:11.

The second point to make is that the New Testament calls the gospel 'the gospel of Christ',[29] or 'the word of Christ'.[30] As a message about Christ, the gospel is 'the gospel of the glory of Christ'.[31] It is the word of Christ about the worth of Christ. In particular, the gospel is about his death and resurrection:[32] it is thus 'the word of the cross',[33] and the proclamation of the resurrection.[34] It presents Jesus as messianic Lord and Saviour, raised from death and exalted to heavenly glory where he reigns over all.[35] So central is he to the gospel that proclaiming the gospel is said to be proclaiming him.[36]

The third point to make about the gospel is that it is 'the gospel of salvation'.[37] It is thus also 'the gospel of peace', 'the word of life', 'the word of reconciliation'.[38] It is the proclamation of what God has done in his Son to save the world. It announces that this salvation is already in operation as a result of Jesus' death and resurrection-exaltation, and also that it is yet to come in its fullness when Jesus returns from heaven.[39] While focusing on what we might call the Easter-events, the gospel also announces the present reign and future return of the risen Lord.[40]

Fourthly, the gospel is 'according to the Scriptures'.[41] It announces the fulfilment of God's End-time purposes and promises.[42] That is why it is also 'the gospel of the kingdom',[43] for the kingdom of God lies at the centre of the promised new age, the time of salvation. The primary

---

[29] Romans 15:19; 1 Corinthians 9:12; 2 Corinthians 2:12; 9:13; 10:14; Galatians 1:7; Philippians 1:27; 1 Thessalonians 3:2; cf. Mark 1:1; Romans 1:9; 2 Thessalonians 1:8.

[30] Romans 10:17; Colossians 3:16.

[31] 2 Corinthians 4:4.

[32] 1 Corinthians 15:3-5.

[33] 1 Corinthians 1:17-18; cf. 1 Corinthians 1:23; 2:2; Galatians 3:1.

[34] Acts 1:22; 4:2, 33; 17:18; Romans 1:4; 1 Corinthians 15:12; 2 Timothy 2:8.

[35] Acts 2:36; Romans 1:3-4; 10:8-9, 17; 2 Corinthians 4:5; 1 Thessalonians 1:5, 9-10; 1 Peter 1:21.

[36] 2 Corinthians 4:4-5; Philippians 1:12-18; Colossians 1:25, 28.

[37] Ephesians 1:13; cf. Acts 13:26; Romans 1:16; Hebrews 2:3; 1 Peter 1:10-12.

[38] Acts 10:36; Ephesians 6:15; Philippians 2:16; 2 Corinthians 5:19.

[39] Ephesians 2:5, 8; Romans 5:9-10; 1 Thessalonians 1:10.

[40] Acts 2:32-36; 3:20-21; 10:42; Romans 2:16; 10:9-13; 2 Corinthians 4:5; 1 Thessalonians 1:10.

[41] 1 Corinthians 15:3-4.

[42] Acts 3:17-21, 24; 10:43; 13:23, 27-35; 26:22-23; 28:23; Romans 1:2; 16:25-26; 1 Peter 1:10-12.

[43] Matthew 4:23; 9:35; 24:14; cf. Luke 4:43; 8:1; Acts 8:12; 20:25; 28:23, 31.

focus of the gospel is the fulfilment that has already come about in Jesus, but it also proclaims that which is yet to come in and with him.[44]

Finally, the gospel is 'the word of faith'.[45] In addition to making an announcement it also makes an appeal – it calls for a response, the response of faith. As we have seen, this faith involves both repentance and obedience. The gospel also involves a promise, that there is salvation for all who have this faith – that is, for all who turn from sin to God and who trust God and his promise.[46]

2.4.   'Gospel' conclusions

It is time for us to stand back and consider what we have learned about the gospel. This will help us to absorb what we need to know about it.

2.4.1.   Gospel of God

The first and most important point we need to make is that the gospel is the gospel of God. It is momentous news from God, his word of truth broadcast to the world. It is thus a divine disclosure, not a human discovery: it is God speaking to us, not us speculating about God. This means that everyone should pay very careful attention to the gospel. Because of its source, it could not be more important: it is the word of God par excellence. A spirituality of the gospel must therefore have the gospel as its root, its foundation.

The gospel is also momentous news about God. Its subject is God, not us. It announces God's great purpose and the work he has done to bring it to fulfilment. This purpose and work were foretold and foreshadowed in the Old Testament Scriptures – so the gospel proclaims the fulfilment of the Old Testament promises and patterns (or 'types'). The gospel thus reveals that we have reached the decisive point in the outworking of God's saving purpose – we have come to the climax of all of his words and works in Israel. We have passed from the era of waiting to the age of fulfilment. The gospel is thus about the meaning of our time. In telling us what God is doing, it also tells us where we are in the unfolding of his purposes. A spirituality of the gospel must therefore be directed to God and shaped by his work.

---

[44]   Acts 10:42; 17:31; Romans 2:16; 1 Thessalonians 1:10.
[45]   Romans 10:8.
[46]   Acts 2:38-41; 3:19-21, 26; 5:31; 10:43; 13:38-39; 20:21; 26:17-18.

2.4.2. *Gospel of Christ*

The second thing we have learned about the gospel is that it centres on the person and work of the Lord Jesus: it is 'the gospel of Christ'. It tells us that God's purpose and work reaches its fulfilment in him. It thus presents him in all his glory as Son of God, Messiah of Israel, and Lord and Saviour of the world. Although it announces his present reign and future return as well, it centres upon his death and resurrection as the great saving events. The gospel is a glorious message about the redeeming, risen, reigning, and returning Lord. A spirituality of the gospel will therefore have the Lord Jesus as its centre and focus.

2.4.3. *Gospel of Salvation*

The third thing we need to say about the gospel is that it is a declaration of what God has done to save the world: it is 'the gospel of salvation'. If we ask why God has done this, the gospel points us in two directions. First and foremost, it points us to him: God did this because he is that kind of God! So the gospel is a message about God's grace, the never-merited, never-limited love in which he gave his Son to win salvation for us. The second way the gospel answers this question is by pointing to us: God did this for us because we desperately need it to be done. The gospel tells us that Christ died for our sins.[47] This alerts us to the fact that there is a dark background to the gospel. What it tells us about God's saving work is glorious news – but only because we are hopelessly lost in our sins and deserving of God's eternal judgment. That God should work to save us rather than bringing his judgment upon us is astounding. That he should rescue us from judgment by turning it upon himself in the death of Jesus is the wonder of all wonders. The more fully we recognize the seriousness of our sin, the more wonderful is the grace that saves us from all that it means. And the more clearly we see the terrible price that God paid to deliver us from sin, the more we see how deadly serious our sin is. A spirituality of the gospel will therefore take a realistic view of our sinfulness. It will also have its roots firmly planted in the grace of God.

2.4.4. *Gospel of faith*

The fourth thing we have learned about the gospel is that it involves both announcement and appeal, both proclamation and invitation – it

---

[47]   1 Corinthians 15:3.

calls for a definite response from everyone who hears it. It offers salvation from sin, and it thus involves a summons to repentance and faith. We can summarize this response as turning from sin and trusting the promise of salvation, saying 'No' to my sinful independence of God and 'Yes' to living under the rule of Jesus as Lord. A spirituality of the gospel will therefore have penitent faith at its heart.

2.4.5.   Gospel of the Scriptures

The fifth and final point we need to make about the gospel is that it is the gospel of the prophets and apostles.[48] It was announced in advance by the prophets: it is 'according to the Scriptures'. It announces that all of God's words and works – all of the promises and patterns – have reached their fulfilment in the person and work of the Lord Jesus.[49] It was declared with authority by the Lord and especially by his apostles. Their calling was to bear witness to Jesus by making the gospel known.[50] The gospel we proclaim is this gospel, the prophetic and apostolic gospel, the gospel of the Scriptures. A spirituality of the gospel will therefore have to be grounded on, and nourished and governed by the Bible.

2.5.   Gospel focus

Now that we have gained an understanding of what the New Testament means by 'the gospel', we can turn to our next task. This is to work out what a 'spirituality of the gospel' will be like – an exploration that will occupy the next three chapters. Before we do this, we must register the most obvious and important implication of our study of the gospel. Whatever else it involves, a spirituality that is shaped and governed by the gospel will be Christ-centred. Jesus Christ is the subject of the gospel. More than that, he is the reason that there is a gospel! So he must be the centre and focus of all of our spirituality. In the New Testament, our faith is directed to him; he is our hope; and he is the one we love.[51] He is the focus of our life and growth: 'Grow in the grace and

---

[48]   See especially Luke 24:44-49; Hebrews 2:3; 1 Peter 1:10-12; 2 Peter 3:2.

[49]   I have attempted to explain how the Old Testament prepares for and points to Jesus, and how the New Testament builds on the foundation laid by the Old Testament, in my book *GPS: God's Plan for Salvation* (Sydney: Aquila Press, 2013).

[50]   Luke 24:48; John 15:26-27; Acts 1:8.

[51]   See, for example, John 14:1; 1 Timothy 1:1; Ephesians 6:24.

knowledge of our Lord and Saviour Jesus Christ'.[52] Indeed, he is our life.[53] And he is the joy beyond our death.[54] Nothing and no one is to matter more to us than he does: 'I consider everything a loss because of the surpassing worth of knowing Christ Jesus my Lord'.[55] And in the end, he is all that we have to say to the world – he is our message: 'We proclaim him'.[56]

Any spirituality that is not centred upon the person and work of the Lord Jesus is thus defective and unacceptable. Martin Luther saw this with great clarity:

> it is certain that he who bypasses the Person of Christ never finds the true God; for since God is fully in Christ, where He places Himself for us, no effort to deal with God without and apart from Christ on the strength of human thoughts and devotion will be successful. Whoever would travel the right road and not go astray with his faith, let him begin where God says and where He wants to be found. Otherwise he will surely miss the goal, and all that he believes and does will prove vain.[57]

Luther's first application of this principle was not to others but to himself. In the light of Christ and the gospel, he judged his own former piety very severely:

> I myself was a monk for twenty years. I tortured myself with prayers, fasting, vigils, and freezing ... What else did I seek by doing this but God, who was supposed to note my strict observance of the monastic order and my austere life? I constantly walked in a dream and lived in real idolatry. For I did not believe in Christ; I regarded Him only as a severe and terrible Judge, portrayed as seated on a rainbow. Therefore I cast about for other intercessors, Mary and various other saints, also my own works and the merits of my order. And I did all this for the sake of God, not for money or goods. Nevertheless, this was heresy and idolatry, since I did not know

---

[52]   2 Peter 3:18.
[53]   Colossians 3:4.
[54]   Philippians 1:21, 23.
[55]   Philippians 3:8.
[56]   Colossians 1:28.
[57]   Martin Luther [1483-1546], *Luther's Works*, fifty-five volumes (St Louis: Concordia/ Philadelphia: Fortress, 1957-86), 24: p 23.

Christ, and did not seek in and through Him what I wanted.[58]

The point is clear: the crucial test of any devotion is not its intensity but its focus. No matter how earnest it may be, seeking God apart from the Christ of the gospel is a serious error. It is not simply invalid; Luther regards it as sinful ('heresy and idolatry'). Since God is known only in and through his Son, true devotion will always be centred on him. So a spirituality of the gospel is a spirituality that is all about the Lord Jesus Christ. We will give careful attention to this vital point in Chapter 12.

Our next chapter considers the fact that a spirituality of the gospel is responsive, which is a direct consequence of beginning with the gospel. We noted at the beginning of the present chapter that this is what God does. It is important for us to recognize that this is also what the New Testament does. There are two ways in which this is true, as we saw at the beginning of this chapter. The first is that Christian life begins when the gospel is proclaimed and believed. The second is that the gospel remains the foundation of the Christian life. That is why the gospel is the basis for the apostles' teaching about how life should be lived. Think, for example, of the way Romans 12 begins. Paul is about to teach the Romans about authentic Christian living. He begins with a 'therefore' (12:1), which shows us that what follows is the fruit that comes from some root. This root is the exposition of the gospel and God's saving work that occupies chapters 1-11 of Romans. He wants his readers to respond rightly to 'God's mercy' in the gospel of Christ. We find something similar in Ephesians. The first half of the letter (chapters 1-3) spells out the riches of God's grace in the gospel; the second half (chapters 4-6) – which also begins with a 'therefore' (4:1) – spells out how to live worthily in view of all that God has done for us and given to us in Christ. Or consider how Paul's exhortations to the Corinthian church are grounded in the gospel. Look, for example, at how he appeals to the gospel in addressing the church's problems over rival factions,[59] sexual immorality,[60] and meat offered to idols.[61] In these and other ways, the apostles treat the gospel as the root from which the fruit of Christian living grows.

---

[58] *Works*, 24: pp 23-24.
[59] 1 Corinthians 1:18-25, 30; 2:2, 7-10; 3:11.
[60] 1 Corinthians 5:7; 6:11, 14, 19-20.
[61] 1 Corinthians 8:6, 11; 9:12, 16, 23.

Where the gospel is not foundational in this way, what people teach about Christian life generally, and Christian devotion in particular, runs into all kinds of difficulties. A good example is provided by William Law's classic, *A Serious Call to a Devout and Holy Life*.[62] This widely influential work, which had a significant impact on the Wesleys and George Whitefield and went into twenty editions on both sides of the Atlantic by the beginning of the nineteenth century, has been hailed as 'one of the most important devotional works of post-Reformation England'.[63] It is difficult to justify this reputation, however. The book begins, not with the gospel, but with the duty of believers to live for God's glory in every part of their lives. Its focus is not the grace to which we should respond but what Law calls 'rules of reason and religion'.[64] For all of its earnestness and obvious sincerity, the book lives up to its author's name: it is more law than gospel! The Scriptures are seen as primarily teaching our duties or 'laws of life'.[65] There are few references to the gospel, and these generally concern its 'duties' or 'precepts'.[66] The glorious message of God's saving grace for sinners is difficult to find. In fact, we are told that God will be merciful only to 'our unavoidable weaknesses and infirmities'.[67] The author insists that there is no such provision for our more deliberate sins[68] – a view which surely misses the whole point of the parable of the prodigal son (to mention only one example). We are also told that 'salvation is only given to those who strive for it'.[69] This striving involves self-denial and intense self-discipline: 'our salvation depends upon the sincerity and perfection of our endeavours to obtain it'.[70] Further, the way 'the sons of Adam' share in the benefits of Christ's atoning work is by 'denying and mortifying their natural appetites, and crucifying the lusts of the flesh'.[71] This is all

---

[62] William Law [1686-1761], *A Serious Call to a Devout and Holy Life*, edited and introduced by J.C. Reid (The Fontana Library: Theology and Philosophy) (London: Collins, 1965 [1728]).

[63] Introduction by J.C. Reid, p 7.

[64] *Serious Call*, p 30; cf. p 21: 'strict principles of reason and piety', 'strict rules of piety and devotion', pp 68-69, 79, 97, 102-3.

[65] *Serious Call*, p 72.

[66] See, for example, *Serious Call*, pp 22, 93, 174.

[67] *Serious Call*, p.31; cf. p 34: 'His mercy is only offered to our frail and imperfect, but best endeavours ...'

[68] *Serious Call*, pp 31, 34.

[69] *Serious Call*, p 33.

[70] *Serious Call*, p 33; cf. p 22: 'self-denial [is] a condition of salvation'.

[71] *Serious Call*, p 240.

much too close for comfort to salvation by good works. By not beginning with the gospel but with our duties, by focusing so strongly not on God's work for us but on our works for him, the book ends up teaching piety as a new law. It is difficult to understand why it is regarded as a spiritual classic.

This example alerts us to a great danger that faces us in this area. It is all too easy to forget the gospel or to leave it behind when we are discussing spirituality. Sadly, there are too many works regarded as classics in which it is difficult to find the gospel. But in order to be true, our devotion must be a fruit of the gospel: it must be a response to God's grace and truth. So what does a 'spirituality of the gospel' look like? What are its hallmarks? What is its shape? What kind of response does it make to God's grace and truth?

3.   A Responsive Spirituality

If I turn on the radio and hear applause, I will immediately think, 'What did I just miss?' That is because applause always comes second; it is a way of responding. So it is with our knowledge of God: our spirituality is *responsive*. This is a direct consequence of the gospel of grace. Although the basic idea here is simple enough, its implications are far-reaching, and it is important that we see them clearly. So we are going to spend this chapter analysing what is meant by a 'responsive' spirituality.

3.1.   *The focus of spirituality*

The first and most important point to make is this: we must not begin with our spirituality. As we saw in the last chapter, we must begin with the gospel. What comes first is not what we do to serve God but what he does to save us.

3.1.1.   *The revealing and redeeming God*

So what kind of spirituality is it that responds to God's grace-filled initiative – the initiative that is announced in the gospel? To answer this question we need to unpack the fact that (as we learned in the previous chapter) the gospel is the word of God about the work of God. What does this tell us? It alerts us, first, to the fact that there are two interwoven and inseparable strands in the way God works. These are what he does as *Revealer* and as *Redeemer*. Our knowledge of God is based on his work of redemption and his word of revelation. We know him only because he is a God who speaks and a God who saves.[1]

3.1.2.   *The sufficient Christ*

The second point we need to make is that all of God's words and works reached their climax in the Lord Jesus Christ. In him we find the fullness of grace and truth – 'grace' pointing us to the finished work of redemption, and 'truth' pointing us to the final word of revelation. Nothing more needs to be said or done, because he is both the Word of

---

[1]   See, for example, Exodus 20:1-3; Psalms 105:1-11, 37-45; 111:1-10; Isaiah 43:10-13; 46:9-13; Ephesians 1:3-14; Colossians 1:9-14.

God and the Lamb of God.[2] The complete sufficiency of his work as both Revealer and Redeemer is guaranteed by the complete supremacy of his person as Son of God and Lord of all. Who he is necessarily means that what he has done does not need to be supplemented and cannot be surpassed.[3] Because there is no greater worth than his, there is no greater work than his either. True devotion therefore magnifies the Lord Jesus, glorying in the unrivalled excellencies of his person and work.

What this means in practice is spelled out in what we can call the first two laws of 'theological mathematics'. The first law states that *whenever you add, you subtract.* Adding more to the Lord Jesus makes him less than he should be. Whenever you put a plus sign after Jesus, you are taking something away from his supremacy and sufficiency. If you need more than Jesus, then he is not enough! Any attempt to supplement Jesus' word or work is a way of saying that he is inadequate as a Revealer or Redeemer. It was exactly this kind of problem that faced the church in Colossae. They were being lured by a teaching that was based on visions and involved worshipping angels[4] as well as strict rules about food and festivals.[5] That is why Paul's letter to the Colossians makes such clear statements about the unsurpassable majesty of the Lord Jesus and the comprehensiveness of the revelation and redemption that we have in him.[6] Paul makes it crystal clear that there is nothing lacking or defective in Jesus' person and work – so that there is neither reason nor excuse for looking outside to someone else or to something extra.

This is one of the cardinal points of Evangelical spirituality. So it is something on which the Reformers insisted. Bullinger, for example, puts it this way:

> they have not yet rightly understood the gospel of Christ, nor sincerely preached it, whosoever do attribute to Christ Jesus our Lord, the true Messiah, either not only, or else not fully, all things

---

[2]   See John 1:1, 14, 29.
[3]   See, for example, John 1:14-18; Romans 5:8-21; Philippians 2:5-11; Colossians 1:15-20; 2:8-15; Hebrews 1:1-4; 7:23-28; 9:24-28; Revelation 1:12-18; 7:9-17; 19:11-16.
[4]   Colossians 2:18.
[5]   Colossians 2:16, 20-23.
[6]   See especially Colossians 1:13-23; 2:2-3, 8-15; 3:1-4, 9-11.

requisite to life and salvation.[7]

Equally clear and direct is the Belgic Confession of 1561:

> We believe that ... the Holy Spirit kindles in our hearts an upright
> faith, which embraces Jesus Christ with all His merits, appropriates
> Him, and seeks nothing more besides Him. For it must follow,
> either that all things which are requisite to our salvation are not in
> Jesus Christ, or if all things are in Him, that then those who possess
> Jesus Christ through faith have complete salvation in Him.
> Therefore, for any to assert that Christ is not sufficient, but that
> something more is required besides Him, would be too gross a
> blasphemy; for hence it would follow that Christ was but half
> a Saviour.[8]

The Puritans also stressed this point, as the following example shows:

> As the eye seeks for no other light than that of the sun, and joins no
> candles with it to dishonour the sufficiency of its beams, so no
> created thing must be joined to Christ as an object of faith. This is a
> dishonour to the strength of this Rock, which is our only
> foundation, this is to undervalue the greatness of the gift, and the
> wisdom of the giver. It is a folly to seek for security anywhere else...
> We cannot trust him too much, nor ourselves too little. God trusted
> him alone, therefore should we ...[9]

The point is made most simply by Paul in the letter written against a
spirituality that subtracts by adding – Christ is all![10]

The second law of 'theological mathematics' states that *whatever you
add is what really counts for you.* That is, while you will pay lip-service to
what precedes the plus sign, the real centre of gravity in your mind and
life is what follows it. So, as happened in Colossae, people whose basis
is 'the gospel + visions' or whose focus is 'Jesus + angels' will give
priority to visions and angels. It was exactly this kind of problem that

---

[7] Heinrich Bullinger [1504-1575], *The Decades,* four volumes (Cambridge: CUP, 1849-52 [1587]), vol 3: p 31f.

[8] The Belgic Confession, Article XXII, in *Reformed Confessions of the 16th and 17th Centuries in English Translation,* compiled with Introductions by James T. Dennison, Jr., two volumes (Grand Rapids: Reformation Heritage, 2010), vol 2: p 436f.

[9] Stephen Charnock [1628-1680], *The Complete Works of Stephen Charnock,* five volumes (Edinburgh: Banner of Truth, 1997), vol 5: p 176.

[10] Colossians 3:11.

confronted the churches in Galatia. They were being threatened by a movement that claimed to affirm the gospel while insisting that there is no salvation without circumcision ('Jesus + circumcision'). That is why Paul's letter to the Galatians is so uncompromising in its insistence that anyone who treats circumcision as a necessity has in fact abandoned the gospel and 'fallen away from grace'.[11] While paying lip-service to God's work as the source of our salvation, the false teachers concerned were putting religious ceremonies – our deeds – in the centre. What really mattered to them was not the cross but circumcision.[12]

3.1.3. The central cross and resurrection

The third thing we need to say is that the heart of all of God's work of revelation and redemption is Jesus' death and resurrection. This is the climax of God's work, the end-point for which all of his work prepared and to which all of his work led. It is also the core of the gospel, the centre of God's word: it is what both the prophets and apostles proclaim.[13] There is no greater redemption still to be accomplished, no greater revelation still to be given – the gospel proclaims the finished work of redemption and forms the final word of revelation. True devotion therefore makes much of the cross and resurrection. It rests on them and rejoices in them as the basis for the mighty salvation in which we participate. It relies on them as the definitive revelation of what God is like and also of what we are like.

3.1.4. The inspiring and illuminating Spirit

Our fourth and final point is that all that has been accomplished for us in the Son is applied to us by the Spirit. He works in us what the Son won for us. This is true of both revelation and redemption: the Spirit takes the objectively completed word and work of God and progressively establishes them in our lives.[14] This means that it is not the role of the Spirit to add to the word of God, to give fresh revelation.

God never intended to abolish his Word, by giving his Spirit ...[15]

---

[11] See especially Galatians 1:6-7; 4:28-5:6; 6:12-16.

[12] Galatians 6:14-15.

[13] Note especially 1 Peter 1:10-12.

[14] See, for example, John 16:13-15; Romans 5:5, 8; 2 Corinthians 1:20-22; 3:17-18; Galatians 3:26; 4:4-6; Ephesians 1:3-10; Titus 3:4-7.

[15] John Flavel, Works, 1: p 132.

There is no Volume Two – such as the Book of Mormon – to come after the Bible; no Revealer – like Mohammed – to follow the Lord Jesus. What the Spirit does is, first, to place revelation in the public domain by his work of *inspiration*. This is what gives us our Bible.[16] Then he sets about lodging it in our minds and lives so that it accomplishes God's saving purpose.[17] This is revelation with a small 'r' – the Spirit's work of *illumination*, enabling us to see what is in the written word, to take it in and live it out.[18] (We will return to this important point in just a few pages.) True devotion therefore makes much of the Bible as God's complete and sufficient word, centred on his Son and breathed out by his Spirit.

3.2. *Gospel Spirituality unpacked*

We have said that true devotion is a spirituality of the gospel, and we have begun exploring what that means. We can now say that a spirituality of the gospel is centred on the saving work of God – what he has done for us in the death and resurrection of his Son. This is a Christ-centred spirituality, an untiring glorying in 'the boundless riches'[19] of his person and work. It is a spirituality of the cross, never losing its sense of wonder at all that God's love has done for us and won for us. It is a spirituality of the resurrection, already enjoying the new life that Jesus' victory has secured for us. It is a spirituality of the word of God, generated, nourished, and directed by the Bible. It is a spirituality of the Spirit of God, relying on him to ground our lives more and more deeply on God's work and word.

---

[16]   2 Timothy 3:16; 2 Peter 1:21.

[17]   See, for example, 1 Corinthians 2:12; Ephesians 1:15-21; 1 Thessalonians 4:1-3, 7-8; Hebrews 3:7-11; 10:15-17.

[18]   Note Calvin's response to people in his day who claimed direct inspiration by the Spirit, dismissing the Bible as a dead letter:
'...the Spirit, promised to us, has not the task of inventing new and unheard-of Revelation, or of forging a new kind of doctrine, to lead us away from the received doctrine of the gospel ... [so] we ought zealously to apply ourselves both to read and to hearken to Scripture if indeed we want to receive any gain and benefit from the Spirit of God... the Word is the instrument by which the Lord dispenses the illumination of his Spirit to believers. For they know no other Spirit than him who dwelt and spoke in the apostles, and by whose oracles they are continually recalled to the hearing of the Word.' (Calvin, *Institutes*, I.ix.1-3 (1: pp 94, 96)).

[19]   Ephesians 3:8.

We can now take the next step in our process of discovering what a spirituality of the gospel is like. In Chapter 2, we learned that the gospel is about what God has done for us and given to us – all out of his grace, his own free, lavish love. This means that our knowledge of God is a gift we have received, not a goal we have achieved. It does not stem from initiatives we have taken; it is the result of what God has done to rescue and restore us. So there is only one source for our fellowship with God – and that is his saving grace.[20] Equally, there is only one means of appropriating that grace – and that is our faith. The gift of salvation is held out to us in the gospel, and faith is the empty hand that grasps that gift.[21]

> [F]aith ... is the hand of the soul, to lay hold of all the graces, excellencies, and high perfections of Christ.[22]

So 'faith' means our reliance upon God's word and work – and our trust in the God who has spoken the word and done the work. True devotion is therefore *a spirituality of grace and faith*.[23] Its core is God's love for us and our trust in him. We will now explore each of these in turn.

3.3. *A spirituality of grace*

What is a 'spirituality of grace'? In the Bible, 'grace' refers to God's way of loving.[24] There are two ways in which this love is unique – it is always free and always rich. It is free because it always comes to us as a gift: 'this is not from yourselves, it is the gift of God'.[25] God loves us not because of what we are like, but because that is what he is like. His love is not a response to what he sees in us – it is a gift not a reward. There is no merit where grace is: it is never deserved. And as a gift, grace is

---

[20]   See, for example, Romans 5:1-11; 2 Corinthians 5:17-21; Ephesians 2:1-9; Titus 2:10-14; 3:4-7; 1 Peter 1:3-5, 18-21.

[21]   See, for example, Acts 15:7-11; Romans 1:17; 3:22-30; 4:16-25; Galatians 2:15-16; 3:22-27; Ephesians 1:13; 2:8-9.

[22]   Richard Sibbes [1577-1636], *Works of Richard Sibbes*, seven volumes (Edinburgh: Banner of Truth, 1973-82), vol 5: p 362.

[23]   For a helpful treatment of prayer as an expression of this spirituality, see Graeme Goldsworthy, *Prayer and the Knowledge of God: What the Whole Bible Teaches* (Leicester: IVP, 2003).

[24]   Note how it is used in parallel with 'love', 'kindness', and 'mercy' (Ephesians 2:4-8; Titus 3:4-7).

[25]   Ephesians 2:8.

always rich: 'the incomparable riches of his grace'.[26] God's love is not about needing or getting; it is all about giving with unimaginable generosity. So there is no limit where grace is: it is never reserved. The God of all grace is not a trickle, or even a torrent, but an avalanche of love! And this is no ordinary love; it is quite unique and completely astounding.

> Grace is love which ... floods with affection the sinner who has deserved anger and resentment, trusts penitent treachery with a confidence that could not have been merited by ages of incorruptible fidelity, confers on a race which has been in revolt honours which no loyalty could have purchased ...[27]

So God's love for us is rich and free, never merited and never limited, always unearned and always unstinting – and a spirituality of grace is shaped by both of these. But before we consider what this means, we need to note that both aspects of God's grace are expressed supremely in his Son. He is the gift of grace. And by him we become rich.[28]

> Christ is God's grace, mercy, righteousness, truth, wisdom, power, comfort, and salvation, given to us by God without any merit on our part.[29]

3.3.1. Grace as gift

How does a 'spirituality of grace' reflect the gift-character of God's grace? It does so first of all by where it focuses. Grace is all about the initiatives God takes to secure his great salvation for us and to impart it to us. As a result, a spirituality of grace-as-gift is focused on God the gracious giver. It is all about what he does for us and with us; it is not about initiatives we take towards him. We always remain the undeserving recipients of his overwhelming kindness – and authentic spirituality will therefore always centre on our recognition of this fact. Heartfelt praise will thus be a constant mark of true devotion: 'I will extol the Lord at all times; his praise will always be on my lips'.[30]

---

[26]   Ephesians 2:7.
[27]   R.W. Dale [1829-1895], *The Epistle to the Ephesians: Its Doctrine and Ethics*, 6th ed. (London: Hodder & Stoughton, 1892), p 178.
[28]   2 Corinthians 8:9; 9:15.
[29]   Luther, *Works*, 14: p 204.
[30]   Psalm 34:1. It is worth noting that more than half of the Psalms speak of praising God.

This means, secondly, that a spirituality of grace-as-gift will always be marked by deep gratitude to God and deep humility before God.[31] We will never see ourselves as elite spiritual athletes who take noble initiatives to and for God, or spiritual warriors who win great victories in God's cause. We do not come to God full of our exploits and what we have achieved; instead, we come as debtors who have been immeasurably enriched by him. In humility, we recognize ourselves to be very low and poor indeed; in gratitude, we magnify what he has done for us, given to us, and made of us through his Son. True devotion will always identify with Mary's words: 'My soul glorifies the Lord and my spirit rejoices in God my Saviour, for he has been mindful of the humble state of his servant'.[32]

Thirdly, a spirituality of grace-as-gift involves deep assurance about our standing before God. We can come to him and relate to him with great confidence.[33] This is not due to the merits of the way we approach him; it is due entirely to the fact that he has opened the way and brought us near: 'we have confidence ... by the blood of Jesus'.[34] This kind of firm, unshakeable assurance cannot be based on the work done *by* me – including my spirituality – for this is never perfect. Nor is it based on the work done *in* me by the Spirit, for this is never complete in this life. Rather, it is based on the work done *for* me by the Son – and because this is both perfect and complete, my assurance is rock-solid. We have already seen that the complete supremacy of Jesus' person means the complete sufficiency of his work. Now we can add that this means the complete security of his people – we could not be more secure because his person and work cannot be surpassed. That is why the New Testament rings with such confidence about where we stand with God.[35] This is one of the choicest fruits of God's grace towards us.

3.3.2. Grace as rich love

Now we turn to consider grace as love that is rich. What is a 'spirituality of grace' seen from this perspective? There are two things we need to

---

[31]   See, for example, Psalms 9:1-2; 145:1-21; 149:4; Isaiah 25:1-8; 66:2b; Jeremiah 9:23-24; Micah 6:8; Matthew 11:25-27; 18:1-4; 1 Corinthians 1:26-31; Ephesians 1:3-14; 5:19-20; Colossians 3:17; 1 Thessalonians 5:18; Hebrews 13:15; James 4:10; 1 Peter 5:6.

[32]   Luke 1:46-48.

[33]   Ephesians 3:12; Hebrews 4:16; 10:19-22.

[34]   Hebrews 10:19.

[35]   See, for example, John 6:37-40; 10:28-29; Romans 8:28-39; 2 Timothy 4:18; Jude 24-25.

say here. The first concerns the character of the Christian life. What does the gospel tell us about this? As we saw in Chapter 2, its message concerns the great salvation God has won for us through his Son. Such are the riches of God's grace that this salvation has a great many dimensions. That is why the New Testament speaks about it from many different angles – being saved means being adopted, cleansed, justified, reconciled, redeemed, regenerated, resurrected, sanctified, and so on. Common to all of these word-pictures is the fact that God's saving work has two sides. One concerns what we are saved out of; the other, what we are saved into. The first has to do with some aspect of sin and what it does to us, while the second is about the corresponding aspect of salvation. So for example, when the New Testament says that we have been resurrected, it is telling us that we have been delivered out of our deadness in sin into a glorious new life.[36] A spirituality of grace gives proper weight to all that salvation means. It does not give undue emphasis to any one of the ways in which the New Testament speaks about salvation; nor does it focus on one side of God's saving work to the neglect of the other. Erring in either of these ways will lead to an impoverished spirituality.

Consider, for example, what happens if our gospel gives great emphasis to the forgiveness of our sins, but not a lot of attention to what we are saved into. In technical terms, this would mean concentrating on justification and neglecting regeneration, for example. What is the likely result of doing so? Instead of giving people a very clear understanding that God gives us a new life, we may well give them the impression that he just gives us another chance. This puts us in the same position as the actor Bill Murray in the movie Groundhog Day – we simply go back to square one and start all over again, day after day after day. But what we have in Christ is more than just a clean slate – we have been given an entirely new identity, a whole new life.

> Our Saviour in his salvation is ... not merely our rescuer but our new life. His work is in the same act reclamation as well as rescue... He does not simply cancel the charge against us in court and bid us walk out of jail, he meets us at the prison-door and puts us in a new way of life.[37]

---

36   Romans 6:1-14; Ephesians 2:1-6; Colossians 2:12-13.

37   P.T. Forsyth [1848-1921], *The Work of Christ* (The Fontana Library: Theology and Philosophy) (London: Collins, 1965 [1910]), pp 151, 163.

So if we are to be faithful to the New Testament, we must give as much emphasis to what we are saved *for* as to what we are saved *from*.

A spirituality of grace-as-rich, nourished by the New Testament, will involve a grand, multi-dimensional view of the Christian life because God's salvation is so rich and comprehensive. Its second feature is what it tells us about the nature of Christian growth. Popular views of this process are often some way from what the Bible teaches. This is because the New Testament's approach is based on the grace of God – and is thus very different from what we might have expected. Perhaps the biggest difference is this: Christian growth does not mean starting with very little and gradually acquiring more. Instead, it means progressively taking hold of what we have already. As Christians of a previous generation used to say, it means 'possessing our possessions'. This is because God has blessed us in Christ with *every* spiritual blessing in the heavenly realms (Ephesians 1:3). This is not Paul's way of saying that God has given us lots of blessings that are – being 'spiritual' – not very real! He means that God has given us the most real and important blessings that there are – and he has not just given us lots of them; he has given us all of them.

Peter makes the same point this way: God 'has given us everything we need for a godly life'.[38] We begin with everything! This is because of 'the riches of God's grace that he lavished on us'.[39] And because we start with everything, Christian growth means *growing into* what we have and where we are; it does not mean *moving on* in order to find more. We see this in Peter's second letter, for example. This begins not only by referring to the richness of God's grace in bestowing upon us everything we need for life and godliness (1:3-4), but also by assuring us that we have a real knowledge of the Lord Jesus (1:2, 8). The letter ends by urging us to keep growing in both 'the grace and knowledge of our Lord and Saviour Jesus Christ' (3:18). It also urges us to take great care that we do not move away from where we are and what we have (3:17).

There is another way of making this quite fundamental point: the greatest breakthrough we experience as Christians is what happens at the very beginning, when we are given new birth,[40] raised from death to

---

[38]   2 Peter 1:3.
[39]   Ephesians 1:7-8.
[40]   John 3:3, 5; James 1:18; 1 Peter 1:3, 23.

new life,[41] adopted into God's family,[42] and so on. As a result, progress in the Christian life is the process of becoming what we are already.[43] That is because the decisive breakthrough is behind us, not ahead of us: 'The old has gone, the new is here!'[44] In the New Testament, this means that Christian growth is not the quest for some gift or change or experience that we lack and must have. Instead, it is the progressive taking hold of, entering into, and expressing, what we are and have already as a result of God's saving grace.

Think for a moment of the process of 'sanctification', that is, the growing in and through which we become holy people. In the New Testament, we read such exhortations as 'Make every effort ... to be holy; without holiness no one will see the Lord'.[45] It is easy to get a false impression from such verses taken in isolation. It sounds as though we begin by being very unholy, and that by persistent effort we gradually become holier and holier. But why isn't this right? The reason is this: before we get to Hebrews 12:14 we have already been told that 'we have been made holy through the sacrifice ... of Jesus Christ once for all'.[46] So holiness is not a distant goal; it is our starting-point! This means that sanctification is not the process of progressively acquiring what we do not have; rather, it is the process of appropriating and growing into what we have from the beginning of our life in Christ.[47] Out of the riches of his grace, God gives us what he wants to find in us; he makes us what he wants us to be. As a result, we grow by becoming what we are – our state is progressively conformed to our status; as we grow, our condition comes to match our position.

3.3.3. Motivation for Christian growth

This is why the New Testament does not generally make use of what we might call 'deficit motivation'. This is more common than it should be as a way of getting Christians to keep growing. Someone who uses 'deficit motivation' tries to motivate me by drawing attention to what I lack, to

---

[41] See, for example, John 5:24; Romans 6:1-13; Ephesians 2:1-6; Colossians 2:12-13; 3:1.

[42] See, for example, Romans 8:14-17, 29; Hebrews 2:10-18.

[43] See, for example, Romans 6:11-13; Ephesians 5:8; Colossians 3:1-14; 1 Thessalonians 5:4-9; 1 Peter 1:22-2:3.

[44] 2 Corinthians 5:17.

[45] Hebrews 12:14.

[46] Hebrews 10:10.

[47] 1 Corinthians 1:2, 30: 6:11; Hebrews 13:12; cf. Leviticus 20:7-8.

what I am not, and by urging me to become what I should be. It is not difficult to see why such an approach would be popular, for we all fail to be what we should be. But it is a very different approach from that taken by the New Testament, which generally uses what we can call 'grace motivation'. To give just one more example, note how in Titus 2:11-14 Paul presents God's saving grace as the basis and source for godly living.

How do these two approaches differ? There are four crucial differences between deficit motivation and grace motivation. The first is that deficit motivation fails to appreciate the distinction between *fruit* and *root*. It attempts to secure fruit by ... calling for fruit. This seems logical enough – until we realize that this is like an orchardist commanding his fruit trees to produce a crop! The way he gets fruit is, of course, by attending to the roots of the trees, fertilizing and watering them. And the way to see the fruit of Christian growth is to focus on the root, the Christian gospel. Deficit motivation looks to my work, to the fruit; grace motivation looks to God's work, to the root. And what happens when I focus on my work? The likelihood is that the more I look at it, the more its imperfections will become obvious – and so I will become more and more uncertain about my standing with God. But when I focus on God's work, its perfections become more and more precious – and I become more and more secure. By the way it tries to bring about growth, deficit motivation undermines my assurance as a child of God and thus impedes my growth.

A second difference is that deficit motivation is all about my *progress*, while grace motivation emphasizes my *position*. What is true of my progress in godliness? I have a very long way to go! My response to God's grace is weak, inconsistent, and very far from perfect. And even if I think in terms of the Spirit's work in me rather than of my progress, that is not yet complete. So the more I look to *where* I am, to my progress, the harder it will be to find assurance – and the less progress I will make. But what happens when I focus on my position? This means concentrating on the fact that God has given me a new status and made me a new person – that he has adopted me, justified me, reconciled me, redeemed me, and so on. Because this is based on the Son's work for me – a work which is finished and perfect – my position is secure. And the more I look to *what* I am, to my position in Christ, the more assurance I will have. This will mean being more and more aware of the riches of God's grace – and this will give me strong and lasting motivation to keep growing. The more I focus on my position rather than my progress, the more progress I am likely to make.

Thirdly, deficit motivation inclines me to look for some great breakthrough that is still *ahead* of me – while grace motivation reminds me that the greatest of all breakthroughs is the one that is *behind* me. Deficit motivation is looking for a transformation that has yet to occur, while grace motivation focuses on the transfer that has happened already. The New Testament tells me that I have been brought from darkness to light, from death to life, from the old to the new[48] – and much more besides. The less weight I give to this great transfer, the weaker will my assurance be – and the less I will be transformed.

Finally, deficit motivation focuses on my *faith*, while grace motivation focuses on my *Saviour*. The more I look to him, the more true faith will grow. However, the more I look to my faith, the more likely I am to fall into one of two opposite problems. The first is to have faith in my faith, to put my confidence in the quality of my faith, usually by overestimating its depth and strength. When this happens, I need to hear the wise words of C.H. Spurgeon: 'Never make a Christ out of your faith ...'[49] The alternative problem is to find that my faith crumbles the more I put it under the microscope. I can thus end up with either false assurance or rapidly shrinking assurance. Either way, I won't be growing as I should be.

3.4. Appropriating God's word and work

We have been considering the fact that true devotion is a 'spirituality of grace'. We have looked at what this means from two angles: grace-as-gift and grace-as-rich. It is now time to analyse the complementary truth that it is a 'spirituality of faith'. What the Bible says about 'faith' can be stated thus:

We confess that the entrance which we have to the great treasures and riches of the goodness of God that is vouchsafed to us is by faith; inasmuch as, in certain confidence and assurance of heart, we believe in the promises of the gospel, and receive Jesus Christ as he is offered to us by the Father and described to us by the Word of God.[50]

---

[48] 2 Corinthians 4:4-6; 1 Peter 2:9; John 5:24; Ephesians 2:1-5; 2 Corinthians 5:17; Colossians 3:9-10.

[49] C.H. Spurgeon [1834-1892], *All of Grace* (New Kensington, PA: Whitaker, 1981), p 57.

[50] The Genevan Confession [1536], in Mark A. Noll (ed), *Confessions and Catechisms of the Reformation* (Grand Rapids: Baker, 1991), p 128.

This has two fundamental ingredients: a spirituality of faith means both *appropriating* God's word and work ('we ... receive Jesus Christ') and *submitting to* God's word and work ('as he is offered to us').

3.4.1. Appropriating faith is essential

Let us consider the first of these, about which we need to make six points. The first is that appropriating is an essential part of faith and what it does. If faith is no more than an empty hand, appropriating is that empty hand grasping the proffered gift. It is that dimension of faith that lays hold on Christ and the gospel.

> True faith is an applying faith... It doth appropriate Christ to itself in particular. Christ is a garment, faith puts him on; Christ is a foundation, faith builds upon him; Christ is a root, faith plants us in him; Christ is our husband, faith yields consent, and consent makes the match.[51]

We see this clearly in Melanchthon's work. After stating that faith means both assent to and trust in God's promise of mercy in Christ, he says that it is 'also the power of laying hold on the promises and applying them to oneself'.[52] This is a point he makes quite often.[53]

> This laying hold on Christ and the gospel promise is vital: without it, I remain outside God's salvation.

> It is not gazing on the lifeboat that saves the shipwrecked sailor, but actually getting into it. It is not knowing and believing that Christ is a Saviour that can save your soul, unless there are actual transactions between you and Christ. You must be able to say, 'Christ is my Saviour, because I have come to Him by faith, and taken Him for my own'.[54]

Without the appropriating that faith does, without the empty hand taking hold of the gift, I stay unconnected with all that the gospel promises.

---

51   Sibbes, *Works*, 5: p 391.
52   *Loci*, p 158.
53   See, for example, *Loci*, p 150 ("This mercy is laid hold on by faith ..."); p 196 (by faith "we lay hold upon our Mediator"); p 198 ("faith ... lays hold on and applies the promise to us").
54   J.C. Ryle [1816-1900], *Holiness: Its Nature, Hindrances, Difficulties, and Roots* (London: James Clarke, 1956 [1879]), p 323.

3.4.2. *Appropriating faith is the character of growth*

The second thing to note here is the character of Christian growth. As we have just seen, this is the process of becoming what we are. Christian growth does not mean gradually acquiring what we do not have, for we begin the Christian life with everything. As a result, our growth is the progressive appropriation of what we have already been given – the process of entering into what we have and are. Our faith has this character because God's grace is so rich. Our appropriating is a response to his lavish generosity.

3.4.3. *Appropriating faith rests on the revelation of the Scriptures*

Thirdly, what applies to our growth in general applies especially to our growth in understanding. God does not reveal his character and purpose and will to us bit by bit, so that we gradually acquire knowledge of who he is and what it means to belong to him. Instead, he begins by giving us everything – in Christ we have *all* the treasures of wisdom and knowledge.[55] The riches of God's grace are such that he has given us *all* wisdom and understanding in making known to us the mystery of his will.[56] This comprehensive revelation is now contained in the Bible, of course. As a result, the Scriptures are not only able to bring us to salvation; they *thoroughly* equip God's servants for *every* good work.[57] So we keep drawing on the Scriptures in order to keep growing in godliness. According to the Waldensian Confession of 1560, believers are those who agree

> to follow the Word of God and pure religion, depending on it and profiting from it all the days of their life, growing and being confirmed in the fear of God, since they need to bear more and more fruit, always advancing in piety.[58]

A whole lifetime of fruitbearing and growing piety will not take us beyond the Scriptures, which give us all that we need. This means that we grow in our knowledge of God not by seeking fresh revelation but by steadily appropriating what has already been revealed.

---

[55]   Colossians 2:3.
[56]   Ephesians 1:7-9.
[57]   2 Timothy 3:15-17.
[58]   *Reformed Confessions of the 16th and 17th Centuries in English Translation*, compiled with Introductions by James T. Dennison, Jr., two volumes (Grand Rapids: Reformation Heritage, 2010), vol 2: p 225f.

For the Lord in the word of truth hath delivered to his church all that is requisite to true godliness and salvation. Whatsoever things are necessary to be known touching God ... touching Christ, our faith in Christ, and the duties of an holy life; all those things ... are fully taught in the word of God.[59]

This means that we keep growing by going to the Bible again and again, progressively mining all of its treasures:

the soul can do without anything except the Word of God ... If it has the Word of God it is rich and lacks nothing ...[60]

We are rich indeed, because everything that we can have now by way of knowledge of God has been given to us in the Bible. It is there for us to make it our own, growing in understanding by persistent appropriation.

3.4.4. *Appropriating faith depends on its focus not its force*

The fourth point we need to make about appropriating faith is that it is not its quantity or quality that counts:

If it never proves great, yet weak faith shall save; for it is not the strength of our faith that saves, but the truth of our faith – not the weakness of our faith that condemns, but the want of faith; for the least faith layeth hold on Christ, and so will save us. Neither are we saved by the worth or quantity of our faith, but by Christ, who is laid hold on by a weak faith as well as a strong. Just as a weak hand that can put meat into the mouth shall feed and nourish the body as well as if it were a strong hand; seeing the body is not nourished by the strength of the hand, but by the goodness of the meat.[61]

What matters is not how strong my faith is but how strong my Saviour is. That is, the crucial thing about faith is not its force but its focus. But while even the frailest faith is enough to connect me with the Lord and all of his great salvation, it is important that my faith continues to grow. This will not happen if I make my faith the centre of attention; it will only happen when it is steadily focused on the Lord himself.

[F]aith does not grow by being pulled up from the roots time and

---

59 Bullinger, *Decades*, 1: p 69. Cf. Calvin's statement that "Scripture is the school of the Holy Spirit, in which ... nothing is omitted that is both necessary and useful to know ... (*Institutes*, III.xxi.3 [2: p 924f]).

60 Luther, *Works*, 31: p 345.

61 John Rogers [c.1570-1636], *The Doctrine of Faith* [1634], quoted in Ryle, *Holiness*, p 127.

again to see how it is getting on... Faith withers and dies when it becomes the centre of attention. There is only one way to promote faith and hence assurance and that is by giving our attention to God more and more and learning to think of ourselves only in the light of His grace and power.[62]

3.4.5. *Appropriating faith works from outside in*

Fifthly, this is just what an appropriating faith does. It is focused outwards, not inwards – that is, it is focused outside of itself, on the objective words and works of God, on what God has said and done in the public domain.[63] Its gaze is directed to God and his gospel, not to me and my soul. So appropriating goes from the outside in, not from the inside out. It is not about discovering or expressing what is internal to me; it is taking hold of what is external to me in order to bring it home and make it my own.[64] True devotion is an *internalizing* of what God has said to us and done for us:

> We can think of spirituality in terms of the *internalization of our faith*. It means allowing our faith to saturate every aspect of our

---

[62] J.C.P. Cockerton, *To Be Sure: Christian Assurance – Presumption or Privilege?* (Christian Foundations 19) (London: Hodder & Stoughton, 1967), p 78f.

[63] Note the obvious parallel with Israel's experience, as expressed by Jon D. Levenson: 'It is significant for our understanding of the nature of the religion of Israel among the religions of the world that meaning for her is derived not from introspection, but from a consideration of public testimony to God. The present generation makes history their story, but it is first history. They do not determine who they are by looking within, by plumbing the depths of the individual soul, by seeking a mystical light in the innermost reaches of the self. Rather, the direction is the opposite. What is public is made private. History is not only rendered contemporary; it is internalized. One's people's history becomes one's personal history. One looks out from the self to find out who one is meant to be. One does not *discover* one's identity, and one certainly does not forge it oneself. He *appropriates* an identity that is a matter of public knowledge.' (*Sinai and Zion: An Entry into the Jewish Bible* (Winston Press, 1985), pp 38f [his italics]).

[64] This runs counter to a prominent view in mystical writings, such as that expressed by Meister Eckhart: "What is truthful cannot come from outside in; it must come from inside out ..." Note also Catherine of Siena: "If thou wouldst arrive at a perfect knowledge of Me the Eternal truth, never go outside thyself." (Both quoted in Donald G. Bloesch, *Spirituality Old and New: Recovering Authentic Spiritual Life* (Downers Grove: IVP/Nottingham: Apollos, 2007), p 68.) See further the discussion in Chapter 9 below.

lives, infecting and affecting our thinking, feeling, and living.[65]

3.4.6. *Appropriating faith is our side of the Spirit's work in us*

The sixth and final point we need to make about appropriating faith concerns the role of the Spirit. We can summarize it this way: what we do in appropriating God's word and work is the flipside of what the Spirit does. He is applying to us and activating in us what we appropriate. This is true of our appropriation of God's word – something we see in Paul's prayer in Ephesians 1, for example. He asks God to give the readers 'the Spirit of wisdom and revelation, so that [they] might know him better' (1:17). He especially wants the Spirit to enlighten their hearts so that they will know their hope, the riches of God's inheritance, and the greatness of God's power (1:18-19). But how will they come to know these things? Not by receiving fresh revelation, but by reading Paul's letter! How, for example, will they realize the greatness of God's power? Paul tells them at once where it is to be seen: God exerted this power 'when he raised Christ from the dead and seated him at his right hand in the heavenly realms, far above all rule and authority, power and dominion, and every name ...' (1:20-21). So they will understand the true extent of God's power by remembering what he did in raising and exalting Jesus. And as they ponder what Paul tells them about this, 'the Spirit of wisdom and revelation' will be making them wise and giving them understanding. As Paul tells Timothy: 'Reflect on what I am saying, for the Lord will give you insight into all this'.[66] On the one side is the believer's activity, carefully thinking over what the Bible says; on the other side is the Lord's activity, giving understanding by the Spirit of what the Bible says. God's word penetrates and takes hold of us by the Spirit and by faith.

And what is true of God's word is also true of his work: this too is embedded in us as his Spirit applies what our faith appropriates. Our status as God's adopted sons is a good example.[67] The New Testament

---

[65]   Alister McGrath, "Loving God with Heart and Mind: The Theological Foundations of Spirituality" in Timothy George & Alister McGrath (eds), *For All the Saints: Evangelical Theology and Christian Spirituality* (Louisville: Westminster John Knox, 2003), pp 13f (his italics).

[66]   2 Timothy 2:7.

[67]   The status the New Testament speaks of applied only to males in Roman society. In Christ this exclusive privilege applies to both males and females.

tells us that God sent his Son in order to make us his sons.[68] Along with everything else that his saving work has won for us, we enter this new status by faith.[69] By this same faith we also receive the promised gift of the Holy Spirit.[70] And the Spirit activates in us what our faith appropriates – by the Spirit we call upon God as our Father;[71] through the Spirit we know ourselves to be God's sons and heirs;[72] in the Spirit we wait to enter completed adoption through our resurrection.[73] In Christ, we are what we are by faith and by the work of the Spirit.

3.5.   Submitting to God's word and work

The second major dimension of a spirituality of faith is that it means *submitting* to God's word and work. As we have seen, true knowledge of God is both based on and generated by his word of revelation and his work of redemption.

3.5.1.   Submitting to God's word of revelation

So what does submitting to God's word of revelation involve? We can state the answer this way: true devotion necessarily involves devotion to the truth. It is not an independent, DIY activity. It is not an arena in which I exercise my democratic rights by forging my own personal spirituality. This flies in the face of quite a widespread view, as many discussions of this subject simply take it for granted that each of us has the right to develop whatever spirituality seems best for us. As a result, such claims as the following are often found:

> in spirituality, there are ultimately no 'rules of the game', even those laid down by the saints, but only 'tips of the trade' ...[74]

The reason we cannot hold such a view will become apparent if you come with me to a town in Northern Ireland. During 'the troubles', its Catholic priest and Presbyterian minister had a history of arguing so bitterly that they eventually reached an unspoken pact to avoid each

---

68 Galatians 4:4-5.
69 Galatians 3:26.
70 Galatians 3:14.
71 Galatians 4:6; Romans 8:15.
72 Romans 8:16-17.
73 Romans 8:23.
74 C.P.M. Jones, "Liturgy and Personal Devotion" in idem, G. Wainwright & E. Yarnold (eds), *The Study of Spirituality* (London: SPCK, 1986), p 6.

other. One morning they happened to round the same corner in opposite directions and bumped into each other. The priest spat out, 'Good morning, you son of the devil!' The minister calmly replied, 'Good morning, father.' And then all the old arguments began in earnest! Eventually the priest threw up his hands and said, 'Alright, alright, alright. You worship God in your way – and I'll worship him in his.' Definitely a low blow! – but the priest undeniably put his finger on something fundamental here. The fact is that our piety, our worship of God, must conform to *his* truth.

We are admitted into a relationship with God that he establishes, shapes, and sustains – and so our spirituality is to be governed by his work and word.

Think about the various trips NASA's space shuttle made to the orbiting space station. The astronauts who had just arrived were able to enter the station only because the space shuttle docked securely in the right place. What made that possible is that the connecting section of the shuttle had been configured to fit exactly into the space-station's docking bay. The shuttle is 'received' by the space-station and connected to it if and only if it conforms to what is there: the character and structure of the space-station determines whether the shuttle can be linked to it, and if so, how. So it is with true devotion. It takes its shape and substance from the work and word of God. It 'docks' with God's truth. Calvin has a clear statement of the basic principle at work here:

> there is a permanent relationship between faith and the Word... Therefore if faith turns away even in the slightest degree ... it does not keep its own nature, but becomes uncertain credulity and vague error of mind. The same Word is the basis whereby faith is supported and sustained; if it turns away from the Word, it falls. Therefore, take away the Word and no faith will then remain.[75]

True fellowship with God is possible, then, only on the basis of loyalty to his word. If we are to know God truly, we do not forge our own spirituality. Rather, our faith and our devotion must be shaped and governed by God's Word:

> faith grounded upon the Word is the mother of right prayer; hence, as

---

[75]   *Institutes*, III.ii.6 (I: pp 548-549).

soon as it is deflected from the Word, prayer must needs be corrupted.[76]

Thus our faith does not assert itself as some kind of creative power; it is responsive, it yields to the truth.

> [S]ince God's word is the foundation of faith, faith cannot wander to and fro, and lean to every word whatsoever: for every opinion conceived without the word of God, or against God's word, cannot be called true faith.[77]

The faith that appropriates God's word and work also submits to God's word and work. One of the chief marks of a spirituality of faith, therefore, is obedience:

> not only faith ... but all right knowledge of God is born of obedience.[78]

The faith that submits to God's word and work sets itself to be obedient to God's will. Our Teacher is also our Lord – and we cannot rightly call upon him if we do not do what he tells us.[79] So true devotion involves obeying the truth.[80] This attitude and practice is what Calvin aptly termed 'spiritual chastity'.[81] Elsewhere he expresses the principle this way:

> let us not take it into our heads either to seek out God anywhere else than in his Sacred Word, or to think anything about him that is not prompted by his Word, or to speak anything that is not taken from that Word.[82]

In every way – and especially in our spirituality – God's word must be our rule and guide:

---

[76]   Calvin, *Institutes*, III.xx.27 (2: pp 886-887).

[77]   Bullinger, *Decades*, 1: p 94.

[78]   Calvin, *Institutes*, I.vi.2 (1: pp 71-72).

[79]   John 13:13-14; Luke 6:46; cf. John 14:15, 21, 23; 15:10; 1 Peter 1:2; 1 John 2:3-5; 5:3.

[80]   Galatians 5:7; 1 Peter 1:22; cf. Psalm 119:8, 17, 34, 44, 56, 57, 60, 67, 88, 100, 101, 129, 134, 145, 167, 168.

[81]   In his *Commentary on the Book of Psalms*, IV: p 240 (commenting on Psalm 106:39):
He denominates as the *works of men* all the false worship which they devise without the Divine sanction; as if he should say, that the holiness, which is truly connected with the worship of God, comes from his word, and that all human inventions and admixtures in religion are profane ... For a strict adherence to the word of God constitutes spiritual chastity.

[82]   *Institutes*, I.xiii.21 (1: pp 145-147). Although the specific focus of his discussion at this point is the Trinity, the attitude expressed is one that Calvin clearly believes should characterize all Christian activity.

a true spiritual life cannot be modelled after our own insight but, rather, must be formed according to God's Word ... We see that the only true measure of diligent and godly exercises is not derived from worldly sources or from our imagination but is found in the Word of the Lord.[83]

It must also be the source of our piety as well as its yardstick. Peter Adam helpfully indicates what this will mean in practice:

Positively, Evangelical and Reformed Christians want to make the most of the 'means of grace' provided by God and explained in the Bible. Negatively, they do not want to be distracted, confused or misled by other religious practices that are not God-given.[84]

3.5.2. Submitting to God's work of redemption

We have now seen what submitting to God's word of revelation means for our spirituality. Now we must ask what submitting to God's work of redemption involves.

From this perspective, true devotion means living as someone who belongs to the Lord. His death not only won salvation for us; it also bought us and made us his. He not only redeems us, he also rules us. So the New Testament tells us that we belong to him because he died and was raised to be our Lord; that we are no longer our own, for we have been bought at a price; that we are no longer to live for ourselves but for him who died for us; that we have been purchased for God by the blood of the Lamb.[85] Submitting to God's saving work thus means submitting to his Son, joyfully accepting his authority and rule over us.

As Jesus Christ is God's assurance of the forgiveness of all our sins, so in the same way and with the same seriousness he is also God's mighty claim upon our entire life.[86]

Jesus Christ our Saviour is also our Lord – and Lord not only of our piety, but Lord of the whole of our lives. So there is to be no divorce

---

[83] Willem Teellinck [1579-1629], *The Path of True Godliness* (Classics of Reformed Spirituality; Grand Rapids: Baker Academic, 2003), p 89.

[84] Peter Adam, *Hearing God's Words*, p 149.

[85] Romans 14:7-9; 1 Corinthians 6:19-20; 7:23; 2 Corinthians 5:15; Revelation 5:9.

[86] Thesis 2, the Barmen Declaration [1934] in Eberhard Busch, *The Barmen Theses Then and Now* (Grand Rapids/Cambridge: Eerdmans, 2010), p 35.

between devotion and discipleship, no area of life that is not submitted to him.

There is another way of seeing all of this. This has to do with the fact that the Bible speaks of our salvation from two sides: it tells us what we have been saved from, and it also tells us what we have been saved for. To focus only on what we have been delivered out of without giving proper recognition to what we have been delivered into is to tell only half the story. Worse than that, it is to stray into what Dietrich Bonhoeffer famously called 'cheap grace':

> Cheap grace is grace without discipleship, grace without the cross ... Costly grace ... is the kingly rule of Christ ... it is the call of Jesus Christ at which the disciple leaves his nets and follows him.[87]

We have been saved by Jesus Christ in order to serve Jesus Christ, delivered out of eternal ruin into grateful discipleship and steadfast allegiance.

In New Testament terms, submitting to God's work of redemption by submitting to the rule of the Lord Jesus is to recognise that we are his slaves. This is implied when the New Testament says that we have been purchased by him.[88] It is also implied when the New Testament calls him our 'Lord', for that is the word for a slave-owner.[89] It is made explicit when the New Testament calls us his 'slaves'.[90] Before we became the slaves of Christ, we were locked in a terrible enslavement to sin. Our slavery to the Lord is a glorious antithesis to that grim slavery from which we have now been delivered.

> As soon as people are set free through Christ from slavery to sin, they enter a new, permanent slavery to Christ. Indeed, the one slavery is terminated precisely in order to allow the other slavery to begin.[91]

This new slavery is a grateful and joyful submission to Christ's rule. He is no domineering ruler, for he is gentle and humble, and his yoke is easy and

---

[87] Dietrich Bonhoeffer [1906-1945], *The Cost of Discipleship* (London: SCM, 1959), p 36.

[88] 1 Corinthians 6:20; 7:23; 2 Peter 2:1; Revelation 5:9; 14:3-4.

[89] So it is the word used at Ephesians 6:5, 9; Colossians 3:22; 4:1.

[90] Matthew 10:24-25; 25:14-30; Luke 17:7-10; John 13:15-16; 15:20; Romans 6:15-23; 1 Corinthians 7:22-23; Ephesians 6:6; Colossians 4:12; 1 Peter 2:16; Revelation 1:1; 2:20; 7:3; 19:2, 5; 22:3, 6.

[91] Murray J. Harris, *Slave of Christ: A New Testament Metaphor for Total Devotion to Christ*, NSBT 8 (Leicester: Apollos, 1999), p 153.

his burden light.[92] And we do not serve him in slavish fear.[93] As his slaves, we are truly free.[94] Indeed, from one perspective, when we become his we are no longer slaves but friends of Christ[95] and sons of God.[96]

In view of all this, why does the New Testament still speak of us as slaves? The point of this metaphor is to highlight our exclusive devotion to Jesus as Lord. As his slaves, we belong exclusively to him – and therefore do not yield to any other Lord. We 'hear Him alone, admire Him alone, love Him alone, follow Him alone'.[97] As his slaves, we belong entirely to him – and so yield our whole selves to him for the whole of our lives. This is what submitting to God's work of redemption means – true devotion means total discipleship.

3.6.   Conclusions and cautions

We have just seen that true devotion is a spirituality of *faith*, a piety that both *appropriates* and *submits* to God's word and work. This completes our analysis of the fact that true knowledge of God is *responsive*. Unfortunately, not all treatments of Christian spirituality – not even those from Evangelical publishers – are like this.

As a particular example will help to make the point clear, I have chosen *Invitation to a Journey: A Road Map for Spiritual Formation*, by M. Robert Mulholland, Jr.[98] This belongs to a series which IVP calls *formatio*. In 'integrating God's Word with spiritual practice', these volumes are said to

> follow the rich tradition of the church in the journey of spiritual formation. These books are not merely about being informed, but about being transformed by Christ and conformed to his image.[99]

This particular volume is helpful in various ways: it recognizes the primacy of grace and is alive to the danger of works-righteousness; it

---

92 Matthew 11:29-30.
93 Romans 8:15.
94 1 Peter 2:16.
95 John 15:15.
96 Galatians 4:7.
97 Huldreich Zwingli [1484-1531], *Commentary on True and False Religion*, edited by Samuel Macauley Jackson and Clarence Nevin Heller (Durham: Labyrinth, 1929/1981), p 92.
98 Downers Grove: IVP, 1993.
99 *Invitation*, p 1.

promotes a whole-of-life approach to spiritual growth as both personal and corporate; it sees conformity to Christ as the goal of Christian growth. But despite these and other pluses, there is a serious flaw running through the whole book. It does not submit to God's word in any consistent or systematic way. It makes use of the Bible – but it does not give the Bible a normative role in the way it develops an understanding of spiritual formation. It is not 'God's Word' but 'the rich tradition of the church' that calls the shots. This becomes evident in a number of ways.

When the author is discussing 'God's transforming work in our lives', he states a 'rule' which is based on what he has discovered 'in my own life and in reading the saints of the church'.[100] It is tradition and experience rather than the Bible that sets the rules to do with God's work! That this is not just a slip of the pen emerges later. When he comes to describe 'the classical pilgrimage toward wholeness in Christ' he simply adopts as a given a four-stage model that relies on 'the fathers and mothers of the Christian spiritual tradition'.[101] Here it is tradition and not the Bible that has the determinative role in establishing the shape and contents of our pilgrimage, that is, of our growth as Christians. Later again, when discussing spiritual disciplines, he gives the controlling voice to 'the mothers and fathers of the church'.[102] Even when he is discussing something as fundamental as our union with God, the Bible has at best a supporting role. The 'two greatest writers on this' are not (as we might have expected) the apostles Paul and John, but 'St. John of the Cross and St. Teresa of Avila'![103] Again, when it comes to 'the classical spiritual disciplines', it is not the Bible but 'Christian tradition' that determines what they are.[104] Most serious of all is the comment about 'the classical discipline of spiritual reading':

> Spiritual reading is the discipline of openness to encounter God through the writings of the mothers and fathers of the church, beginning with the Scriptures. In spiritual reading the text becomes a means of grace through which we encounter ... God ...[105]

---

[100] *Invitation*, pp 38-39.
[101] *Invitation*, pp 79, 82.
[102] *Invitation*, p 136.
[103] *Invitation*, p 98.
[104] *Invitation*, p 104.
[105] *Invitation*, pp 110-111.

Here the Bible is only one amongst many texts which can become a means of grace leading us to God. It is not in a class of its own, as the true and authoritative word of God; it is only *primus inter pares*, first among equals. The prophets and apostles are not unique bearers of revelation; they are submerged within the wider company of 'the mothers and fathers of the church'.

The approach taken by this book is not the path of true devotion, one crucial mark of which is

> a burning affection and insatiable thirst for the divine Word, and a persistent desire to hear, understand and practise it ...[106]

Very different is our response to 'the holy treatises of the fathers', which are acceptable only insofar as they are 'agreeing with the Scriptures':

> Neither do we think that we do them any wrong in this matter; seeing that they all, with one consent, will not have their writings matched with the canonical Scriptures ...[107]

In contrast to what we see in Mulholland's work, then, a properly responsive spirituality is characterised by a humble and thoroughgoing submission to the Bible.

We have been discussing the fact that true devotion is *responsive*. It is not autonomous or self-sustaining; it is generated by God and his gospel. We have seen that it is a *spirituality of grace*, drawn from us by the amazing love of God. We have considered how, as a *spirituality of faith*, it is meant to be shaped and governed by the work and word of God. We have examined briefly a modern discussion of spirituality from an Evangelical publisher, and noted ways in which it fails to be properly responsive to God's grace and truth. This brings us to the point where we can consider a second fundamental characteristic of a spirituality of the gospel: the fact that it is *paradoxical*.

---

[106] The Confession of the Spanish Congregation of London (1560/61), Chapter 19, in *Reformed Confessions of the 16th and 17th Centuries in English Translation*, compiled with Introductions by James T. Dennison, Jr., two volumes (Grand Rapids: Reformation Heritage, 2010), 2: p 394.

[107] The Second Helvetic Confession (1566), Chapter 2, in *Reformed Confessions*, 2: p 812.

4.   A Paradoxical Spirituality

True knowledge of God is *paradoxical.* I am referring to the fact that, consistently, we have to see it from two sides – it is not a case of either this or that, but of both this and that. *This is a direct consequence of the structure of God's saving work and our present position in it.* What does the Bible have to say about this?

The most helpful way of answering this question simply is to concentrate on a particular passage. Colossians 3:1-5 provides a good example of what we are looking for:

> Since, then, you have been raised with Christ, set your hearts on things above, where Christ is, seated at the right hand of God. Set your minds on things above, not on earthly things. For you died, and your life is now hidden with Christ in God. When Christ, who is your life, appears, then you also will appear with him in glory. Put to death, therefore, whatever belongs to your earthly nature ...

We begin by noting the three things the passage says about the Lord Jesus. The first is that he has been raised (v.1a); the second is that he is now seated at God's right hand (v.1b); and the third is that he is to be revealed (v.4) – he has been raised, he is reigning, and he will return.

Next, we need to note that we are involved in all three of these facts about him. The key word here is 'with': as believers, we have been raised *with* Christ (v.1a); our life is now hidden *with* him in God (v.3); and we are going to be revealed *with* him (v.4). What is this telling us? It means that our true identity is who we are in Christ. This identity was secured when, by believing the gospel, we died with Christ (v.3; cf. 2:20) and were raised with him.[1] It is now hidden from the world, but the day is coming when the truth about us will be made public.[2] We live in-between, with the conferring of our identity behind us and its revelation ahead of us. Our life in Christ is like a bridge suspended between two pylons – at one end is Jesus' death and resurrection, and at the other, his return.

---

[1]   See also Romans 6:3-11.
[2]   See also Romans 8:16-19; 1 John 3:1-2.

4.1. The paradox of time

What the passage is telling us here is part of the larger New Testament picture, which reveals that there are three dimensions – three tenses – in God's great salvation. According to the New Testament, salvation is past, present, and future: believers have been saved, are being saved, and will be saved.[3] So am I saved? The answer is both Yes and No! I have already been saved – but equally, I have not yet been saved. I live between salvation commenced and salvation completed. This does not mean that the future is uncertain, or that we are meant to be unsure about our destiny, for the salvation that has taken place already guarantees what is yet to come.[4] And God can be trusted to bring to completion the saving work he has already begun.[5]

These three aspects of salvation correspond to what the gospel says about Jesus as the one who died and was raised, who now reigns as Lord, and who will return from heaven. These great facts of salvation-history are not all on the same level, however. The decisive ones, those which occupy the centre of the gospel, are Jesus' death and resurrection.[6] In the same way, there is a decisive turning-point in the salvation-history of each believer. This is the past event of our entry into God's salvation, when we were united with Jesus' death and resurrection by believing the gospel. This is so decisive and far-reaching that the New Testament regards it as the end of one life and the beginning of a new one.[7] That is why it divides our lives between what was true 'once' and what is true 'now'.[8] This is the basis on which we are taught to put a stop to the way we used to live, and to adopt a new way of life.[9] We are to cease being what we used to be, for that is not what we are now. Instead, we are to become what we are, for we have

---

[3] See, for example, Ephesians 2:5, 8; 1 Corinthians 1:18; Romans 5:9-10.

[4] See especially Romans 5:9-10; 8:31-34.

[5] John 6:37-40; 1 Corinthians 1:8-9; Philippians 1:6; 1 Thessalonians 5:23-24.

[6] 1 Corinthians 15:3-4.

[7] John 3:3-8; 5:24; Romans 6:4-6; 7:4-6; 2 Corinthians 5:17; Galatians 5:19-25; Ephesians 2:1-5; 4:22-24; James 1:18; 1 Peter 1:3, 23; 2:2-3.

[8] Romans 7:6; 1 Corinthians 6:9-11; Ephesians 2:1-5, 11-13; 5:8; Colossians 1:21-22; 3:7-8; Titus 3:3-5; 1 Peter 2:9-10; cf. Galatians 1:13-16, 22-24.

[9] Romans 6:1-23; 1 Corinthians 5:7-8; Ephesians 4:17-24; 5:3-11; Colossians 3:5-17; Titus 3:1-8; 1 Peter 1:13–2:3.

taken on a new identity and begun a new life: 'you were once darkness, but now you are light in the Lord. Live as children of light ...'[10]

Our passage has connected us with Jesus' death and resurrection, his reign, and his return. By being bound up with him in this way, our faith is given a double focus. We are told that we are to look heavenward, with the risen and reigning Jesus as our focus (vv.1-2); we are also to look forward, with the returning Jesus as our focus (v.4). This is how we are to live in between resurrection and revelation[11] – between the past fact of our death and resurrection with Jesus and the future fact of our revelation with him when he returns. That Christian believing is bifocal in this way is also the point of Hebrews 11:1: 'Now faith is confidence in what we hope for and assurance about what we do not see.' In this in-between time faith means looking *above* to what we do not see – especially the reigning Jesus – and *ahead* to what we hope for – especially the returning Jesus.

4.2. The paradox of focus

According to the Colossians 3 passage, there is a second way in which we live in-between. The first is on the horizontal axis, with the contrast between the past, the present, and the future, while this second one is on the vertical axis. It concerns the contrast between the heavenly and earthly realms. Paul says that we are to seek (v.1) and to focus on (v.2) what is above. At first glance, this seems to confirm the accusation sometimes made against Christians that we are 'so heavenly-minded that we are of no earthly use.' But when we are reading the Bible, we should never be content with a glance! When we take another look at the passage, two things become clear. The first is this: the reason that we are to seek and set our minds on what is above is that this is where Christ is, seated at God's right hand (vv.1-2). In other words, what must capture our hearts and minds is the Lordship of Jesus. We are not fixated on 'heaven' in some abstract or escapist sense; we are focused on the exalted, reigning Jesus, the Lord of glory. Secondly, the 'earthly' reality we must steadily ignore (v.2) and resolutely put to death (v.5) is not our life in this world. What we must set ourselves against is ... sin! This becomes clear when Paul lists the kind of things that count as

---

[10]   Ephesians 5:8.

[11]   Cf. 1 Peter 1:3-9, 13.

'earthly': 'sexual immorality, impurity, lust, evil desires and greed ...' (v.5; cf. vv.8-9). Why must I kill these off? Because I have died and been raised, so that my life is hidden with Christ in God (vv.1a; 3). So I am to kill off that to which I have died – the earthly life I live now must be in line with my new, heavenly identity. I am to cease being what I used to be, and instead I am to live out what I am now. Because I am a new person, I am to live a new life.

Elsewhere in the New Testament I learn that I am to live out my life on earth as a citizen of heaven, as an exile who does not belong here.[12] My way of life is governed by where I belong (the heavenly realm) rather than where I live now (the earthly realm). This means being out of step with the world around me – something that the world does not understand and does not like.[13]

The key point of this Colossians 3 passage, whether I consider its horizontal or vertical axis, is that the Christian life is lived *in-between*. It is this that gives it its paradoxical character, because from every angle it is a two-sided reality. And what we have seen in this passage is true throughout the New Testament. We have noted a few examples along the way, but now we need to go further. How is our life in Christ depicted as a two-sided and thus paradoxical reality?

4.3. *Living in tension*

We begin by noting that this applies to what is said about the Lord Jesus himself. As we have seen, he is at the Father's side in heaven[14] – and yet he is also in our hearts by his Spirit.[15] He is both here indwelling us and also there interceding for us. And although he is with us here and now,[16] he is going to come for us on the last day, to take us to be with him.[17] And because we are united with him, we are caught up in this two-sided reality. We have been raised with him and seated with him in the

---

12 Philippians 3:20; Hebrews 11:13-16; 1 Peter 1:1, 17; 2:11.
13 See John 15:18-20; 16:2-3; 1 Peter 4:3-4, 12-16.
14 Colossians 3:1; note also Romans 8:34; Ephesians 1:20; Hebrews 10:12; 12:2; 1 Peter 3:21-22.
15 John 14:18-20, 23; Ephesians 3:16-17.
16 See, for example, Matthew 18:20; 28:20; Acts 18:9-10; 2 Timothy 4:17.
17 John 14:3; 17:24; Acts 1:11; 3:20-21; Philippians 3:20; 1 Thessalonians 4:16; 2 Thessalonians 1:7-10; 2:1, 8; Titus 2:13; Hebrews 9:28.

heavenly realms.[18] But we are also waiting for him to come from heaven, when at last we will be with him.[19] Through him, we confidently enter God's presence now[20] – but we will not stand before him until the last day.[21] We have clothed ourselves with Christ – but we are yet to bear his image.[22] We are united with him – he is the head of the body whose parts we are; he is the vine whose branches we are; he is the cornerstone of the building whose stones we are.[23] Yet there is a separation between us, such that in special ways and at special times he can come near, to be with us.[24] And the list could go on.

In this in-between time our participation in God's salvation is already real – but it is not yet final. As we have seen, salvation has three dimensions: we have been saved; we are being saved; and we will be saved. So in this era, our life in Christ means both having and not having, already rejoicing but still waiting, both being comforted by our security and warned against complacency. We still live in the conditions of the Old Age, the domain where the results of the first act of rebellion are still being felt. Both inside us, in our natures, and outside us, in our environment, the disintegrating processes set in train by this rebellion continue. And yet, at the same time, we already belong to the New Age, and the processes of reintegration are at work within us and between us. We are under renovation: God's saving purpose is being worked out in our lives.

The New Testament uses many images and ideas as it presents the two-sided character of our life in Christ. For example: we are already holy people, accepted and owned by God – but on the one hand, he is progressively making us holy, and on the other, we must continue to become holy, for without holiness no one will see the Lord.[25] Also, we have already been redeemed – and yet we are still waiting for our redemption.[26] We have already come to the heavenly city – but we are

---

[18]   Ephesians 1:20-23; 2:4-7.

[19]   1 Thessalonians 4:16-17; 2 Thessalonians 2:1.

[20]   See, for example, Ephesians 2:18; 3:12; Hebrews 4:16; 10:19-22.

[21]   See, for example, 2 Corinthians 4:14; 1 Thessalonians 3:13; Jude 24.

[22]   Galatians 3:27; 1 Corinthians 15:47-49; cf. Romans 13:14; Philippians 3:21.

[23]   Ephesians 1:22-23; 4:15-16; John 15:1-8; 1 Peter 2:4-6.

[24]   Acts 18:10; 23:11; Philippians 4:5; 2 Timothy 4:17; James 5:9; Revelation 3:20.

[25]   See, for example, 1 Corinthians 1:2; Hebrews 10:10; Ephesians 5:25-26; Hebrews 2:11; 2 Corinthians 7:1; 1 Thessalonians 4:3, 7; Hebrews 12:14; 1 Peter 1:14-15.

[26]   See, for example, Luke 21:27-28; Romans 3:24; 8:23; Galatians 4:5; Ephesians 1:7, 14; Colossians 1:14; Hebrews 9:12.

waiting for it to come.[27] The promised new creation is a reality in which we participate now – but it will only arrive on the last day.[28] And so the list could continue.

4.3.1. *Feelings and fellowship with God*

All of this has a direct bearing on our fellowship with God. Our knowledge of him is real, but it is not yet complete – and there are always two sides to this relationship so long as we are in this world. The apostle John presents the paradox like this: the Lord Jesus is in us and we are in him[29] – and yet he has gone to the Father.[30] In Paul, there are more than one hundred and sixty places in which he says that we are 'in Christ' or 'in the Lord'. He also says that Christ is in us[31] – and yet that he is in heaven,[32] from which he will come,[33] or be revealed,[34] or appear.[35] So as well as being in him, at present we are also away from him – and yet despite this, we have direct access to God and can confidently enter his presence.[36] In Matthew the disciples are told that they will not always have Jesus with them (26:11), and yet that he is with them always (28:20)! In this in-between time, our relationship with the Lord is thus uniquely paradoxical.

While this is especially true of our life in Christ, there is a two-sidedness about all life with God. So the Old Testament too is full of examples of the paradoxes in our knowledge of God. We find a striking instance in Psalm 63. In verse 1 David says,

> You, God, are my God, earnestly I seek you; I thirst for you, my whole being longs for you …

But then in verses 7 and 8 he says,

> Because you are my help, I sing in the shadow of your wings. I cling

---

[27] Hebrews 12:22-24; 13:14; cf. Philippians 3:20.
[28] 2 Corinthians 5:17; 2 Peter 3:10-13.
[29] John 14:20; 15:4-5; 1 John 2:24, 28; 3:24; 4:12-13, 15-16; 5:20.
[30] John 7:33; 13:1, 3; 14:12, 28; 16:5, 10, 17, 28; 17:5, 11, 13, 24.
[31] Romans 8:10; 2 Corinthians 13:5; Galatians 2:20; Ephesians 3:17; Colossians 1:27.
[32] Acts 3:21; Ephesians 1:20-23; Philippians 3:20; Colossians 3:1; 1 Thessalonians 1:10; 4:16; 2 Thessalonians 1:7; cf. Hebrews 1:3; 8:1; 10:12; 12:2; 1 Peter 3:22.
[33] 1 Corinthians 4:5; 15:23; 1 Thessalonians 2:19; 3:13; 4:15; 2 Thessalonians 1:10; 2:1, 8; cf. James 5:7-8; 1 Peter 1:13; 2 Peter 3:4; 1 John 2:28; Jude 14.
[34] 1 Corinthians 1:7; cf. 1 Peter 1:7, 13.
[35] 1 Timothy 6:14; 2 Timothy 4:1, 8; Titus 2:13; cf. Hebrews 9:28; 1 Peter 5:4; 1 John 3:2.
[36] 2 Corinthians 5:6; cf. Philippians 1:23; 1 Thessalonians 4:17; Ephesians 2:18; 3:12.

to you; your right hand upholds me.

In his experience, God is both present and absent, close at hand and yet distant. David seeks God, and God shelters David. He longs for God because he is dry and empty – and he sings of God because he is held and helped. But the transition from verse 1 to verses 7-8 does not signal a permanent breakthrough, such that a season of thirst gives way to endless song. David went through other periods of spiritual dryness and deep longing: he thirsted for God again.[37] And he experienced other precious times of balm in his barrenness, sheltered again under God's wings and held fast by his right hand.[38] His life with God continued to have two sides – all day long he praised God; all day long he went about mourning.[39] Day after day he had sorrow in his heart – and yet his heart rejoiced in God's salvation.[40]

What David experienced is also true of our life in Christ: our knowledge of God in this in-between time is marked by longing as well as satisfaction, distance as well as nearness. It is joyful, as his love becomes more real and precious to us;[41] it is painful, as he expresses his love for us by disciplining us.[42] In love he comforts us in our tears and strengthens us in our trials.[43] In love he also holds back, permitting us to stumble and requiring us to endure.[44] As a result, *our experience of God and his love is not uniformly linked to one particular feeling or emotion.* His love is both expressed and experienced in many ways. It therefore registers at many points on the spectrum of emotions. So there is no special God-feeling, different from all of our other feelings. This needs to be emphasized, for it is easy to go wrong at this point. If I treat a certain kind of feeling as my God-feeling, I am limiting God's involvement in my life only to those times when I have this feeling and to those places which give it to me. In practice, I will no longer see him as the God of my whole life. And I will spend lots of time and effort

---

[37] See Psalm 143:6; cf. Psalms 13:1; 22:1-2; 69:1-3. This was not true only of David, of course: see Psalm 42:1-2.

[38] Psalms 57:1; 18:35; 20:6; 138:7; 139:10.

[39] Psalms 35:28; 38:6.

[40] Psalm 13:2, 5.

[41] See, for example, Romans 5:1-5; Philippians 2:1-2.

[42] See, for example, 1 Corinthians 11:32; Hebrews 12:7-11; Revelation 3:19.

[43] See, for example, 1 Corinthians 1:8; 2 Corinthians 1:3-7, 21; 7:5-6; Philippians 2:27; 2 Thessalonians 3:3.

[44] See, for example, Luke 22:31-34; Revelation 2:10; 13:10; 14:12.

trying to bring on this special feeling and to hang onto it for as long as possible. Sadly, this means that in the end I will come to resemble a 'junkie', always seeking the next 'God-hit'. Contrast this with the approach we see in the Psalms, for example: 'my hope is in you all day long ... I will extol the Lord at all times ... Trust in him at all times ... My mouth is filled with your praise, declaring your splendour all day long... I will sing to the Lord all my life ...'[45] God does not belong only to some times and some places and some emotions, for he is the God of the whole day and of my whole life. I am meant to be responding to him and relating to him through all of the ups and downs and ins and outs that make up my life.

4.4. The duality of death and life

What does all of this mean for us? What is life in Christ actually like? It takes a whole New Testament to answer this question, so we have room to consider only some of its most fundamental features. Perhaps the most basic of all is the fact that both life and death are at work in us. At one level, this is simply a reflection of our mortality. Even though the Spirit of him who raised Jesus from death is imparting life to us, we still experience the gradual decaying of body and mind as we move steadily closer to our inevitable death – inwardly we are being renewed day by day, but outwardly we are wasting away.[46] But there is a more fundamental reason why this is our experience: our lives bear the imprint of Jesus' death and resurrection.[47]

The Christian life is all about death: it bears the mark of the cross. The death of Jesus marks the beginning of our Christian life, for that is when we die *with* him.[48] But it also marks the whole of our life in Christ, for we are to continue dying *with* him and *for* him every day.[49]

The cross is laid on every Christian... When Christ calls a man, he

---

[45] Psalms 25:5; 34:1; 62:8; 71:8; 104:33.
[46] Romans 8:10-11, 23; 2 Corinthians 4:16; 5:4-5; Colossians 3:10.
[47] Romans 6:1-11; 2 Corinthians 4:10; Philippians 3:10; Colossians 2:20; 3:1.
[48] See, for example, Romans 6:3-8; 2 Corinthians 5:14; Galatians 2:20; 6:14; Colossians 2:20; 3:3.
[49] See, for example, Mark 8:34-35; 10:35-45; Luke 14:25-33; John 12:24-26; Acts 20:23-24; Philippians 2:19-22, 29-30; Hebrews 10:32-34; 13:12-13; 1 Peter 2:20-21; 4:12-16; Revelation 2:1-3, 8-10.

bids him come and die... Discipleship means allegiance to the suffering Christ...[50]

This is a necessary mark of authentic discipleship, for Jesus made it clear that there is no way of following him that bypasses the cross: 'whoever does not carry their cross and follow me cannot be my disciple'.[51] This happens in two ways: we carry the cross passively, in the sufferings we endure for his sake,[52] and actively, in the sacrifices we make for his sake.[53] Neither of these is meritorious, for in both of them we are simply following Jesus. This means walking in the way of the cross: 'Whoever wants to be my disciple must deny themselves and take up their cross daily and follow me'.[54] This is not just for a small spiritual elite; it is for every disciple ('whoever'). And it is not just for exceptional moments; it applies every day ('daily'). This is the pattern of the disciple's life.

> To follow the way of the cross means to show the same sacrificial love that Jesus showed when he went to the cross. The same self-denial. The same submission to God. The same willingness to suffer. The same service of others.[55]

The whole of the Christian life is cross-shaped. Therefore, if 'we desire to be Christians, we must not seek to be free from the cross ...'[56]

Being Christian is all about life as well as death: the Christian life is also shaped by the resurrection. In one sense, this is reserved for the last day: our final destiny is to be raised *like* Jesus.[57] But in another

---

[50] Bonhoeffer, *The Cost of Discipleship*, pp 79, 80.

[51] Luke 14:27.

[52] See, for example, Matthew 5:10-12; Romans 8:17; 2 Corinthians 1:5; Philippians 1:29; 1 Thessalonians 1:6-7; 2:14-15; 3:3-4; 2 Thessalonians 1:4-5; 2 Timothy 2:3, 8-9; Hebrews 10:32-34; 13:12-13; 1 Peter 4:13; Revelation 1:9; 2:3; 7:14.

[53] See, for example, Mark 10:28-30; Luke 14:25-27, 33; Philippians 2:30; 2 Timothy 1:7-8; Hebrews 11:24-26.

[54] Luke 9:23.

[55] Tim Chester, *The Ordinary Hero: Living the Cross and Resurrection* (Nottingham: IVP, 2009), p 50.

[56] John Calvin, *The Gospel according to St John 11-21 and the First Epistle of John* (Calvin's New Testament Commentaries; Grand Rapids: Eerdmans, 1959 [1553]), p 133 (on John 16:33).

[57] 1 Corinthians 6:13b-14; 15:20-26, 42-49; 2 Corinthians 4:14; Philippians 3:20-21; Colossians 1:18; 1 Thessalonians 4:14-16; Revelation 1:5.

sense, we have already been raised *with* him into new life.[58] So resurrection is not just our future destiny; it is also our present position. Like our cross-bearing, this too is a reality to be renewed every day – daily, we are to say No to sin and Yes to God as people who have been brought out of death and into life.[59] So while we share in Jesus' sufferings and death, we also share in his victory and his reign – every day as well as at the End.

4.4.1. *Suffering and glory*

One of the ways the New Testament expresses this duality of death-and-life is through the contrast between *suffering and glory*. For the Lord Jesus, suffering was followed by glory.[60] The cross and all of its horrors gave way to the glories of the resurrection – a pattern that is also expressed in other ways in the New Testament. In Hebrews 12:2, for example, we read this of Jesus: 'For the joy set before him he endured the cross, scorning its shame, and sat down at the right hand of the throne of God.' First there was the cross and its shame; then there was his enthronement and its joy.

What is true of the Lord is also true of the believer: we share in his sufferings now in order that we may also share in his glory, the glory that is yet to be revealed.[61] It is not that suffering is the price we have to pay for glory, as though heavenly glory is our reward for earthly trials. Rather, as for Jesus, so for us, the only path to glory passes through suffering: 'We must go through many hardships to enter the kingdom of God'.[62]

In this in-between time, there is also a sense in which suffering and glory are intertwined, so that our life in Christ is marked by both at the same time. We find a good example in what John tells the seven churches: he shares with them 'the suffering and kingdom and patient endurance that are ours in Jesus'.[63] Although the kingdom would not come in its fullness until the End,[64] they were participating in it already.[65]

---

[58] Romans 6:10-11; Ephesians 2:6; Colossians 2:12-13; 3:1; 1 Peter 1:3.

[59] Romans 6:1-4, 11-13; cf. John 5:24; Ephesians 2:4-5.

[60] See, for example, Luke 24:26; Hebrews 2:9-10; 1 Peter 1:11, 18-21.

[61] Romans 8:17-18; cf. also Romans 5:2-3; 2 Corinthians 4:17; 1 Peter 4:13; 4:19-5:1; 5:10; James 1:12; Revelation 2:9-10.

[62] Acts 14:22.

[63] Revelation 1:9.

[64] Revelation 11:15-18.

The glory of the kingdom was a present reality as well as a future certainty. That is why John and his churches responded to their sufferings with patient endurance. They persevered because their sufferings were not the whole story – they knew both the cross and the crown, both suffering and glory.

4.4.2. Weakness and power

The duality of death-and-life is also seen in the New Testament contrast between *weakness and power*. This is seen first in the Lord Jesus: 'he was crucified in weakness, yet he lives by God's power'.[66] For him, the weakness that marked everything to do with his crucifixion was followed by the power of his resurrection. The same transition will also be seen in us. The weakness of our present form of embodiment is to be replaced by resurrection power.[67] So, speaking of the body, Paul says, 'it is sown in weakness, it is raised in power'.[68] Yet this is not just reserved for the future, for the power of the coming new age of resurrection is already at work in us. As a result, our life in Christ is marked by power-in-weakness.

This paradoxical pattern is evident in Paul's life and ministry. His message concerned Jesus Christ crucified [weakness] and risen [power]. His ministry had the same components: on one side was his own weakness; on the other side was the Spirit's power.[69] Neither of these excluded or replaced the other – Paul remained weak while the Spirit continued displaying his power. This pattern lies at the heart of Paul's understanding of apostolic ministry: he lived and served in this power-in-weakness.[70] This was not something of his own devising; he had learned it in a very dramatic and painful experience.[71] The Lord responded to his request to be delivered from his 'stake' in the flesh with the following assurance: 'My grace is sufficient for you, for my power is made perfect in weakness'.[72] We learn of these events only because Paul was forced to defend this pattern of ministry in his

---

[65]   Revelation 1:6; 5:10.
[66]   2 Corinthians 13:4.
[67]   1 Corinthians 6:14; Philippians 3:21.
[68]   1 Corinthians 15:43.
[69]   1 Corinthians 2:1-5.
[70]   1 Corinthians 4:9-13, 20-21; 2 Corinthians 4:7-12; 6:3-10; 11:23-33.
[71]   2 Corinthians 12:7-8.
[72]   2 Corinthians 12:9a.

dealings with the church in Corinth. The Corinthians were not tolerant of his weaknesses, and much preferred the strengths displayed by a group of 'super-apostles'.[73] In the face of this very different view of apostolic service, Paul insisted:

> I will boast all the more gladly about my weaknesses, so that Christ's power may rest on me. That is why, for Christ's sake, I delight in weaknesses, in insults, in hardships, in persecutions, in difficulties. For when I am weak, then I am strong.[74]

As Paul saw it, there was an important principle at stake here. The weaknesses that were so apparent in him made it clear that the powerful impact of his ministry of the gospel was not due to him: 'we have this treasure in jars of clay to show that this all-surpassing power is from God and not from us'.[75]

This paradoxical blend of weakness and power, suffering and strength, is not unique to Paul. The Philippians are to follow his example, as he sets himself to know the power of Jesus' resurrection and also to share in his sufferings.[76] He prays that the Colossians will be strengthened 'with all power according to his glorious might so that [they] may have great endurance and patience' in the face of their hardships and weaknesses.[77] He commends the Thessalonians for their perseverance and faith in the face of persecution and trials and also prays that they might experience God's power.[78] He urges Timothy to join him in suffering for the gospel in view of the fact that the Spirit gives us power.[79] Peter reminds his readers that they are shielded by God's power even though they are also suffering trials.[80] Such passages make it clear that power-in-weakness lies at the heart of authentically Christian life and service. In this in-between time, we experience God's power not so much in being kept *from* hardships and weaknesses but in being kept *in* them. His power is seen most often in our perseverance, when we triumph not by rising above our trials but by staying true in them.

---

[73] 2 Corinthians 10:1–13:10.
[74] 2 Corinthians 12:9b-10.
[75] 2 Corinthians 4:7.
[76] Philippians 3:10, 17.
[77] Colossians 1:11.
[78] 2 Thessalonians 1:4, 11; 2:16-17.
[79] 2 Timothy 1:7-8.
[80] 1 Peter 1:5-6.

4.4.3. Grief and Joy

Another way we meet this death-and-life pattern in the New Testament is in the combination of *grief and joy*. Even in the midst of suffering and grief, we experience joy.[81] From one perspective, this joy is an anticipation of the joys that await us at the End. We are 'joyful in hope' and therefore 'patient in affliction'.[82] From another perspective, joy is a sign of the Spirit's presence and power. So the Thessalonians 'welcomed the message in the midst of severe suffering with the joy given by the Holy Spirit'.[83] Our joy reflects the fact that we are never abandoned or alone, even in the midst of the most severe trials. As Samuel Rutherford observed:

> Christ and His cross are not separable in this life; howbeit Christ and His cross part at heaven's door, for there is no house-room for crosses in heaven. One tear, one sigh, one sad heart, one fear, one loss, one thought of trouble, cannot find lodging there: they are but the marks of our Lord Jesus down in this wide inn, and stormy country, on this side of death... I think it a sweet thing that Christ saith of my cross, 'Half mine;' and that He divideth these sufferings with me, and taketh the larger share to Himself ...[84]

Perhaps the clearest and simplest way of speaking about this paradoxical two-sidedness of life in Christ comes from Jesus himself:

> I have told you these things so that in me you may have peace. In this world you will have trouble.[85]

So we have peace with God – but we live in a war-zone. Also, we are more than conquerors through him who loved us – but we must fight daily against sin, the world, and the devil.[86] We are likely to suffer hardships of many kinds[87] – failure (our own and other people's), opposition, and possibly even martyrdom – but the Lord will rescue us

---

[81] See, for example, Matthew 5:11-12; Acts 5:41; Romans 5:1-5; James 1:2; 1 Peter 1:6.

[82] Romans 12:12.

[83] 1 Thessalonians 1:6.

[84] Samuel Rutherford [1600-1661] in Hamilton Smith (ed.), *Gleanings from the Past: Extracts from the Letters of Samuel Rutherford* (London: The Central Bible Truth Depot, n.d.), pp 109-10.

[85] John 16:33.

[86] See, for example, Ephesians 6:10-18; 1 Timothy 6:12; 2 Timothy 4:7; James 4:4; Hebrews 12:4; 1 Peter 2:11; 5:8-9.

[87] See, for example, Mark 13:5-13; Acts 14:22; 2 Timothy 3:10-13.

from every evil and save us into his heavenly kingdom.[88] We must stand firm, holding fast to what we have[89] – but we must also press on towards the prize that is waiting for us.[90] We are running a marathon – and we must not grow weary and give up; we must persevere until the end.[91] This two-sided character of Christian life and service is expressed memorably by Paul:

> As servants of God, we commend ourselves in every way: in great endurance; in troubles, hardships and distresses; in beatings, imprisonments and riots; in hard work, sleepless nights and hunger ... dying, and yet we live on; beaten, and yet not killed; sorrowful, yet always rejoicing; poor, yet making many rich; having nothing, and yet possessing everything.[92]

This moving testimony serves to remind us that a crucial mark of authentic spirituality is that it is robust enough to deal realistically with suffering.[93]

4.5. Already and not yet

Where does all of this lead us? The crucial point to emerge from our discussion is that true devotion is a spirituality of *already and not yet*. We live between real participation in the great salvation God has already won and complete participation when he makes that salvation full and final. The powers of the promised new age are already at work in the present era even though that new age has not yet come in its fullness. So both the new and the old are intertwined in this in-between time. As

---

[88] 2 Timothy 4:18; cf. 1 Corinthians 1:8; 2 Peter 2:5-9.

[89] See, for example, 1 Corinthians 15:58; Galatians 5:1; Philippians 1:27; Colossians 1:23; 2 Thessalonians 2:15; 1 Timothy 1:18-19; Titus 1:9; 1 Peter 5:12; 1 John 2:24; 2 John 9; Revelation 2:25; 3:3, 11.

[90] See, for example, 1 Corinthians 9:24-25; Philippians 3:12-14; 2 Timothy 4:8; Hebrews 10:35-36; James 1:12; Revelation 2:10.

[91] See, for example, Mark 13:13; Acts 20:24; Galatians 6:9; 2 Thessalonians 3:5; 2 Timothy 4:5-8; Hebrews 6:11-12; 12:1-3; Revelation 2:3.

[92] 2 Corinthians 6:4-5, 9-10; cf. also 2 Corinthians 4:8-9: 'We are hard-pressed on every side, but not crushed; perplexed, but not in despair; persecuted, but not abandoned; struck down, but not destroyed'.

[93] See the chapter entitled "Hard Gaining: The Discipline of Endurance" in J.I. Packer, *A Passion for Holiness* (Cambridge: Crossway, 1992), pp 239-71.

a result, our relationship with God in the present is paradoxical and two-sided: as we have seen, it is characterized by a great many dualities.

4.6.   Keeping the right balance

Why have we given this such emphasis? For two reasons. First, because some discussions of spirituality give the impression that they are chafing under the constraints of life in this in-between time and are attempting to break out of them. In effect, spirituality becomes the quest to experience the End ahead of time. But this can never be right. Yes, it is entirely right to seek everything God has to give us at present – but this does not include deliverance from the way things are now. There is no spiritual practice or discipline capable of taking us to the End early. Deep and unbroken intimacy with God is what lies ahead of us, in the age to come.[94] In the here and now there is no way of escaping the two-sidedness that characterizes our experience of God. So long as we are in the body we are away from the Lord[95] – and it is not the role of spirituality to bridge that gap.

Secondly, we have given such emphasis to the two-sided, paradoxical character of our life in Christ because problems arise whenever one side is highlighted at the expense of the other. We find an example in a modern study of Christian spirituality in which the author argues that in addition to being our King, 'God also desires to be our friend, our companion, our confidant'.[96] There is nothing intrinsically wrong with using the image of friendship in this way, for the Bible too uses it. It must be said, however, that it does not use it very often.[97] Nor does the Bible endorse all the ways in which this image can be used. The study we have just mentioned employs the friendship-analogy as follows:

> A relationship with God has many similarities to friendship on the human plane, involving some form of give-and-take communication.[98]

---

[94]   1 Corinthians 13:12; Revelation 21:3; 22:4.
[95]   2 Corinthians 5:6.
[96]   Klaus Issler, *Wasting Time with God: A Christian Spirituality of Friendship with God* (Downers Grove: IVP, 2001), p 21 (original in italics).
[97]   See Job 29:4; Isaiah 41:8; John 15:13-15; James 2:23; cf. Jeremiah 3:4; James 4:4.
[98]   *Wasting Time*, p 153.

> Cultivating a personal relationship requires a dynamic, experiential communication between two persons ...[99]

On this basis the author makes an important claim: 'When we are ready to listen, God the Spirit speaks to us ...'[100] He portrays God as engaging us in conversation, just the way that friends do. This forms a significant part of the author's understanding of the way our relationship with God works.[101]

> If we wish to deepen our relationship with God, we must grow in our ability to hear God's direct voice to us ... as it comes from within ...[102]

There is a problem here, for the Bible itself does not use the friendship idea this way.[103] This underlines the importance of taking great care with how we use it, so that we do not claim more than we should.[104] While there may well be some similarities, we must also note the ways in which our relationship with the Lord differs from a normal human friendship. Not to do so will almost certainly mean developing inappropriate expectations that cannot be met. That this point needs to be made can be seen in passages like this:

> Is it not our deepest longing to experience the kind of friendship with God portrayed in the Gospels, of walking with Jesus ...?[105]

The author wants to assure his readers that this longing can and will be met in our present experience. But this is a claim we must dispute. It does not fit with what we have learned in this chapter about the two-sided, in-between character of our relationship with God. Yes, the Lord is with us – but not in exactly the same way he was with his disciples. That way of being present came to an end when he left them to go to the Father (note especially Luke 24:44; John 16:4-7). They would no longer have him walking and talking with them as he did during his ministry.

---

[99] *Wasting Time*, p 181.

[100] *Wasting Time*, p 181.

[101] This is the theme of his sixth chapter (*Wasting Time*, pp 151-82).

[102] *Wasting Time*, p 180.

[103] There are other significant problems with this view, as we will see in Chapter 7.

[104] That the idea can be used in ways that are not at variance with Scripture is illustrated in the works of J.C. Ryle, who often refers to the Lord Jesus as our "Friend". However, he is careful not to go beyond what the Bible says about this relationship. See especially his chapter, "The Best Friend" in *Practical Religion* (London: James Clarke, 1959 [1878]), pp 221-32.

[105] *Wasting Time*, p 152.

There is therefore no way in which we can recreate that experience. In addition, we must accept the fact that while we are in the body, we are away from the Lord.[106] It is not now, but only at the End, that we will know him face-to-face.[107]

We have now considered some of the primary ways in which true knowledge of God is *paradoxical*. Our life in the present is shaped by both the past and the future, by both the 'already' of God's saving work and also its 'not yet'. We have seen that knowing the Lord means focusing above us and also ahead of us. He is present with us – but we are waiting for him. We are living on earth as citizens of heaven. Our relationship with him involves both life and death, suffering and glory, weakness and power, grief and joy. This brings us to the point where we can explore a third characteristic of true devotion: the fact that it is *relational*. What kind of relationship with God is opened for us by the gospel?

---

[106] 2 Corinthians 5:6.
[107] 1 Corinthians 13:12.

5. A Relational Spirituality

True knowledge of God is *relational*. It is a personal knowing, a relationship between persons. *This is a direct consequence of the character of God.* God's nature as Trinity consists of persons in eternal mutual relationship, knowing and being known, loving and being loved, indwelling and being indwelt. So God is internally relational, with Father, Son, and Spirit in perfect relationship with each other. And because we are made to image God,[1] we are made for relationship, with each other and also with God. So the Bible begins with God relating to the first human beings.[2] It ends with God coming to be fully present with his redeemed people, who now see his face.[3] Throughout, the Bible's focus is how God creates and sustains real relationship between himself and his people.

At one level, there is no great surprise in the fact that God relates to us – this is what we were made for. But the way he does this is simply staggering. Consider what the Lord Jesus prayed for us:

> I pray ... for those who will believe in me through their [sc., the apostles'] message, that all of them may be one, Father, just as you are in me and I am in you. May they also be in us so that the world may believe that you have sent me. I have given them the glory that you gave me, that they may be one as we are one – I in them and you in me – so that they may be brought to complete unity... I have made you known to them, and will continue to make you known in order that the love you have for me may be in them and that I myself may be in them.[4]

This tells us that God binds us to himself in a deep personal relationship. This relationship is like those that are internal to him. Just as the Father is in the Son and the Son is in the Father, so the Son is in us and we are in God. Nothing less than the love that the Father has for the Son is in us, and the glory the Father gave the Son has been given to us. It is as though the inner life of the Triune God is so rich that it spills over into his relationship with us. We are caught up in the most basic and fundamental of all

---

[1]   Genesis 1:26-27.
[2]   Genesis 1:28-30; 2:15-22; 3:8-9.
[3]   Revelation 21:3; 22:4.
[4]   John 17:20-23, 26.

realities: the relationships that make God who he is. To have a part in something so good, so rich, and so real is an immense privilege. That is why, as we saw when considering the spirituality of grace, those who know God will always be marked by an amazed and humble gratitude.[5]

Since the God we know is internally relational, three Persons in perfect permanent relationship, knowing him cannot be anything less than relational. But what does this actually mean? What kind of relationship do we have with God? What does it means to 'know' God? It takes an entire Bible to answer these questions, so we cannot hope to do them justice in one brief chapter! What we are going to do is to focus on three fundamental points the Bible makes.

5.1.   A personal relationship

The first is that knowledge of God is personal – as we have just seen, it is a real personal knowing.[6] Hence, in the Bible 'knowing' is followed by 'whom' as well as by 'that'. The Bible focuses our attention on who we know as well as on what we know.[7] But how are these two related – what is the connection between the 'who' and the 'what', the personal and the propositional?

The first thing we need to say is that, biblically, the two cannot be separated. Consider Colossians 2:6-7:

> just as you received Christ Jesus as Lord, continue to live your lives in him, rooted and built up in him, strengthened in the faith as you were taught ...

This tells us that Christian life begins and continues as a twofold relationship to the Lord and to his word: it is 'in him' and 'in the faith'. Our commitment is not to either Jesus or the gospel, but to both Jesus and the gospel. The Lord I know is the Jesus of the gospel: it is the gospel that brings us together. We see this from the other side in Galatians 1:6:

> I am astonished that you are so quickly deserting the one who called

---

[5]   See, for example, Psalms 9:1-2, 7-11; 34:1-9; 40:1-5, 9-10; 71:14-24; 95:1-7; 116:1-19.

[6]   John 14:7-9; 16:3; 17:3; 1 Corinthians 1:21; Galatians 4:8-9; Philippians 3:10; 1 Thessalonians 4:5; 2 Thessalonians 1:8; Titus 1:16; 2 Peter 1:2-3, 8; 2:20; 3:18; 1 John 2:3-4, 13-14; 4:7-8; 5:20.

[7]   See, for example, Psalms 36:10; 46:10; Ezekiel 37:12-14; John 17:3, 25; Galatians 4:8-9; Philippians 3:10; 2 Timothy 1:12; 1 John 5:20.

you to live in the grace of Christ and are turning to a different gospel ...

To abandon the gospel is to desert God – which clearly means that to hold fast to him we must hold fast to the gospel. Believing the gospel and knowing God are thus like two sides of the same coin:

see that what you heard from the beginning remains in you. If it does, you also will remain in the Son and in the Father.[8]

It is the 'what' of revelation that makes the 'who' of relationship possible. Yes, we can know God – but only in the way he has made himself known.

God does not will to be known in any way other than how He has revealed Himself – in His Word and through His Son.[9]

These two are closely bound together – just as it is not possible to come to the Father except through the Son,[10] so it is not possible to come to the Son except through the gospel.[11] Calvin makes the point this way:

the true knowledge of Christ [is] if we receive him as he is offered by the Father: namely, clothed with his gospel. For just as he has been appointed as the goal of our faith, so we cannot take the right road to him unless the gospel goes before us.[12]

It is only the word that enables us to know the Lord; it is only the gospel that leads faith to its goal. But not only does it bring me to him, the gospel also brings him to me. We can see this by considering Paul's prayer that 'Christ may dwell in our hearts through faith'.[13] In expounding this passage, Calvin asks,

How may this be? For we cannot mount up so high. He is in the glory of heaven, and we are grovelling here in the world ... Seeing then that there is so long a distance between him and us, how can he dwell in us?[14]

His answer is as follows:

the gospel is of such power as to unite us to God's Son, at least

---

8   1 John 2:24.
9   Melanchthon, *Loci*, p 372.
10   See, for example, Matthew 11:27; John 8:19; 14:6; 2 Corinthians 4:4, 6; 1 John 2:23.
11   See, for example, John 17:20; Romans 10:13-17; Ephesians 1:12-13; Colossians 1:5-7; 2:6-7; 1 John 2:24; 2 John 9.
12   *Institutes*, III.ii.6 (1: pp 548-549).
13   Ephesians 3:17.
14   Calvin, *Ephesians*, p 289.

provided that we receive it by faith ... Jesus Christ dwells in us by faith and ... if we receive him as he offers himself with all his grace in the gospel, it is ... in order that he should dwell in us by the power of his Holy Spirit... It is true that he really comes down to us by his Word ...[15]

By the Spirit and through faith we are united to Christ through the gospel. It is the gospel that that brings him to me – just as it is the gospel that takes me to him. So whichever way we look at it, our knowledge of God-in-Christ is bound up with our knowledge of his word. As we saw in Chapter 3, true devotion means devotion to the truth.

So knowing *that* and knowing *who* cannot be separated – but nor can they be equated. Knowing about God is not the same as knowing him. I can accept the truth of propositions about God without knowing the God of whom they speak. That is the 'faith' of the demons.[16] Biblical faith, by contrast, is not only a believing *that*; it is also a believing *in*.[17] It involves both conviction and commitment, both assent (*assensus*) and trust (*fiducia*). It is more than a response to truth; it is engaging with a Person. Christian commitment is thus not ideological. Christians are not captivated by a system of ideas, in love with a body of doctrine. Christian spirituality is relational. The convictions that are precious to us matter precisely because they are the means by which we know and love the person of the Lord Jesus.

Because true knowledge of God is personal, it is also direct. God has no grandchildren! I cannot piggyback on someone else's knowledge of God – if I do not know him for myself, I do not know him. This means that there is no one who can go to God for me, so that I don't need to come to him myself. God has provided the only mediator I need, the only mediator I can have: in him and through faith in him we may approach God with freedom and confidence.[18]

This is the great privilege we have under the new covenant: 'they will all know me, from the least of them to the greatest'.[19] And this is one of the obvious differences between the old and new covenants:

---

[15]   *Ephesians*, pp 289-91.
[16]   James 2:19.
[17]   See, for example, John 3:16, 18; 11:25-27; 20:31; 1 John 5:1, 5, 10, 13.
[18]   Ephesians 3:12; cf. Ephesians 2:18; 1 Timothy 2:5-6; Hebrews 4:14-16; 7:25; 10:19-22; 1 Peter 3:18.
[19]   Jeremiah 31:34.

The kingdom of Christ ... interposes no sacrificial tribe or class between God and man ... Each individual member holds personal communion with the Divine Head. To Him immediately he is responsible, and from Him directly he obtains pardon and draws strength.[20]

There is no priesthood under the new covenant because all believers have priestly status, with direct access to God-in-Christ.[21] Using this privilege by coming to God is what lies at the heart of true devotion.[22]

This personal knowledge of God means a spirituality of faith, hope, and love. These are the primary ways in which the Bible speaks about our present relationship with God.[23]

5.2.   A relationship of faith

On our side, it is a relationship anchored in our faith: the God we know is the God in whom we believe.[24] As we have seen, this means both conviction (believing that) and commitment (believing in), responding both to God's truth and to God's Person. The basis of this faith is the words of God the Revealer and the works of God the Redeemer. We can trust him because he has made himself known by his words and works.

5.2.1.   Faith and faithfulness

Three important things the Bible says about faith are relevant here. The first is the close connection between faith and faithfulness. In the New Testament, both are represented by the same Greek word. This points to the fact that there is considerable overlap in their meaning. Indeed, from one perspective, faith is faithfulness.[25] So there is a close connection between faith and loyalty. Faith is not a vague credulity or a

---

[20]   J.B. Lightfoot [1828-1889], "The Christian Ministry" in *Saint Paul's Epistle to the Philippians* (Grand Rapids: Zondervan, 1953), p 182.

[21]   Hebrews 10:19-20; 1 Peter 2:5, 9; Revelation 1:6; 5:10; 20:6.

[22]   Psalms 5:7; 73:28; 95:1-2; 100:2; Hebrews 4:16; 7:19, 25; 10:22; James 4:8.

[23]   Note Romans 5:2-5; 1 Corinthians 13:13; Galatians 5:5-6; 1 Thessalonians 1:3; 5:8; 1 Peter 1:3-8.

[24]   See, for example, John 3:16, 18, 36; 6:29, 35; 14:1; Acts 10:43; 11:17; 16:31; 20:21; 26:18; Romans 4:17, 24; 10:11, 14; Galatians 2:20; Ephesians 1:15; 3:12; Philippians 1:29; Colossians 1:4; 2:5; 1 Timothy 1:16; Titus 3:8; Philemon 5; Hebrews 6:1; 1 Peter 1:8, 21; 1 John 5:10, 13.

[25]   Note Ephesians 1:1; Colossians 1:2.

spasmodic religious impulse; it is loyal trust. Those who believe are those who stay true, holding fast to God and his word.[26] As we have seen, they practice 'spiritual chastity'.

> Faith leans upon one God, clings to One, trusts in One, hopes on One, flies to One for refuge, knows for certain that it will find with One everything that it needs.[27]

Secondly, faith and obedience are closely connected. So Paul refers to the 'obedience of faith'.[28] And instead of referring to believing the gospel, the New Testament can speak of obeying it.[29] Faith is not a meritorious initiative or some autonomous religious energy; it 'docks' with the truth of the gospel. Thirdly, there is a strong link between faith and perseverance. Those who believe are steadfast, those who stay firm and keep on keeping on.[30] Faith is not fickle or flagging, but resolute and tenacious – not like the changing moods of the uncommitted, but like the pledged loyalty of a lifelong marriage.

Where does faith get this staying power? It does not come from within faith itself, as though it is self-sustaining and self-sufficient. As we saw in Chapter 3, faith is receptive and responsive. It does not stand alone, but rests on a foundation. More than that, it draws its life from its base – it is a fruit, dependent on the root:

> faith needs the Word as much as fruit needs the living root of a tree... faith vanishes unless it is supported by the Word.[31]

It persists and grows only so long as it is directed to God's words and works, and especially to God's Son. In all of this it relies upon God's Spirit, who goes on activating faith within us as we go on adhering to the gospel. Along with every other aspect of salvation, this faith is the gift of God.[32]

---

[26]   Matthew 24:45; 25:21, 23; Romans 3:2-4; Colossians 1:23; 1 Thessalonians 3:8; 2 Thessalonians 2:15; Hebrews 3:1-6; 1 Peter 5:12; 3 John 3; Revelation 2:10, 13; 13:10; 14:12.

[27]   Zwingli, Commentary, p 271.

[28]   Romans 1:5; 16:26.

[29]   Romans 10:16 (literally: see ESV); 2 Thessalonians 1:8; Hebrews 4:6; 1 Peter 4:17.

[30]   Matthew 10:22; 24:13; 1 Corinthians 15:58; 16:13; 2 Corinthians 1:21, 24; Galatians 5:1-6; Ephesians 6:14; Philippians 1:27; Colossians 1:11; 2 Thessalonians 1:3-4; Hebrews 12:2-3; James 5:8; 1 Peter 5:9-10; Revelation 1:9; 2:3.

[31]   Calvin, Institutes, III.ii.31 (1: pp 576-579).

[32]   Ephesians 2:8.

5.2.2. Faith and God's promises

Now to a second point the Bible makes about faith. This concerns the close connection between our faith and God's promises.[33] We see this clearly in the story of Abraham, whom the Bible treats as a kind of prototype of the Christian believer.[34] God gave him a remarkable promise: his descendants were to be as numerous as the stars in the sky.[35] We are then told that 'Abraham believed God'.[36] He did so by trusting the promise God had just given him. We then learn that the connection between promise and faith is of great importance, because we are told that God 'credited it to him as righteousness'. Whatever else this means, it tells us that Abraham did the right thing by responding to the promise with faith. Calvin sees the connection this way:

> faith properly begins with the promise, rests in it, and ends in it... Therefore, if we would not have our faith tremble and waver, we must buttress it with the promise of salvation, which is willingly and freely offered to us by the Lord ...'[37]

For us, the fundamental promise upon which faith is grounded is the promise contained in the gospel – the promise that offers God's salvation and thus expresses God's mercy. Accordingly, faith means trusting that God is merciful:

> we need the promise of grace, which can testify to us that the Father is merciful; since we can approach him in no other way, and upon grace alone the heart of man can rest.[38]

It also means trusting that the promise-giver will prove to be a promise-keeper. Faith thus rests also upon the faithfulness of God.[39] So our faith lays hold of the salvation held out in the gospel, trusting that God is

---

[33] Genesis 15:5-6; Psalm 106:12, 24; Romans 4:13-21; Galatians 3:14, 22; Hebrews 4:1-3; 6:12; 10:23; 11:9, 11, 13.
[34] Romans 4:11-12, 16-24; James 2:20-24.
[35] Genesis 15:5.
[36] Genesis 15:6.
[37] Institutes, III.ii.29, 30 (1: pp 575-576); cf. Melanchthon, Loci, pp 138-45, 150-58.
[38] Institutes, III.ii.7 (1: pp 549-551).
[39] Exodus 34:6; Deuteronomy 7:9; 32:4; Joshua 21:45; 23:14; 1 Kings 8:24, 56; Psalms 33:4; 36:5; 40:10; 89:1-14; 100:5; 117:2; 145:13; 146:6; Isaiah 25:1; Lamentations 3:23; 1 Corinthians 1:9; 10:13; 2 Corinthians 1:18; 1 Thessalonians 5:24; 2 Thessalonians 3:3; 2 Timothy 2:13; Hebrews 10:23; 11:11; 1 Peter 4:19; 1 John 1:9; Revelation 1:5; 3:14; 19:11.

both merciful and faithful. This means trusting that, as soon as we believe what the gospel announces, we have entered into the salvation God has won for us and now offers to us. In this way our faith grasps the 'already' of the gospel proclamation. It is the means by which we participate in the present reality of God's salvation.

5.2.3. Faith and hope

A third important aspect of faith as the Bible presents it is the distinction between faith and sight. For the Bible, living by faith is the opposite of living by sight. That is because faith means fixing our eyes on what is unseen, and being sure about what we do not see.[40] This has to do with where we are in the outworking of God's saving purpose – faith also concerns the 'not yet' of the gospel. Only on the last day will we begin seeing all that we have taken on trust for now.[41] Above all, this means seeing the God in whom we have believed.[42] But before the last day, God and his great salvation remain unseen. As a result, our faith is bifocal – it is not only assurance about what we do not see, but also confidence in what we hope for.[43]

As we go through the roll of honour in Hebrews 11 of those who lived by faith, Moses is held out as an example of what this faith is like. He was confident of what he hoped for: he was looking forward to his reward. As a result, he chose disgrace rather than the treasures of Egypt (11:25-26). He also had assurance about what we do not see: he was looking upward, seeing him who is invisible. As a result, he risked the wrath of Pharaoh and left Egypt (11:27). What was true of Moses should also be true of us – for us too faith means looking *above* to what we do not see and *ahead* to what we hope for (11:1).

There is thus a very close connection between faith and hope – something which Calvin saw clearly:

> hope is nothing else than the expectation of those things which faith has believed to have been truly promised by God. Thus, faith believes God to be true, hope awaits the time when his truth shall be manifested ... faith is the foundation upon which hope rests, hope nourishes and sustains faith... Hope strengthens faith, that it may

---

[40]   2 Corinthians 4:18; 5:7; Hebrews 11:1; 1 Peter 1:8.
[41]   Romans 8:18-25.
[42]   Matthew 5:8; John 17:24; Hebrews 12:14; 1 John 3:2; Revelation 22:4.
[43]   Hebrews 11:1.

not waver in God's promises, or begin to doubt concerning their truth. Hope refreshes faith, that it may not become weary. It sustains faith to the final goal ...[44]

5.3.   A relationship of hope

This brings us to the second aspect of this knowledge of God: namely, the fact that it is a relationship of hope. The God we believe in is the God in whom we hope.[45] As we have seen, hope is faith looking forward in anticipation of what God is going to do,[46] patiently but eagerly waiting for God's promises to reach their fulfilment.[47] So hope means waiting upon God.[48] It is our recognition that we must wait before faith becomes seeing and hope becomes possession. It is our confidence that the waiting will be worth it. It is our reliance upon God to bring our waiting to an end at the right time. Hope is thus faith's response to the 'not yet' of the gospel – to the fact that our full and final entry into all that salvation means happens only at the End.

5.4.   A relationship of love

This is, thirdly, a relationship of love: the God we believe and hope in is the God we love.[49] Our love for God is not an initiative but a response, the response we make to his grace: 'We love because he first loved us'.[50] This is a response to the gospel, to the grace displayed in the saving events: 'This is love: not that we loved God, but that he loved us and sent his Son as an atoning sacrifice for our sins'.[51] This is a response that finds expression in such ways as obedience to the Lord and love for one

---

[44]   *Institutes*, III.ii.42 (1: pp 590-591).

[45]   2 Corinthians 1:10; Ephesians 1:12; 1 Thessalonians 1:3; 1 Timothy 1:1; 4:10; 6:17; 1 Peter 1:21; 3:5.

[46]   Romans 4:16-18; Hebrews 11:1, 8-10, 24-26.

[47]   Romans 8:23-25; Galatians 5:5; 1 Thessalonians 1:10; 5:8-9.

[48]   Psalms 27:14; 33:20; 37:7; 119:166; 130:5-8; Isaiah 8:17; 30:18; 51:4-6; 64:4-5; Lamentations 3:22-26; Hosea 12:6; Micah 7:7; Hebrews 9:28.

[49]   Exodus 20:6; Deuteronomy 5:10; 6:5; 7:9; 10:12; 11:1, 13, 22; 30:6, 16, 20; Joshua 22:5; 23:11; Nehemiah 1:5; Psalms 5:11; 18:1; 31:23; 97:10; 116:1; 145:20; Isaiah 56:6; Daniel 9:4; John 14:15, 21, 23, 28; 16:27; Romans 8:28; 1 Corinthians 2:9; 8:3; 16:22; Ephesians 6:24; 1 Peter 1:8; 1 John 2:5, 15; 4:20-21; 5:2-3.

[50]   1 John 4:19.

[51]   1 John 4:10.

another.[52] But above all, it is a response to the person of the Lord Jesus.[53] It is here more than anywhere else that we come to the heart of relational spirituality, with our love for him answering his love for us.

A spirituality of faith and hope emphasises the fact that we have taken everything on trust. So there is, in a sense, a gap between us and all that we believe, which we will not see or possess fully until the End: 'those things which we know through faith are nonetheless absent from us and go unseen'.[54] In particular, this spirituality draws attention to the fact that in this life we are at a distance from the God in whom we trust. A spirituality of love, by contrast, emphasises the bond of communion between ourselves and the Lord we love. There is thus a paradox here: 'though you have not seen him, you love him'.[55] Our relationship with the Lord means both distance and closeness, both waiting and having, both longing and loving. We are united without being together; at a distance without being divided.

5.5.   A unique relationship

This brings us to the end of our first point: that relationship with God is personal. Now we turn to consider a second fundamental point the Bible makes – the fact that our knowledge of God is *not the same as our knowledge of one another*. While it is essential to grasp that our knowledge of God is personal, it is equally necessary to recognize that it is not the same as our other relationships. There are similarities, because God is truly and fully personal – but there are also important differences, for God's way of being personal is not identical with ours. To note only the most obvious examples: unlike God, we are embodied persons – and only God is a Trinity of personal relationships. As a result of such differences, our knowledge of God will be both like and unlike human relationships – even the closest of them, whether those between husbands and wives, or between parents and children.

There are in fact two sides to this issue, as we saw in Chapter 4. On the one hand, our relationship with God is closer than any other relationship we do have or could have, and yet on the other hand, there

---

[52]   John 14:15; 1 John 4:10-11, 19-21; 5:3.
[53]   John 14:15, 21, 23, 28; 16:27; 1 Corinthians 16:22; Ephesians 6:24; 1 Peter 1:8.
[54]   Calvin, *Institutes*, III.ii.14 (1: pp 559-560).
[55]   1 Peter 1:8.

is an important sense in which our present relationship with him is not as close as our closest relationships. As we have seen, the Lord is in us and with us – and yet also above us, as the exalted and enthroned Lord, and ahead of us, as the returning Lord. So although it is deeply personal, our relationship with him in the here-and-now is also, in a way, distant. There is an intimacy it does not have and cannot have yet. That is why the Bible compares our present relationship with the Lord to betrothal, the period before their wedding when a couple were pledged to each other and thus belonged to each other but did not yet live together.[56] From this perspective, my knowledge of God is more like the relationship I had with my fiancée when we lived in separate towns than it is like the relationship I have had with her since we married. And yet, of course, there is an important sense in which all such analogies fail in the end, for we are dealing with something that is quite unique.

Failure to give adequate weight to everything the Bible says about it can easily lead to false expectations about our relationship with God. If we underplay the fact of our present union with God-in-Christ, we are likely to portray spirituality as a long and difficult quest, in which union with God is a far-distant destination reached only by a spiritual elite. This is obviously a long way from the spirituality of grace, which rejoices in the free gift of a secure relationship with God that is based on his work, not ours. We must give proper weight to the way the Bible affirms and celebrates the fact of this union – a relationship so close and deep that it involves our mutual 'in-ness': we are in the Lord, and he is in us. But at the same time, we must be careful that we do not give the impression that this union involved some kind of merging of identities. Perhaps the best way of avoiding this problem while giving due emphasis to the personal nature of our union is to speak of the 'communion' between believers and God-in-Christ.[57] The relationship is not one in which our personal identity disappears; rather, it is a real fellowship between persons.[58]

On the other hand, if we do not make sufficient allowance for the fact of our present distance from God, we are likely to claim too much about how our relationship works. In particular, we will not give enough

---

[56] 2 Corinthians 11:2; Revelation 19:7-9; cf. Matthew 25:1-13.
[57] The importance of this distinction will become evident in Chapters 6 and 9 below.
[58] Note especially 1 Corinthians 1:9; 1 John 1:3.

weight to the ways in which it is different from intimate, face-to-face relationship. It is not uncommon for popular works on spirituality to fall into this trap, by using our fellowship with each other as the basis on which to describe our communion with God. One way of doing this is to describe our relationship with God as a friendship – a potential problem we noted in the previous chapter. Yes, there are ways in which it is like a rich, close friendship, but there are also ways in which it differs radically from any such relationship. We see the same problem surfacing in some of the songs we Christians have sung. Consider the following examples:

> He lives, he lives, Christ Jesus lives today;
> He walks with me and talks with me along life's narrow way.

> He walks with me, and he talks with me,
> And he tells me I am his own ...

The intention of such words was to express the deeply personal nature of our relationship with the Lord Jesus. They were perhaps a reaction against a merely formal profession of faith which lacked any real engagement with the Lord himself. The problem with them is that they claim more than they should. They imply that the relationship we have with the Lord now is just like that which the disciples enjoyed during his ministry – but they forget that the Bible tells us that he is now enthroned in heaven, and that we are to set our minds there.[59] Yes, there is a very real sense in which he is with us – but we are not yet with him.[60] God does make his home with us now – but we have to be away from the body before we are at home with him – and it is only at the End that God will be fully and finally present with his people.[61] So there is both closeness and distance in the present form of our relationship with the Lord. As a result, it is as misleading as it is helpful to claim that he walks and talks with us.

5.6. A relationship of the heart

The third fundamental point the Bible makes about true knowledge of God is that it is a matter of the *heart*.

---

[59] Colossians 3:1-2.
[60] See Matthew 18:20; 28:20; 2 Corinthians 5:6-8; 1 Thessalonians 4:17.
[61] John 14:23; 2 Corinthians 5:8; Revelation 21:3.

Consider Paul's well-known words in Romans 10:9-10:

> If you declare with your mouth, 'Jesus is Lord,' and believe in your heart that God raised him from the dead, you will be saved. For it is with your heart that you believe and are justified ...

Here the heart is where I do my believing. In the words of Proverbs 3:5 ('Trust in the Lord with all your heart ...'), it is where I do my trusting.[62] It is also where the Bible locates our thinking, understanding, and knowing[63] – as well as such things as our loving, desiring, grieving, and rejoicing,[64] and our decisions and motives.[65]

Clearly, the Bible uses 'heart' in a much wider way than we tend to do. For us, it is normally the opposite of 'head', and means emotion as distinct from reason – the affective and intuitive dimensions of our personality rather than the cognitive; right-brain instead of left-brain. Some discussions of spirituality wrongly assume that where the Bible speaks of the 'heart' it is using this distinction. But it generally has quite a different distinction in mind. For the Bible, the heart is the real, inner me as distinct from the merely visible me. We see this, for example, in Romans 2:28-29:

> A person is not a Jew who is one only outwardly, nor is circumcision merely outward and physical. No, a person is a Jew who is one inwardly; and circumcision is circumcision of the heart ...[66]

The distinction here is between the body and the 'heart', that is, between the outer and inner dimensions of my self, my identity as a person. The heart is thus the core of my self – as when we refer to what someone is like 'at heart'. Or consider how I might say that I have taken something 'to heart'. In saying this, I am not referring directly or primarily to my feelings – but because I am talking about what really matters to me, my

---

[62] See also Luke 24:25; Psalms 28:7; 112:7; Jeremiah 17:5.

[63] See, for example, Psalms 19:14; 77:6; Proverbs 2:2; Ecclesiastes 7:22; Isaiah 6:9-10; Mark 2:8; Luke 2:35; Ephesians 1:18; Hebrews 4:12.

[64] See, for example, John 5:42; 1 Peter 1:22; Matthew 5:28; Romans 10:1; Romans 9:2; 2 Corinthians 2:4; Acts 2:46; 14:17.

[65] See, for example, Psalm 33:11; Proverbs 6:14, 18; 16:1, 9; 19:21; 20:5; 1 Corinthians 4:5; 2 Corinthians 9:7.

[66] Note also Deuteronomy 30:14, 17; 1 Samuel 1:13; 12:20, 24; 16:7; Psalms 14:1; 15:2; 17:3; 19:14; 24:4; Proverbs 2:1-2; 3:1; 4:20-23; Matthew 5:28; 6:21; 15:17-20; Luke 6:45; Acts 16:14; 1 Corinthians 4:5; 2 Corinthians 5:12; Ephesians 6:5-6; Hebrews 3:7-12.

emotions will normally be involved. Instead, I am referring to 'what makes me tick': what is in or on my heart are my strongest convictions, my deepest concerns, or my greatest passions.[67]

It is in this sense that true devotion is a matter of the heart. As Calvin puts it:

> the Word of God is not received by faith if it flits about in the top of the brain, but when it takes root in the depth of the heart ...[68]

He is not talking about whether biblical truth has reached my emotions as well as my reason. He is talking about how deeply it has penetrated into the real me, into the person that I am. His concern is that our hold upon the truth should not be shallow and superficial. Instead, he wants to encourage a deep engagement with God's word, a receptivity and responsiveness that are as real as possible.

So, biblically, true devotion is wholehearted. That is, true knowledge of God penetrates to the heart, and true response to God comes from the heart.[69] A heart-knowledge of God is one in which the word and work and worth of God are not incidental to me but fundamental, the central realities of my life. And because knowing him is of surpassing worth and matters more to me than anything else, my whole person is caught up in this relationship.

5.6.1 The place of emotions

So what part do my emotions play in wholehearted devotion? What should I expect? There are two errors we must avoid here. The first is when we have unrealistic expectations about what our emotions will do. This often takes the form of looking for a perfect correlation between my thoughts and my feelings. So if I am reading a part of the Bible that speaks about how much God loves me, I might expect strong feelings to arise quite naturally – feelings of wonder and gratitude, praise and happiness. Or if I am confessing my sins to God, I might expect to be weighed down by feelings of guilt and shame and sadness. What is the

---

[67] That is why the Bible can speak about prayer as "pouring out our hearts" to God: see Psalm 62:8; Lamentations 2:19.

[68] *Institutes*, III.ii.36 (1: pp 583-584); cf. similar comments in I.v.9 (1: pp 61-62); III.vi.4 (1: pp 687-688).

[69] See, for example, Deuteronomy 6:5; 10:12; 11:13; 30:6, 10; Joshua 22:5; 1 Samuel 12:20, 24; 2 Chronicles 34:31; Ezekiel 36:26; Acts 11:23; Romans 1:9; 15:6; Ephesians 6:6; 1 Peter 3:15.

problem here? – apart from the fact that all too often this doesn't happen! Why are these expectations unrealistic? Because I am part of a fallen creation, and the disintegrating effects of our fallenness impact on my emotions just as much as they do on every other part of me. My body is subject to wear-and-tear and vulnerable to infections – and my feelings have no immunity from similar processes of decay. As a result, they often do not behave as I think they should. Sometimes I have little or no feeling when emotion would be appropriate; sometimes my emotions are out of all proportion to what aroused them. On one occasion, I can be moved by a song about God and his grace towards me, but the next time I sing it, I might feel nothing at all – except disappointment at my lack of emotion! Also, I have learned by experience that I have less emotional balance when I am very tired, for my emotions are closer to the surface and harder to control. In these and other ways my feelings do not work as I would like them to.

So is there anything I can do about all of this – or do I just have to put up with the fact that my emotions are often unpredictable and uncontrollable? I do have to be realistic about the fallen-ness of my emotions, but there is no reason to be fatalistic about this fact. I should ask God to be at work on my emotions, so that they are being rescued and restored like the rest of me. I should let the Bible teach me about emotions, so that I develop a godly perspective towards them. (This is one of the contributions that the Psalms in particular can make.[70]) I should look forward to the new creation, when at last my emotions too will be redeemed, and I will always feel exactly what I should feel.

The other error we need to avoid is the opposite of the first one. If that means expecting too much of our emotions, this error involves expecting too little. At one level, this can mean passive resignation to a Christian life without much emotion. At another level, it can take the form of a suspicion of emotions – the belief that we would be better off without them, as they only get in the way! There are several things we need to say about this approach. The first is that it fails to see that

---

[70] Speaking of the Psalms, Calvin says, '[T]here is not an emotion of which anyone can be conscious that is not here represented as in a mirror. Or rather, the Holy Spirit has here drawn to the life all the griefs, sorrows, fears, doubts, hopes, cares, perplexities, in short, all the distracting emotions with which human minds are wont to be agitated.' (John Calvin, *Writings on Pastoral Piety*, edited and with translations by Elsie Anne McKee in *The Classics of Western Spirituality*; (New York: Paulist, 2001), p 56.)

emotions are a good gift from the God who created us.[71] The fact that, like the rest of the creation, our emotions have been damaged by sin does not make them bad. They are defective but not deplorable – and they are being redeemed. So while they do not yet function perfectly, they can still be received as a good gift.[72]

Secondly, we have been created in God's likeness.[73] There is reason to think that our emotions are part of what this means, for the God of the Bible is an emotional being – he loves, hates, desires, delights, rejoices; he is pleased or angry; and so on.[74] But unlike ours, God's feelings are not tainted or twisted by sin – so they are never in any way selfish or improper, but are always pure and good. The day is coming when this will also be true of human emotions. In the meantime, our feelings can be a blessing just as much as they can be a problem. There is certainly no reason to dismiss them as an inferior or unfortunate aspect of our personality.

Thirdly, when we look more closely at this view, those who disparage the right-brain, the affective and intuitive side of our personality, are usually highly left-brain people! They are inclined to suspect or even disdain our emotions because they place great confidence in our minds. But along with our emotions, the mind shares in our fallenness – as well as in God's work of rescuing and restoring us. It does not become infallible, any more than our emotions do – but on the way to full and final redemption, enlightened by God's Spirit and instructed by God's word, both our thoughts and our feelings become capable of responding to God and his gospel. Both have a necessary role to play in wholehearted devotion.

The fourth and final point to make about this error is that there is one respect in which it comes close to the truth. One of the lessons we all have to learn about living by faith is that there are times when we must sit loose to our emotions and hold fast to our convictions. Sometimes our feelings can be giving us the wrong messages and pushing us in the wrong direction. This is when faithfulness will mean choosing not to heed them. Asaph provides a good example in

---

[71]   Genesis 1:31.
[72]   Note 1 Timothy 4:4-5.
[73]   Genesis 1:26.
[74]   See, for example, Psalm 136; Deuteronomy 12:31; Psalm 51:6; Psalm 149:4; Isaiah 62:5; Psalm 135:6; Psalm 95:10.

Psalm 77. He begins with his *emotions*, reporting the fact that he felt wretched (vv.1-4). In his distress he pleaded with God to help him. We then discover what is making him feel so terrible, for he goes on to report his *questions* (vv.5-9). He reveals the doubts and struggles that went along with his awful feelings – questions that are very troubling because they threaten to undermine his confidence in God and his love (vv.7-9). So what is he to do? The crucial step is what he does next: he focuses on his *convictions* (vv.10-20). He sets himself to meditate on what God has done – that is, to remember and consider the mighty works of God (vv.11-12). And with that, he ends his psalm. He does not answer his troubling questions or explain his wretched feelings – because although he might not know what the answer is, he now knows what it isn't! It is not the case that God has run out of mercy and compassion; he has not given up on his promises; he has not abandoned his people. By reflecting on God's saving work (v.15), Asaph is reminded of what is true about God and his grace. And that is what he will hold on to, even in the face of his feelings and his doubts. What Asaph has done in this psalm is what we will sometimes have to do in order to be faithful. There are times when we will have to ignore or refuse our feelings in order to hold fast to God and his truth.

5.7. *Conclusions and consequences*

It is time to review where we have been. In addition to the fact that for now it is exercised at a distance, we have seen that relational knowledge of God is personal and direct, and a matter of the heart. One of the most important consequences of all of this is the simplicity and directness that marks our fellowship with God. This is such a basic characteristic of Bible-based spirituality, and so different from other approaches, that there have been times in church history when Bible-believing Christians have been accused of not having a spirituality at all.

> In the name of faith, the Reformers destroyed superstition. In consequence, they were attacked as impious and even atheistic. Was there a Protestant spirituality? Many said there was not, for they could not credit the *simplicity* which true faith engendered.[75]

---

[75] P.F. Jensen, "Faith" in B.G. Webb (ed), *Responding to the Gospel: Evangelical Perspectives on Christian Living*, Explorations 9 (Adelaide: OpenBook, 1995), pp 1-14 (at p 8: his italics). Cf. Adam, *Hearing God's Words*, p 21.

The Reformers were very clear about superstition and why it was a problem:

> superstition is false religion, which doth not serve God but somewhat else for God, or not God alone, or not rightly or lawfully... Unlawful service proceedeth from the will and imagination of men; and it is contrary to the word and ordinance of God. For God is then lawfully served, when he is served according to his own will and word.[76]

A piety that deviated from the Bible, by omitting what the Bible requires or requiring what the Bible omits, amounted to superstition and had to be condemned. So, as we noted in Chapter 2, Martin Luther speaks in very strong terms against his own former piety:

> Yes, all that the world undertakes ... counts for nothing before God; as, for instance, the zeal, the spirituality, the self-chosen worship of all ... the pope's saints... For more than twenty years I was a pious monk, read Mass daily, and so weakened myself with fasting and praying that I would not have been long for this life had I continued... I myself must now stamp and condemn it as sin committed in idolatry and unbelief.[77]

The great problem with his devotion was not any lack of earnestness, but the fact that it failed the test of 'spiritual chastity'. It was not in conformity with the word of God; it was 'self-chosen worship'[78] and thus idolatry.

> [A]mong us Christians all those people are idolatrous ... who have invented or are following new ways of worshiping God, without his commission or command, simply out of their own pious inclination ... let everyone see to it that he is certain his worship and service of

---

[76] Bullinger, *Decades*, 3: pp 232, 237.

[77] *Works*, 24: p 229. The same approach can also be seen in Zwingli:
'Whatever ... has been given out by the Romanists, without the authority and testimony of the divine Word, as pious, holy, and acceptable to God, like fictitious indulgences, the extinguishing of the fires of purgatory, forced chastity, a variety of orders and superstitious customs, which it would be tiresome to enumerate: all this is sin and an abomination in the sight of God.' (Huldreich Zwingli, *A Short and Clear Exposition of the Christian Faith* [1536], in *On Providence and Other Essays* (Eugene: Wipf & Stock, 1999 [1922]), p 266.)

[78] This is an allusion to Colossians 2:23, where Paul condemns a defective piety that was influencing the Colossians.

God has been instituted by God's word, and not invented by his own pious notions or good intentions.[79]

The point is clear: true devotion is shaped and controlled by the Bible. As Zwingli puts it, 'those only are truly pious who hang upon the utterances of God alone'.[80]

In contrast with the piety from which the Reformers were distancing themselves, the spirituality they found in the Bible was very direct and simple. It was not a complex and demanding quest for an elusive union with God. At its heart was the gift of personal relationship with the God of all grace.

We have now reached the end of our exploration of a spirituality of the gospel. I began by arguing that true knowledge of God is based on the gospel, nourished by the gospel, and shaped by the gospel. We then considered how it is responsive, paradoxical, and relational. These are a direct consequence, respectively, of the gospel of grace, of the shape of God's saving work, and of the nature of the Triune God. So true devotion is a spirituality of grace and faith; a spirituality of the Son of God, the Spirit of God, and the word of God. It is a spirituality of faith, hope, and love; a spirituality of the heart; and a spirituality for the in-between time in which we live. One discussion of Evangelical spirituality summarizes it this way:

> Lived doctrine centred on Christ, growth towards maturity measured by Christ, and moral renewal after the image of Christ provide the goals of the Christian spiritual life. But the love of God requires active response, a serious pursuit of holiness and obedience. Godliness is neither painless nor inevitable. Christian spirituality therefore presupposes the practice of spiritual discipline. The life of grace is nourished by the means of grace. Disciplined regular devotion is a declaration of love, a daily affirmation of loyalty, an indication of spiritual desire, an admission of need and above all an act of worship which acknowledges the sovereignty of God over the entire life.[81]

---

[79] Luther, *Works*, 35: pp 270, 273.
[80] *Commentary*, p 93. He adds, with reference to Catholic piety, 'It is false religion or piety when trust is put in any other than God... They are impious who embrace the word of man as God's.' (pp 97f).
[81] James M. Gordon, *Evangelical Spirituality* (London: SPCK, 1991), p 4.

How does all of this help us to be wise and discerning in our response to the great smorgasbord of spirituality being set before us today? How does it give us a way of testing the various models that are presented and claims that are made in contemporary writings on this subject? The answer will become clearer if we compare the character of this biblical spirituality with the approach I have called 'the mystical way'. That is the task we will tackle in the next five chapters of the book.

PART II: THE MYSTICAL WAY

'The greatest problem of the world today is ... our lack of mysticism'.[1]

'The Christian of the future will be a mystic or he will not exist at all'.[2]

'We may be mystics, or we may be Christians. We cannot be both'.[3]

'Faith opposes the mystical interpretation with a sharp, plain 'No''.[4]

In order to decide which of these claims is right, we need to have a clear idea of what they are talking about. But unfortunately, it is not easy to define mysticism. That is why one wit claimed that 'it begins with mist and ends with schism'! The problem is that the word is used to refer to a variety of beliefs and practices within Christendom and in other religions as well. Like mist, it is very hard to pin down; like schism, this is a subject that tends to divide people. As the quotations above make clear, some people are all in favour of mysticism while others are strongly against it. In view of these various difficulties, what is the point of using this term? What do we mean by 'the mystical way'?

We are going to limit the discussion in this section of the book to mysticism as it is found within Christendom. So we will not consider any of the ways in which mysticism is encountered in other religions – or experienced by people of no religion. Secondly, our focus will be limited to mysticism at street-level. We are not concerned here with esoteric discussions among the experts that do not reach the ordinary Christian. Nor are we investigating classical mysticism and the works which give expression to it – unless they are well-known at popular level. What we are going to do here is to examine some basic ways in which a mystical approach shapes Christian devotion. An analysis of the mystical tradition within Christendom – its history, its classical expressions, and its practices – is beyond the scope of this book.

---

[1] William Johnston, quoted in the Introduction by Halcyon Backhouse to Mother Julian of Norwich, *Revelation of Divine Love* (London: Hodder, 2009 [1393]), xxiv.

[2] Karl Rahner, quoted in Carl McColman, *The Big Book of Christian Mysticism: The Essential Guide to Contemplative Spirituality* (Charlottesville: Hampton Roads, 2010), p 6.

[3] B.B. Warfield, *Biblical and Theological Studies*, edited by Samuel G. Craig (Philadelphia: P&R, 1952), p 462.

[4] Emil Brunner, *Man in Revolt: A Christian Anthropology* (Cambridge: Lutterworth, 1957), p 253.

In order to proceed, then, we need a clear definition of Christian mysticism. Here is where we encounter another difficulty, for there are two different ways in which the term is used.

One applies it to the relationship every believer has (or should have) with God. In effect, 'mystical' means genuinely personal – it denotes real fellowship: 'all experience of a knowledge of God and of fellowship with God is mystical in nature'.[5] It is in this sense that the Puritans spoke of a 'mystical union' between Christ and the believer.[6]

The other use of the term limits it to an experience only some believers have. This is the approach we will follow, because if the word applies to everyone in general it does not apply to anyone in particular – it just becomes too vague to be useful. So, without getting bogged down in technicalities, it will suit our limited purposes here to define mysticism as follows:

> The mystical element in Christianity is that part of its belief and practices that concerns the preparation for, the consciousness of, and the reaction to what can be described as the immediate or direct experience of God.[7]

The principal characteristics of this experience are directness, inwardness, and oneness. In the first place, then, mysticism means direct and unmediated experience: it means 'consciousness of the direct presence of God'.[8] This makes it different from the more usual kinds of consciousness:

> this mode of the divine presence is said to be given in a direct or immediate way, without the usual internal and external mediations

---

[5]   Arie de Reuver, *Sweet Communion: Trajectories of Spirituality from the Middle Ages through the Further Reformation* (Grand Rapids: Baker Academic, 2007), p 22. He defines mysticism as "the faith-knowledge that comes over a person by the word and the Spirit and includes an intimate communion with God himself", and says that it exists "wherever the effect of the word of God is a personal encounter between God and the soul worked by the Holy Spirit." It applies to "fellowship with God in Christ through the word and Spirit." (*Sweet Communion*, pp 22, 23).

[6]   For a useful study of this theme, see J. Stephen Yuille, *The Inner Sanctum of Puritan Piety: John Flavel's Doctrine of Mystical Union with Christ* (Grand Rapids: Reformation Heritage, 2007).

[7]   Bernard McGinn, *The Presence of God: A History of Western Christian Mysticism, Volume I: The Foundations of Mysticism* (New York: Crossroad, 1991), p xvii.

[8]   Evan B. Howard, *The Brazos Introduction to Christian Spirituality* (Grand Rapids: Brazos, 2008), p 19.

found in other types of consciousness.[9]

It thus reaches beyond words and ideas and, as a result, can more readily be attested than described.

Secondly, this experience is marked by intense inwardness:

In the mystical ethos we meet God in the innermost part of the soul, sometimes called the cave of the heart. We find God by journeying to the center of the soul, which comprises the point of contact between the divine and the human.[10]

Thirdly, this experience is the goal of the mystical quest – the *unio mystica*, union with God. This is the theistic understanding of what appears to lie at the heart of all mysticism:

Mysticism is the art of union with Reality. The mystic is a person who has attained that union in greater or lesser degree ...[11]

If these are the hallmarks of Christian mysticism at popular level, how do they shape the understanding and practice of Christian devotion? That is what we will focus on in this section of the book. We will begin by considering how the mystical experience is treated in popular-level works on Christian spirituality (Chapter 6). We will then examine three of the most influential features of this mysticism – its view of how God speaks to us (Chapter 7), its way of prayer (Chapter 8), and its focus on the inward journey (Chapter 9). We will conclude this part of the book by considering how the Protestant Reformers reacted to the piety in which they were reared, including the teaching of the mystics (Chapter 10). In Chapters 6–9, we will note the principal features of the mystical approach, and then outline some reasons for caution about where it is heading. This will mean assessing the views and practices concerned by the teaching of the Bible, our supreme authority in all matters of faith and practice.

We will also rely heavily on the teachings of the Reformers and the Puritans. In part, this reflects the fact that I am more familiar with these writings than I am with those from other periods of church history. But

---

[9] McGinn, *Presence*, xix.

[10] Donald G. Bloesch, *Spirituality Old and New: Recovering Authentic Spiritual Life* (Downers Grove: IVP Academic/Nottingham: Apollos, 2007), p 52.

[11] Evelyn Underhill [1875-1941], *Practical Mysticism: A Little Book for Normal People* (Guildford: Eagle, 1991 [1914]), p 2 (original in italics).

there is another reason for this focus, and that is the fact that these writers had to face and resolve the issues that concern us in this part of the book. To ignore them would therefore mean depriving ourselves of great wisdom and riches. It would also leave us less familiar than we should be with fundamental elements of the Evangelical heritage.[12] Yet, as always, we must ensure that we test what they say. It is not the words of church leaders, no matter how highly esteemed, but the words of the prophets and apostles that we must live by. Our devotion, like every other aspect of our life in Christ, must be governed by the Bible.

---

[12] To say this is to imply an answer to a question that has been the subject of debate amongst historians: namely, where do the roots of Evangelicalism lie? I think the Reformers and the Puritans are important parts of its family tree. On this see John Coffey, "Puritanism, Evangelicalism and the Evangelical Protestant Tradition" in Michael A.G. Haykin and Kenneth J. Stewart (eds), *The Emergence of Evangelicalism: Exploring Historical Continuities* (Nottingham: Apollos, 2008), pp 252-277.

6.   Experiencing God

We have just seen that at its core Christian mysticism is the quest for direct, unmediated experience of God: it is

> a search for and experience of immediacy with God. The mystic is not content to know *about* God, he longs for union *with* God.[1]

Popular-level presentations of this approach treat God's presence as something that is felt, rather than merely believed in. So A.W. Tozer, for example, refers to 'the man who has passed on into the divine Presence in actual inner experience'.[2] In another connection, he speaks of this in terms of the superiority of 'knowledge by direct spiritual experience':

> Through the indwelling Spirit the human spirit is brought into immediate contact with higher spiritual reality. It looks upon, tastes, feels and sees the powers of the world to come and has a conscious encounter with God invisible... To such a man God is not a conclusion drawn from evidence nor is He the sum of what the Bible teaches about Him. He knows God in the last irreducible meaning of the word know. It may almost be said that God happened to him... the Triune God wills to dwell in the redeemed man's heart, constantly making His presence known ...[3]

A very influential book on prayer makes the same point more simply: 'God's presence is real. You can feel it because it is with you wherever you go ...'[4] Another makes the following claim: 'We can train ourselves to sense the presence of the indwelling Christ ... just as Mary did when God's Son was forming in her womb ...'[5]

This approach is not found only in contemporary works, of course. A fourteenth-century English mystic says, '[B]e quite sure that you shall

---

[1]   Andrew Louth, *The Origins of the Christian Mystical Tradition: From Plato to Denys* (Oxford: Clarendon, 1981), p xv (his italics).

[2]   A.W. Tozer [1897-1963], *Man, The Dwelling Place of God* (Blacksburg, VA: Wilder, 2009), p 106.

[3]   *Man, The Dwelling Place of God*, p 38.

[4]   Bill Hybels, *Too Busy Not to Pray: Slowing Down to be with God*, 3rd edition (Nottingham: IVP, 2008), p 170.

[5]   Joyce Huggett, *Open to God* (London: Hodder & Stoughton, 1989), p 27.

never see God clearly in this life; but, by his grace, you may feel his presence if it is his will'.[6] And the Quaker theologian Robert Barclay said that in their meetings

> the great work of one and all ought to be to wait upon God, and returning out of their own thoughts and imaginations, to feel the Lord's presence ... Yea, though there be not a word spoken, yet is the true spiritual worship performed and the body of Christ edified, yea it may and hath often fallen out among us that divers meetings have past without one word, and yet our souls have been greatly edified and refreshed, and our hearts wonderfully overcome with the secret sense of God's Power and Spirit ...[7]

6.1. Questions about popular mysticism

What should we make of this strand of Christian piety? How far should we go down the road of this popular mysticism? I think the traffic lights need to flash amber here for five reasons.

6.1.1. Is there a God-feeling?

The first difficulty with this approach is its claim that the presence of God in my life is marked by a particular feeling, distinguishable from other feelings. This view must be challenged. As we discovered in Chapter 4, our present location in-between the Old Age and the New Age means that the experience of God's presence and activity in our lives is not limited to one type of feeling but involves many different feelings. One important consequence of this fact is indicated in an astute observation by the Puritan Thomas Brooks:

> It is a very great mistake among many weak, tender-spirited Christians, to think that they have no communion with God ... except they meet with God embracing and kissing, cheering and comforting up their Souls: And oh that all Christians would remember this once for all, *viz.* that a Christian may have as real communion with God in a heart-humbling way, as he can have in a heart comforting way ... A Christian may have as choice communion with God when his eyes are full of tears, as he can have

---

6   *The Cloud of Unknowing* (London: Hodder, 2009), p 19.

7   Robert Barclay [1648-1690], *An Apology for the True Christian Divinity* [1678]: The Eleventh Proposition: Concerning Worship, §VI.

when his heart is full of joy ...[8]

Brooks' point is clear: our fellowship with God should not be dependent on outward circumstances. It can therefore be experienced in various ways in different situations. The underlying reason for this is also clear: God's presence is never withdrawn from his children.

How do we know this? Is it because we always feel his presence? No, it is because he has given us a clear promise to this effect: 'Never will I leave you; never will I forsake you'.[9] This means that he is with us when life hurts us, just as much as when life is good. So even if we feel wretched because life has turned out badly, we can and should recognize and even rejoice at his presence.[10] This is very unlikely to happen, however, if we identify the presence of God with a particular kind of feeling. That is because what we think of as the God-feeling will inevitably be a good feeling. After all, who is going to equate the presence of God with something unpleasant? But good feelings are generally dependent on good times – we do not usually feel good when life is going wrong. So instead of trusting that he is with us always, as he has promised, in practice we will limit God's presence to the times when we have our God-feeling. As a result, we will effectively exclude him from involvement in many areas and periods in our lives:

God will be there when we feel joy or peace, but will be deemed absent when we feel sadness and inner turmoil.[11]

There is a sad irony here, for one of the ways God is involved in our lives is in disciplining us. But although this is painful rather than pleasant, it is an expression of his love for us.[12] And just as God's presence is never withdrawn from his children, so his love for us is constant and unwavering: 'the Lord's unfailing love surrounds the one who trusts in him'.[13] But because he expresses it in various ways, including discipline, our experience of his love is not always pleasant.

---

[8] Thomas Brooks [1608-1680], *The Works of Thomas Brooks*, six volumes (Edinburgh: Banner of Truth, 1980), 3: p 288.

[9] Hebrews 13:5; also Deuteronomy 31:6, 8; Joshua 1:5; 1 Kings 8:56-57; 1 Chronicles 28:20; Psalm 9:10; cf. Matthew 28:20.

[10] See especially Habakkuk 3:17-18.

[11] Dennis P. Hollinger, *Head, Heart and Hands: Bringing Together Christian Thought, Passion and Action* (Downers Grove: IVP, 2005), p 99.

[12] Hebrews 12:5-11.

[13] Psalm 32:10.

Yet even when we are hurting, God is present, loving us and working for our eternal good. We know that this is true in every situation and circumstance, since God works for our good in all things.[14] It is not that all things are good, but that through the presence and power of God, all things do good: 'even winter seasons contribute to the fruitfulness of the earth'.[15] This is an obvious dimension of the Christian life in which I will miss the presence and activity of God if I rely on a special God-feeling that can come only when all is well.

None of this is to deny the wonderful ministry of the Holy Spirit, filling us with love, joy, and peace.[16] But in this in-between time and in this fallen world, these gifts often come to us in the context of trouble, suffering, and grief.[17] As a result, our experience of God's love for us and presence with us is two-sided – more often than not, it means peace-in-trouble and joy-in-grief.[18] We know life as both bitter and sweet: 'Each heart knows its own bitterness, and no one else can share its joy'.[19] So here and now God's presence with us does not generate unmixed and unwavering God-feelings. Because of the Spirit's work in our lives, we do experience love, joy, and peace – along with other 'holy affections'.[20] But because of our continuing sinfulness, and our continuing participation in this fallen world, we do not experience these affections as pure or constant. So to expect and rely on a special God-feeling is to set myself up to be dispirited or else to be misled about my spiritual condition.

6.1.2. What to make of feelings?

There is a second reason for amber lights here – another consequence of living in this in-between time. God has set about the work of restoring us, progressively delivering us from the disintegrating effects of sin. Yet until the work of reintegration is completed, we have to learn to live with the unfortunate fact that our convictions and our emotions

---

[14]   Romans 8:28.
[15]   Matthew Henry [1662-1714], *The Pleasantness of a Religious Life* (Fearn: Christian Heritage, 1998 [1714]), p 130.
[16]   Galatians 5:22.
[17]   See, for example, Lamentations 3:19-33; Romans 5:3-5; 1 Peter 1:6-8.
[18]   See, for example, John 16:33; 1 Thessalonians 1:6.
[19]   Proverbs 14:10.
[20]   "True Religion, in great part, consists in Holy Affections." (Jonathan Edwards, *The Religious Affections*, p 23).

are often 'out of sync'. C.S. Lewis' wily old devil Screwtape writes about this to his nephew Wormwood:

> Has no one ever told you about the law of Undulation? ... the repeated return to a level from which they repeatedly fall back, a series of troughs and peaks. If you had watched your patient carefully you would have seen this undulation in every department of his life – his interest in his work, his affection for his friends, his physical appetites, all go up and down. As long as he lives on earth periods of emotional and bodily richness and liveliness will naturally alternate with periods of numbness and poverty.[21]

As a result, one of the earliest discipleship lessons we have to learn is that living by faith often means tenaciously trusting God and his word when our feelings are pushing us very hard in the opposite direction. The New Testament tells us that we live by faith and not by sight.[22] Perhaps we need to add that we live by faith and not by feel!

6.1.3. Dependence on feelings

Thirdly, those who believe that direct experience of God takes the form of a particular feeling make themselves vulnerable by doing so. If this feeling is seen as the primary way – or, even more dangerously, the only way – in which I know that God is with me, I become dependent on the activities, or places, or people, or sensory stimuli that convey this feeling to me. Conversely, I must avoid anything (or anyone!) that diminishes or dispels the feeling. Eventually, as we noted in Chapter 4, this puts me in a position that is uncomfortably close to that of a drug addict. And like someone in that tragic condition, I may well find it hard to resist anything that promises to provide the 'hit' I need. In other words, I will be less capable than I should be of exercising discernment about the ideas and methods that produce the desired result. I may thus end up in a state of spiritual promiscuity – because the world we live in is always offering me plenty of opportunities to stray. But as we discovered in Chapter 3, true devotion is a spirituality of faith, a vital component of which is submitting to the word of God. True devotion is not the arena of DIY activity; it is marked by what Calvin called 'spiritual chastity'.

---

[21]   C.S. Lewis, *The Screwtape Letters* (London: Collins, 1942), pp 44f.

[22]   2 Corinthians 5:7.

6.1.4. What others experience

Fourthly, there is another way of describing the vulnerability created by the belief that God's presence is a particular feeling. What can be thought of as 'promiscuity' at the level of personal piety is 'universalism' at the level of theological analysis.[23] This pressure begins as soon as we look over the fence, when we discover that it is not only in our own backyard that such things are to be found. The reality is that people of other religions – and people of no religion – use similar methods or techniques, and get similar results.

The story of Thomas Merton serves as a salutary warning here. One of the evangelical theologians we quoted in the Introduction has developed a very high regard for Merton as a guide to deeper, more authentic relationship with God. So, on the one hand, he enthusiastically commends him:

> Thinking Christians cannot avoid Thomas Merton; he is that imposing a spiritual and prophetic voice of the twentieth century. Some have described Merton as the most influential intellectual and spiritual figure of our time...[24]

But on the other hand, he is clearly embarrassed by the outcome of Merton's spiritual journey:

> Merton spent most of his life as a priest in a Trappist monastery in Kentucky... Later in life, Merton became attracted to the spirituality of the East. He searched for common ground between Christianity and Eastern religions, such as Buddhism and Hinduism. He suspected that Christian contemplation and Zen meditation pursue the same goal – the unmasking of the false or illusory self and the discovery of the true self... After extensive dialogue with Eastern masters, Merton saw no contradiction between Buddhism and Christianity. When Merton journeyed to the East to visit the Dalai Lama, he said he went not to preach, but to discover truth in dialogue... When Merton writes on Christian issues ... he remains on rather solid ground... Things are different when Merton delves

---

[23] By "universalism" I mean the belief that all religions involve true knowledge of God or the expectation that all people will be saved.

[24] Demarest, *Satisfy Your Soul*, p 274.

into Eastern religions ...[25]

However, it is difficult to see how universalism can be resisted once I adopt the belief that God is experienced in a specific sensory-visceral way – because Christians are not the only people who have 'experiences' when they use mystical practices! (I do not mean, of course, that everyone who has read any of the books I have quoted or used any of the practices I have described is a universalist. I am referring to the inner logic of Christian mysticism's core principle, and thus to its in-principle outcome rather than to its actual result in people's lives. Few of us are completely consistent, taking all of our assumptions to their logical conclusions.)

6.1.5. How we know God

There is a fifth reason for caution here. This has to do with the fact that what is being advocated and claimed is direct, immediate experience of God. Consider, for example, these words of A.W. Tozer:

> The Bible assumes as a self-evident fact that men can know God with at least the same degree of immediacy as they know any other person ... The same terms are used to express the knowledge of God as are used to express knowledge of physical things. 'O *taste* and *see* that the LORD is good' (Psalm 34:8, emphasis added)...[26]

This experience is immediate in that it is thought to occur directly, just like our knowledge of each other. When we are together, I know you because I can see you and hear you and touch you. It is only if we are apart that we have to rely on means – such as phoning and emails – to get to know each other. But we get to know one another far better when we are together and do not have to rely upon such means. And (so the claim goes) since God is both personal and present, we can and should know him in this direct way, without anything coming between us – that is, without needing to rely upon any means. What is the problem with this way of seeing things?

We need to remind ourselves at this point that true devotion is a spirituality of the gospel. Yes, there is a relationship with God that is real and personal – a spirituality of the gospel is relational: we really do know God (Chapter 5). But this is also a responsive spirituality – we

---

[25] Demarest, *Satisfy Your Soul*, p 276.

[26] A.W. Tozer, *The Pursuit of God* (Milton Keynes: Authentic Media, 2009), p 31.

know him only in and through the gospel; we know him only by faith (Chapter 3). Our knowledge of God is thus dependent on means. And the quest for direct, immediate experience of God is an attempt to have what I cannot have in this life. It is only when I 'depart' (that is, when I die) that I will be with Christ.[27] It is only when he comes at the end of this age that we will all see him.[28] Only then, in the new creation, will God be fully and permanently present; only then will we see him face to face.[29] In the meantime, we love him and believe in him without seeing him.[30] In this world the only seeing of him that we do is in the gospel and by faith. In other words, this is a 'seeing' that comes by hearing. Paul makes this point in Galatians 3, for example, when he reminds his readers that they saw Jesus as crucified (v.1) by hearing the gospel (v.2). We see this again in 2 Corinthians 4:2-6, as John Piper indicates:

> By means of the glory of Christ in the gospel, and for the sake of the glory of Christ in the gospel, God restores our sight only in the presence of Christ in the gospel. In this way, when our eyes are opened and the light shines, it is Christ whom we see and enjoy and glorify... Christ is not visually present for us to see. He is presented today in the Word of God, especially the gospel... Therefore we can say that seeing the glory of Christ is what happens in the heart when the hearing of the gospel is made effective by the Spirit.[31]

I have given five reasons for caution about the mystical approach to experiencing God. I have also indicated that our confidence about God's presence with us is based on the solid rock of his promise, not the shifting sand of our feelings. But is this the whole story? Surely all believers have had times when they have sensed God's nearness in a special way, when they have perceived God's presence rather than merely believed in it. So it is not a case of either faith or feelings, but of both faith and feelings – isn't it?

Here too we need to return to our fundamental starting-point: that true devotion is a spirituality of the gospel. We need to begin our answer

---

[27]   Philippians 1:23.
[28]   1 John 3:2; Revelation 1:7.
[29]   See Revelation 21:3; 1 Corinthians 13:12; Revelation 22:4.
[30]   1 Peter 1:8.
[31]   John Piper, *When I Don't Desire God: How to Fight for Joy* (Wheaton: Crossway, 2004), pp 64-65 (his italics).

to this important question by reminding ourselves that we are united to God-in-Christ by responding to the gospel in faith.[32]

> Such ... are the causes of Christ's presence in his people. The Spirit and the word, on his side; on their side, a living faith... [It is] a spiritual union with Christ which the Spirit is the agent in accomplishing and faith the means of maintaining.[33]

6.2.   Knowing God's presence

This leads us to our second point: that in this spiritual union there is a knowing that is proper to faith, a knowing that relies upon God's word. This is not so much a sensing or feeling of God's presence as a recognition of it, an awareness that he is present in accordance with his promise.[34] This knowing is what Richard Baxter calls a 'believing apprehension':

> To walk with God, is to live as in his presence, and that with desire and delight... we believe and apprehend that wherever we are, we are before the Lord ... Our walking with God then is not only a sense of that common presence which he must needs afford to all; but it is also a believing apprehension of his gracious presence, as our God and reconciled Father, with whom we dwell, being brought near unto him by Christ; and who dwells in us by his Spirit.[35]

At its heart, this apprehension, this recognition, is a matter of faith and not of feelings. It is about trusting a promise rather than sensing a presence. So it has got more to do with what I know than how I feel.

Why does this matter? Is it really all that important? And aren't we in danger of splitting hairs here – after all, how much difference is there between an 'awareness' and a feeling? These are important questions, and they deserve a good answer. What follows is my attempt to provide that answer.

---

[32]   See Romans 10:8-17; 2 Corinthians 5:17–6:2; Galatians 3:1-9, 13-14, 26-29; 4:4-8; Ephesians 1:13; 1 Peter 1:1-5, 10-12, 21-25; 1 John 1:1-3; 4:9-16; 5:9-13.

[33]   Hugh Martin [1822-1885], *The Abiding Presence* (Fearn: Christian Focus, 2009), pp 193, 202.

[34]   See Psalms 46:7, 11; 73:23, 28; 91:15; 118:6-7; 139:18.

[35]   Richard Baxter [1615-1691], *The Practical Works of Richard Baxter: Selected Treatises* (Peabody: Hendrickson, 2010), pp 193-4.

6.2.1. Living by faith

What is at stake here is this fundamental Biblical principle: that our calling is to live by faith, taking God at his word and trusting him.[36] This is especially true of our devotion to God, which as we saw in Chapter 3, must be a spirituality of faith. Why does this need to be emphasized here? The reason is that the quest for direct experience of God can lead us astray at this point. That is because our experiences rather than our faith can become the focus in our walk with God. Again, we take our example from A.W. Tozer:

> we have in our hearts organs by means of which we can know God as certainly as we know material things through our familiar five senses... The soul has eyes with which to see and ears with which to hear. Feeble they may be from long disuse, but by the life-giving touch of Christ they are now alive and capable of sharpest sight and most sensitive hearing. As we begin to focus on God ... [a] new God-consciousness will seize upon us and we shall begin to taste and hear and inwardly feel God ...[37]

What is the problem here? It is the claim that we can experience God – we can feel him – through the spiritual equivalent of the physical senses. But isn't this so? Why else, for example, does David urge us to 'taste and see that the LORD is good'?[38] Yes, the Bible expects us to know God in a way that is intensely real – but for now, this is a reality that we participate in only by faith: 'If we taste the Lord, we taste through faith'.[39] So, commenting on 1 Peter 2:3 (a verse which alludes to Psalm 34:8), Alexander Nisbet observes that

> the way of believers' partaking and feeling of this graciousness or sweetness of the Lord be spiritual, arising in their hearts from their exercising of their faith in God as favourable to them through Christ ... All those tastes of the graciousness and sweetness of Christ which the saints may expect in this life are to be looked for in and through the Word ...[40]

---

[36] 2 Corinthians 5:7.

[37] *The Pursuit of God*, pp 32, 37.

[38] Psalm 34:8.

[39] Evagrius of Pontus [345-399], in Craig A. Blaising and Carmen S. Hardin (eds), *Psalms 1-50* (ACCS, Old Testament VII; Downers Grove: IVP, 2008), p 262.

[40] Alexander Nisbet [1623-1669], *An Exposition of 1 & 2 Peter* (Edinburgh: Banner of Truth, 1982 [1658]), p 64.

It is through the word of God, the gospel, that we are given new birth;[41] it is through the same word that, as newborn babies, we taste the Lord's goodness.[42] What comes to us through the word, we receive by faith. So, preaching on this latter passage, Charles Spurgeon recognizes that faith is

> the soul's eye by which it sees the Lord. Faith is the soul's ear by which we hear what God the Lord will speak. Faith is the spiritual hand which touches and grasps the things not seen as yet... Faith also is the soul's taste by which we perceive the sweetness of the Lord, and enjoy it for ourselves.[43]

Faith is the key. When the Bible speaks as though we have spiritual senses – so that we taste the Lord's goodness, for example – it is speaking metaphorically about what faith does. And here and now it is not by feelings but by faith that we know God.

> They that have lived most in communion with God have lived most in the exercise of faith; trusting him with all they have, in all they fear, for all they want. Walking in communion with God is a walking by faith, not by sense ... While you stay yourselves on God, and go leaning on him, you are near him; he is near you, you are in fellowship with him.[44]

Not to recognize that our communion with God is a 'walking by faith' amounts to a confusion about where we are. In effect, it is to want now what we can have only at the End, when faith will give way to sight, and we will know God directly and immediately.

But is there no place for feelings? Won't it feel good to taste that the Lord is good? And in addition to believing in God, aren't we meant to

---

[41]   1 Peter 1:23-25.

[42]   1 Peter 2:2-3.

[43]   C.H. Spurgeon, *The Metropolitan Tabernacle Pulpit*, 36: p 558 [1890]. Cf. what David Clarkson [1622-1686] says about faith:

'Faith is the *hand* of the soul; so it receives Christ himself, who is the gift of God, John iv.10. It is the *arm* of the soul; so it embraces Christ, Cant. iii.4. It is the *eye* of the soul; so it looks upon Christ, as the stung Israelites upon the brazen serpent, John iii.14, 15. It is the *mouth* of the soul; so it feeds upon Christ the bread from heaven, John vi.32-34. It is the *foot* of the soul; so it comes to Christ, Matthew xi., John vi...' (*The Works of David Clarkson*, three volumes (Edinburgh: Banner of Truth, 1988), 1: p 77 (his italics).)

[44]   Clarkson, *Works*, 3: p 182.

love him, fear him, rejoice in him, and so on? The answer is, Yes, of course. So what place do feelings have in our walk with God? This is a large and difficult topic, but we have room only to consider three important issues raised by this question.[45] The first is that our insistence on putting faith before feelings does not mean that faith is something dry and cerebral. It means much more than giving assent to certain truths. That is not saving faith, for even the enemy goes this far.[46] True faith means not only believing the Lord, but also believing in him and upon him.[47] It is thus a matter of the heart: 'The heart of faith is wanting, till faith hath taken possession of the heart.'[48] It means confidence in, reliance on, and commitment to the Lord himself. To believe is to come to him;[49] to follow him;[50] to look to him;[51] to receive him;[52] to take refuge in him;[53] to rely on him;[54] to trust him;[55] and so on. So faith is a deeply personal response to and engagement with God-in-Christ.

6.2.2. Living in our personalities

This brings us to the second point we need to make. This concerns the fact that our personality-type has a significant influence on the way we express and experience the faith we have been speaking about. The fact is that we are wired differently – some of us are very intense by nature, while others are quite phlegmatic; some are very left-brain, others very right-brain; some wear their heart on their sleeves, others are very private people ... and so on. There are many kinds of people in the world, many personality-types. It is important not to treat these as

---

45   Note our discussion of emotions in Chapter 5.

46   James 2:19.

47   Believing him: John 5:46-47; 8:45-46; 10:37-38; believing in him: John 6:29; 9:35-36; 12:37, 44; 16:9; 17:20; believing (up)on him: Acts 11:17; 16:31; Romans 4:24; 1 Timothy 1:16.

48   Richard Baxter, *Works*, p 590. See Psalms 28:7; 112:7; Proverbs 3:5; Luke 24:25; Romans 10:9-10; etc.

49   Matthew 11:28; John 6:35-37, 64-65; 7:37; 1 Peter 2:4; etc.

50   Numbers 14:24; 32:10-12; Deuteronomy 13:4; 2 Chronicles 34:31; Hosea 11:10; Mark 8:34; 10:21, 28; John 8:12; 12:26; 21:19, 22; Revelation 14:4; etc.

51   Psalms 34:5; 105:4; 123:2; John 6:40; 12:44-45; etc.

52   John 1:12; Colossians 2:6.

53   Psalms 2:12; 5:11; 7:1; 11:1; 16:1; 18:2, 30; 34:8, 22; 118:8-9; etc.

54   2 Chronicles 13:18; 14:11; 16:8; Psalm 71:6; Isaiah 10:20; 48:2; 50:10; 2 Corinthians 1:9; 1 John 4:16; etc.

55   Psalms 9:10; 20:7; 32:10; 40:3-4; Proverbs 3:5; Isaiah 25:9; 26:3-4; Romans 10:11; 1 Peter 2:6-7; etc.

confining or inflexible, for God is able to make deep and lasting changes in each one of us. Yet we all have a natural tendency to engage with God and the gospel in line with how we function as individuals. So, just as we give and receive human love differently, there will be differences in the way we express our love for God and his grace. For some of us, who are 'heart'-people, the most important thing is that his love for us is real; for others, the 'head'-people, what matters is that it is true. The strongest tendency in some will be to feel this as deeply as possible; in others, to understand it as fully as possible. Each of these approaches is valid – so long as it doesn't try to exclude the other but, on the contrary, seeks to include it. Each type of personality has its own strengths and weaknesses, its benefits and dangers – and each will appropriate and express the realities of faith differently to some degree, even though each should be aiming to make a full-orbed, wholehearted response to the Lord and his word. We referred above to the fact that faith is 'a deeply personal response'. The point we are making here is that the texture of that response depends on the person whose response it is. So saying that it is 'deeply personal' is not the same as saying that it is deeply introverted – or thoroughly extroverted either, for that matter. It is unhelpful, and in the end unfair, to give the impression that authentic spirituality involves the kind of intensity that only some are likely to experience. People with a more matter-of-fact approach to life also have a place in the family of God!

6.2.3. Root then fruit

The third point we need to make about faith and feelings is this: feelings can serve as a confirmation of our faith, but they are not meant to be its foundation. This applies especially to our knowledge of God's presence with us. Here God's promise is the foundation, the root, while our sense of his presence is the confirmation, the fruit. Again, Spurgeon has some helpful comments on this matter:

> Faith doth not come by feeling, but through faith arises much of holy feeling, and the more a man lives in the walk of faith, as a rule, the more will he feel and enjoy the light of God's countenance. Faith hath something firmer to stand upon than those ever-changing frames and feelings which, like the weather of our own sunless land, is fickle and frail, and changeth speedily from brightness into gloom. You may get feeling from faith, and the best of it, but you

will be long before you will find any faith that is worth the having, if you try to evoke it from frames and feelings.[56]

The root has to do with an unvarying fact: that in accordance with his promise, God is present with his people.[57] But the fruit – our sense of his presence – is not stable and enduring like this. Comparing it to the British weather, Spurgeon says that it is 'fickle and frail' – it comes and goes. Sometimes it is very clear; sometimes it is muted – and sometimes it seems to vanish completely. One of faith's earliest lessons is that in such times we hold fast to the root: we go by what we know rather than how we feel. So we hold fast to the fact that God is with us even when he doesn't seem to be near.

> God is present everywhere, but especially with his saints; and not only when they are apprehensive of him, but when they perceive no evidence of his presence... the sun may shine and I not see it; there may be fire in the room and I not feel it; so God may be really present with his people when he is not sensibly present with his people...[58]

God's promise tells us that he is present even if we have no sense that this is so – and we believe it even if we are unable to perceive it. As we noted earlier in this chapter, we walk by faith, not by feel.

6.3. Fluctuating feelings

Why does our sense of God's presence fluctuate? Why does he seem to be very near at some times and yet so far away at other times? There are several reasons for this. One of the most obvious is that sometimes life goes wrong, and we find ourselves afflicted by suffering of one kind or another. Perhaps the worst aspect of being in pain is that it tends to eclipse our sense of God's presence: 'Why, LORD, do you stand far off? Why do you hide yourself in times of trouble?'[59] Yet we know that even in such times God is still with us: 'Even though I walk through the darkest valley, I will fear no evil, for you are with me'.[60] Although our

---

[56]   C.H. Spurgeon, *The Metropolitan Tabernacle Pulpit*, 18: p 40 [1872].

[57]   Matthew 28:20; Hebrews 13:5; cf. Deuteronomy 31:6, 8; Joshua 1:5.

[58]   Thomas Brooks, *Works*, 5: pp 539, 541.

[59]   Psalm 10:1; See also Psalms 22:1, 11, 19; 35:22-25; 38:21-22; 71:10-13.

[60]   Psalm 23:4.

suffering makes him seem far away, we know that God is near, ready to hear us and help us.[61]

> Though the saints have not always the comforting presence of God in their afflictions, yet they have always the supporting presence of God in their afflictions ...[62]

Because of his promise, faith knows that he is holding us fast – even if he doesn't seem to be holding us close.

Another reason we do not always sense God's presence is that there are times – too many of them! – when we go wrong. Our weakness in the face of the world, the flesh, and the devil interferes with the sense that God is with us.

> If we were wholly freed from the effects of a depraved nature, the snares of an evil world, and the subtle temptations of Satan, our actual communion with God would be always lively, sensible, and fervent... But so long as we are liable to security, spiritual pride, indolence, an undue attachment to worldly things, and irregular distempered passions, the Lord is pleased to afford, increase, suspend, or renew the sensible impressions of his love and grace, in such seasons and measures as he sees most suitable to prevent or control these evils, or to humble us for them.[63]

Sometimes our sense of God's presence is squeezed out when we pay undue attention to the clamour of the world. Sometimes we forfeit this sense by proving to be ungodly and unfaithful – hence David's prayer: 'Do not cast me from your presence ...'[64]

A third reason that our sense of God's presence fluctuates is that while we live in this body and in this world, our moods and emotions are very changeable. The one constant about them is that they are not constant! They ebb and flow in ways we understand – and for reasons we can only guess at. They are affected by such factors as the sunlight, our sleep patterns, our body's biochemistry, and our upbringing. While

---

[61] Psalms 34:15-22; 69:13-18; 85:4-9; 119:150-151; 145:18-20; Isaiah 50:7-9; Lamentations 3:55-58.

[62] Thomas Brooks, *Works*, 5: p 542.

[63] John Newton [1725-1807], *The Works of John Newton*, six volumes (Edinburgh: Banner of Truth, 1985), 1: p 308.

[64] Psalm 51:11; See also Psalms 25:16-18; 38:1-4, 15-18, 21-22; Isaiah 59:2.

our feelings are subject to so much change, our sense of God's presence also comes and goes.

> [T]he evidence yielded by feeling is singularly fickle. When your feelings are peaceful and delightful, they are soon broken in upon, and become restless and melancholy. The most fickle of elements, the most feeble of creatures, the most contemptible of circumstances, may sink or raise our spirits: experienced men come to think less and less of their present emotions as they reflect upon the little reliance which can be safely placed upon them... Feelings are a set of cloudy, windy phenomena which cannot be trusted in relation to the eternal verities of God.[65]

A fourth reason is that in his wise and holy sovereignty, the Spirit varies his dealings with us:

> They who, by that faith which is of the operation of God, are thus united to him in Christ, are brought thereby into a state of real habitual communion with him. The degree of its exercise and sensible perception on our parts, is various in different persons, and in the same person at different times; for it depends upon the communications we receive from the Lord the Spirit, who distributes to every man severally according to his will, adjusting his dispensations with a wise and merciful respect to our present state of discipline.[66]

So, sometimes the Spirit diminishes or even withholds our sense of God's presence in accordance with our condition. This suggests that we should regard the sense of God's presence as a gift and not an entitlement. And as a gift, it can be given in varying proportions or even withdrawn:

> The Holy Spirit is a sovereign and free agent who dispenses his favours in what measure he pleases and at what times he will.[67]

A fifth reason why our sense of God's presence varies is that we do not keep reminding ourselves of his promise and responding to it. As a result, our awareness of his presence decreases and can vanish

---

[65] C.H. Spurgeon, *The Metropolitan Tabernacle Pulpit*, 61: p 473 [1915].

[66] John Newton, *Works*, 1: p 308.

[67] Isaac Watts [1674-1748], *A Guide to Prayer* (Edinburgh: Banner of Truth, 2001 [1715]), p 157.

altogether. What can we do about this? The solution is very simple. In the first place, I need to think of God more often!

> Entertain frequent and delightful thoughts of God. Such will present us to God, and make him present with us. While they are in our minds, he is in our hearts ... Christ enters into our hearts, when thoughts of Christ enter; and the meditation of him, in effect, is his inhabitation in us.[68]

In particular, I need to re-focus my attention on God's promise, and thus on the fact of his presence. In this way I become conscious again that he is with me. Then I need to express that awareness by turning to him more often.

> He walks as in the presence of God that converses with Him in frequent prayer and frequent communion; in all his necessities, in all doubtings; that opens all his wants to Him; that weeps before Him for his sins; that asks remedy and support for his weakness; that fears Him as a Judge; reverences Him as a Lord; obeys Him as a Father; and loves Him.[69]

This frequent turning to God does not mean setting aside many prayer-times throughout the day; rather, it means creating many Nehemiah-moments.[70] The more I relate to God, the more I act on my awareness of the fact of his presence, the more likely I am to have a sense of that presence. But it is important to remember the root-and-fruit principle here: it is the fact of God's presence that gives me some sense of it, the promise that undergirds the perception. When I have a sense of God's presence, that confirms my conviction that he is always present in accordance with his promise – but I am to live by that faith, and not by how I feel.

In this chapter we have been arguing that if the Bible is a sufficient and reliable guide to true devotion, then the mystic's quest for felt experience of God involves some significant problems. There is much more that could be said about this important subject, but we must now turn our attention to another feature of popular mysticism: its approach to prayer. Once again, we will aim to assess what is being taught here by what the Bible teaches.

---

[68]   David Clarkson, *Works*, 3: p 181.

[69]   Jeremy Taylor [1613-1667], *The Rules and Exercises of Holy Living*, abridged with a preface by Anne Lamb (New York: Harper & Row, 1970 [1651]), p 25.

[70]   Nehemiah 2:4-5.

7.   The Voice of God

One of the most important features of the mystical path is its approach to prayer. At the heart of this approach is the claim that prayer involves listening to the voice of God:

> Jesus Christ is alive and here to teach his people himself. His voice is not hard to hear; his vocabulary is not hard to understand. But we must learn how to hear his voice and obey his word. It is this ability to hear and obey that is the heart and soul of ... meditative prayer.[1]

7.1.   Prayer as a dialogue

For the mystic, true prayer is not a monologue but a dialogue: it

> begins in listening and seeking to hear the Word of God. It consists in a response to the voice of God speaking within the depths of our soul.[2]

This understanding of prayer is not confined to classical expressions of mysticism; it is advocated in many popular-level works:

> Prayer is a two-way conversation between God the Father and one of us, his children... when prayer is a one-way conversation, it is a very dull and boring experience. And that is exactly what prayer is to most people... prayer [is] transformed when it moves from a monologue to a dialogue – when you listen to God speak after you have spoken or when you listen to him speak before you utter a word.[3]

> To listen to God in prayer is to look up to Him with the intuitive-thinking organ the Bible calls the heart. Through the eyes and ears of the heart we see and hear God; through it we apprehend the transcendent ... To listen in prayer for the voice of the Lord is to find the mind of Christ; it is to gain transcendent wisdom, a wisdom that includes understanding, guidance, knowledge, exhortation, and

---

[1]   Richard Foster, *Meditative Prayer* (London: MARC Europe, 1983), p 3.
[2]   Donald G. Bloesch, *The Struggle of Prayer* (Colorado Springs: Helmers & Howard, 1988), p 54.
[3]   Peter Lord, *Hearing God* (Grand Rapids: Baker, 1988), pp 205-6.

consolation ... The Christ-life within listens for the voice of the Father.[4]

Although there are some important differences between the authors just quoted, they coincide at this point: we experience God as the One who speaks directly into our souls – and true prayer involves listening to his voice.

7.1.1.   What kind of dialogue?

What are we to make of this view of prayer? Are we meant to experience prayer as a dialogue, a two-way conversation? The answer must be a qualified 'Yes':

> Be much with God in holy dialogue, letting him speak to you by His Word while you speak back to Him by your prayers and praises.[5]

There is a dialogue with God that should be an essential part of our daily life – but it happens with prayer, not in prayer. Prayer is our part of this dialogue, in which we respond to what God says to us in Scripture. In response to his word, we speak and he hears – prayer goes from our minds or mouths to God's ears.[6] It is this responsive view of prayer, rather than the dialogue view, that is found consistently in writers from the Reformed and Evangelical tradition. In addition to the example just quoted from the nineteenth century, here is one from each of the sixteenth, seventeenth, eighteenth, and twentieth centuries:

> Next to the preaching of the Gospel, in which God speaks to us and offers us all his grace and goods, the greatest and foremost work we can do is to speak to Him *in turn* through prayer and to receive what He gives us.[7]

The Word will direct you, quicken and encourage you, unto prayer.

---

4   Leanne Payne, *Listening Prayer: Learning to Hear God's Voice and Keep a Prayer Journal* (Grand Rapids: Baker, 1994), pp 122, 125.

5   C.H. Spurgeon, *An All-Round Ministry: Addresses to Ministers and Students* (Edinburgh: Banner of Truth, 1960 [1900]), p 340.

6   See, for example, Psalms 5:1-3; 17:1, 6; 54:2; 66:17-20; 88:1-2; 116:1-2.

7   Luther, *Works*, 24: p 389 (my italics). Cf. also:
'In the first place, one must hear the Word, which is given to us by God. Here we do nothing, but we only take hold of what has been offered. In the second place, one must pray and implore God's help after the Word has been heard and taken hold of ...' (Luther, *Works*, 5: p 373).

By the Word, God speaks to you; by prayer, you speak to him.[8]

The Bible is a letter God hath sent to us, prayer is a letter we send to him ...[9]

One of the great privileges of a believer is to have fellowship with almighty God. We do this by listening to him speak to us from his word and by speaking to him through prayer.[10]

Obviously, the basis for this approach to prayer is a particular view of where and how God speaks to us. Or to say this in another way, the basis is a particular view of revelation and the Bible. We will take this up again after we have considered the next point.

7.1.2. The location of revelation

There is a second problem with the dialogue view of prayer. Although its exponents often acknowledge the primacy of the Bible, they too easily shift the location of revelation from the Bible to the believer's heart. This leads to all kinds of claims to know what God wants, many of which bypass the Bible completely. We find a striking example in the way a popular book on prayer begins:

> God has graciously allowed me to catch a glimpse into his heart, and I want to share with you what I have seen. Today the heart of God is an open wound of love. He aches over our distance and preoccupation. He mourns that we do not draw near to him. He grieves that we have forgotten him. He weeps over our obsession with muchness and manyness. He longs for our presence. And he is inviting you – and me – to come home ... The key to this home, this heart of God, is prayer... Believe me. The Father's heart is open wide ...[11]

---

[8] Nathaniel Vincent [1639-1697], The Spirit of Prayer, in The Puritans on Prayer (Morgan, PA: Soli Deo Gloria, 1995), p 173. Cf. George Swinnock [1627-1673], The Works of George Swinnock, five volumes (Edinburgh: Banner of Truth, 1992), I: p 107: 'As Scripture is God's letter, wherein he openeth his mind to man, so prayer is man's letter, wherein he openeth his mind to God'.

[9] Matthew Henry [1662-1714], The Secret of Communion with God (Grand Rapids: Kregel, 1991 [1712]), p 19.

[10] Jerry Bridges, The Practice of Godliness (Colorado Springs: NavPress, 1983), p 62.

[11] Foster, Prayer, pp 1, 2. These words form part of the introduction entitled, "Coming Home: An Invitation to Prayer" (pp 1-4).

This is an astonishing claim! In effect, the author puts himself in the position of a prophet or apostle. He believes that he is revealing God's 'heart' to us. And he urges us to act upon this revelation, by responding with our praying to God's desire for us to come home to him. In seeking to draw us into prayer, he goes on to quote Samuel Coleridge, Julian of Norwich, Richard Rolle, and Charles Wesley, and to describe an experience had by a friend of his. There is no reference at all to the Bible in this introduction to the book.[12]

Perhaps the nearest analogy for what is being advocated here, and a very clear indication of its dangers, is the origin of the Quaker movement.[13] In the strenuous conflict between the Quakers and the Puritans, one of the core issues was that of revelation. The Quakers denied – indeed, they scorned – the Puritan teaching that the Spirit speaks and reveals Christ in Scripture. They insisted instead that the Spirit speaks in the believer. This meant that, in practice, they treated the Bible as a dead letter. So one of the early Quakers described their meetings as follows:

> We met together often and waited upon the Lord in pure silence, from our own words, and all men's words, and hearkened to the voice of the Lord, and felt his word in our hearts, to burn up and beat down all that was contrary to God, and so we obeyed the Light of Christ in us, and followed the motions of the Lord's pure Spirit ...[14]

They had no need to use the Bible because God spoke to them directly. Their founder George Fox even went so far as to compare himself with the prophets and apostles, claiming to be inspired by the Spirit to the same degree:

> These things I did not see by the help of man, nor by the letter, though they are written in the letter, but I saw them in the light of the Lord Jesus Christ, and by his immediate Spirit and power, as did

---

[12]   This sets the tone for the book as a whole. It devotes a chapter to each of twenty-one different forms of prayer. There is no systematic attempt to derive these ways of praying from the Bible: each of the chapters begins with a quotation from someone who has written about prayer. The Bible is referred to along the way, but usually to illustrate a point that has been derived from somewhere else.

[13]   It is worthy of note that the author we have just quoted is a Quaker.

[14]   Quoted in Geoffrey F. Nuttall, *The Holy Spirit in Puritan Faith and Experience*, 2nd ed. (Oxford: Blackwell, 1947), p 69.

the holy men of God, by whom the Holy Scriptures were written.[15]

A study of where this theology and practice led the Quakers serves as a very clear warning about its dangers.[16]

Against this approach, it needs to be said (as one of the Puritans said in response to the Quakers):

> God's people are led by the Spirit, when they are led by the word inspired by the Spirit,... and they are taught by God, when taught by his Book: No Spirit of Christ doth abstract any man's faith from the Word of God ...[17]

In his *Nature of Saving Conversion* [1719], the New England Puritan Solomon Stoddard argues that the Spirit

> reveals things to us by opening our eyes to see what is revealed in the Word; but the Spirit doth not reveal new truths, not revealed in the Word... If God do but help us to receive the Revelation in the Word, we shall have comfort enough without new Revelation.[18]

The conflict between these views is not limited to the beginnings of the Quaker movement, of course. Others both before and after them have found it necessary to make the same point the Puritans insisted on. So Calvin says that

> the Spirit ... has not the task of inventing new and unheard-of Revelation, or of forging a new kind of doctrine, to lead us away from the received doctrine of the gospel, but of sealing our minds with that very doctrine ... [so] we ought zealously to apply ourselves both to read and to hearken to Scripture if indeed we want to receive any gain and benefit from the Spirit of God ... [for] the Word is the

---

[15] The Journal of George Fox [1624-1691], in *Quaker Spirituality: Selected Writings*, edited and introduced by Douglas V. Steere (Classics of Western Spirituality; New York: Paulist, 1984), p 69. Fox also speaks of himself as having 'a message and a word from the Lord as the prophets and apostles had and did' (p 81).

[16] See especially Adam, *Hearing God's Words*, pp 179-202; T.L. Underwood, *Primitivism, Radicalism, and the Lamb's War: The Baptist-Quaker Conflict in Seventeenth-Century England* (Oxford Studies in Historical Theology; New York: OUP, 1997), especially chapters 2-4, 7.

[17] Richard Hollinworth [1607-1656], *The Holy Ghost on the Bench, Other Spirits at the Bar: Or the Judgment of the Holy Spirit of God upon the Spirits of the Times, Recorded in Holy Writ.* (London: Luke Fawn, 1656), p 25.

[18] Quoted in Jonathan Edwards, *The Religious Affections*, p 158.

instrument by which the Lord dispenses the illumination of his Spirit to believers.[19]

Commenting on John 16:13, Luther says that

Christ sets bounds for the message of the Holy Spirit Himself. He is not to preach anything new or anything else than Christ and His Word. Thus we have a sure guide and touchstone for judging the false spirits. We can declare that it surely does not indicate the presence of the Holy Spirit when a person proclaims his own thoughts and notions and begins to teach in Christendom something apart from or in addition to what Christ taught... now that the apostles have preached the Word and have given their writings, and nothing more than what they have written remains to be revealed, no new and special revelation or miracle is necessary.[20]

Then in 1774 we find the Evangelical leader John Newton saying that

the Holy Spirit does influence the hearts of all the children of God ... they are inspired, not with new Revelation, but with grace and wisdom to understand, apply, and feed upon the great things already revealed in the Scriptures ...[21]

This point about the relationship between Scripture and the Spirit was also made from the opposite angle. So in his Journal, John Wesley says that a certain individual

was doubtless a pious man, but a thorough enthusiast; guided, in all his steps, not by the written word, but by his own imagination; which he calls the Spirit.[22]

Several years later he had occasion to refer to this man again:

He was ... greatly devoted to God. But he was a consummate enthusiast. Not the word of God, but his own imaginations, which he took for divine inspirations, were the sole rule both of his words and actions. Hence arose his marvellous instability ... Upon the whole, I do not know that I ever read a more dangerous writer; one who so wonderfully blends together truth and falsehood; solid piety,

---

[19] Calvin, *Institutes*, I.ix.1-3 (1: pp 94, 96).
[20] *Works*, 24: pp 363, 367.
[21] *Works*, 1: p 489.
[22] John Wesley [1703-1791], *The Works of John Wesley*, fourteen volumes (Grand Rapids: Zondervan, 1872), 4: p 50 (for Tuesday, July 4, 1775).

and wild enthusiasm.[23]

There are two convictions at work here: the Bible is God speaking to us, and the Spirit works by and with the word of God.[24] These are foundational to Evangelical spirituality, which relies on the Bible to discover how God wants us to express our devotion to him. This applies especially to our practice of prayer:

> God's word must be the guide of your desires and the ground of your expectations in prayer ...[25]

When we make the Bible our guide and ground in this way, the effect is to move us away from the mystical view of prayer as a two-way conversation. Prayer is our response to the word God speaks in Scripture, not to his voice in our hearts. Thus the dialogue view of prayer has not been a feature of Evangelical spirituality.

7.2. *Listening to God*

Some popular works go further than this dialogue view of prayer, however, maintaining that hearing God's inner voice is a vital component of authentic Christian living as a whole.[26] Thomas à Kempis' famous work makes the point this way:

> Blessed is the soul that hears the Lord speaking within it, and receives comfort from His Word. Blessed are the ears that hear the still, small voice of God, and disregard the whispers of the world. Blessed are the ears that listen to Truth teaching inwardly, and not to the voices of the world... Blessed are those who enter deeply into inner things, and daily prepare themselves to receive the secrets of heaven.[27]

---

[23]   *Works*, 4: p 131 (for Saturday, July 4, 1778).

[24]   On which see Peter Adam, *Written For Us: Receiving God's Words in the Bible* (Nottingham: IVP, 2008), Part 4.

[25]   Matthew Henry, *Communion with God*, p 16.

[26]   See the extensive expositions in Klaus Bockmuehl, *Listening to the God who Speaks: Reflections on God's Guidance from Scripture and the Lives of God's People* (Colorado Springs: Helmers & Howard, 1990); Joyce Huggett, *Listening to God* (London: Hodder, 1986); and Dallas Willard, *Hearing God: Developing a Conversational Relationship with God* (Downers Grove: IVP, 1999).

[27]   Thomas à Kempis [1380-1471], *The Imitation of Christ* (Penguin Classics; Harmondsworth: Penguin, 1952), p 89.

Coming nearer to our own time, Frank Buchman, the founder of Moral Re-Armament, maintained that

> the lesson the world most needs is the art of listening to God... Definite, accurate, adequate information can come from the mind of God to the minds of men. This is normal prayer.[28]

There is a real problem here: the implication that the written word in Scripture is not complete without the whispered word in the soul. We see this in a recent book called *The Power of a Whisper*.[29] At first glance, this appears to regard the Bible as the comprehensive source from which all of God's 'whispers' come to us:

> God, in his kindness, has provided you and me with a lifetime of whispers, found between the covers of the Bible... through his Word, every Christ-follower has full access to what he wants us to know – about himself, his character and the life he is calling us to live.[30]

But the book turns out to be full of anecdotes about 'whispers' that are taken to be heaven-sent even though they do not come from Scripture:

> God listens when we speak through prayer, and we are to listen when he speaks through his whispers... By the still, small voice of God, our lives are flooded with personal assurance, correction, insight, guidance from above.[31]

> The goal of the Christ-following life is to grow to the point that we live in God's reality ... And that's a way of life we'll only maintain consistently by hearing from heaven on a regular basis.[32]

The author does not hesitate to draw the Quaker-style conclusion:

> Just like the kings and prophets and apostles who have gone before us, you and I can hear straight from God.[33]

---

[28] Frank Buchman [1878-1961], quoted in Bockmuehl, *Listening*, p 8.
[29] Bill Hybels, *The Power of a Whisper: Hearing God, Having the Guts to Respond* (Grand Rapids: Zondervan, 2010).
[30] *Whisper*, p 140.
[31] *Whisper*, pp 44, 50.
[32] *Whisper*, p 89.
[33] *Whisper*, p 59.

And like the Quakers, he does not regard this as something for the exceptional few; it is seen as the key to authentic Christian living:

> The heart and soul of the Christian life is learning to hear God's voice and then developing the courage to do what he asks us to do.[34]

The inevitable result of this approach will be what is was with the Quakers: lip-service will still be paid to the importance of the Bible, but in practice it will be regarded as a dead letter, and there will be a marked preference for what the Spirit is thought to be saying here and now.[35]

7.2.1. The sufficiency of Scripture

Against this approach we must set the consistent teaching of the Reformed and Evangelical tradition. Based on the Bible's own testimony, this affirms the sufficiency of Scripture: everything we need in order to know God and to live with him and for him is given to us in the Bible. The first Helvetic Confession [1536] states the point this way:

> Biblical Scripture ... alone deals with everything that serves the true knowledge, love and honour of God, as well as true piety and the making of a godly, honest and blessed life.[36]

One of the Anglican Homilies, compiled during the reign of Elizabeth I, puts it equally simply and succinctly:

> [T]he Holy Scriptures are God's treasure house, wherein are found all things needful for us to see, to hear, to learn, and to believe,

---

[34] Bill Hybels, *Too Busy Not to Pray: Slowing Down to be with God*, 3rd edition (Nottingham: IVP, 2008), p 125.

[35] So the Quaker theologian Robert Barclay says that 'the Spirit, and not the Scriptures, is the foundation and ground of all Truth and knowledge, and the primary rule of faith and manners' (*An Apology for the True Christian Divinity*: The Third Proposition: Concerning the Scriptures, §II). And William Penn [1644-1718] says that the Quakers will not allow 'any book, or literal rule or judge, to come between that indwelling spirit of light, life, and wisdom from God, and the soul, as its rule of faith and practice'. (A Discourse of the General Rule of Faith and Practice and Judge of Controversy [1673], in *The Select Works of William Penn*, three volumes, 4th edition (London: Phillips, 1825), 2: p 25.

[36] Quoted in Timothy Ward, *Words of Life: Scripture as the Living and Active Word of God* (Nottingham: IVP, 2009), p 111.

necessary for the attaining of eternal life.[37]

The Westminster Confession of Faith [1648] is equally clear and direct:

The whole counsel of God concerning all things necessary for His own glory, man's salvation, faith and life, is either expressly set down in Scripture, or by good and necessary consequence may be deduced from Scripture: unto which nothing is at any time to be added, whether by new Revelation of the Spirit, or traditions of men.

This conviction is also stated clearly by the Puritan theologian John Owen:

All divine truths necessary to be known and to be believed, that we may live unto God in faith and obedience, or come unto and abide in Christ, as also to be preserved from seducers, are contained in the Scripture ...[38]

[T]he Holy Spirit of God hath prepared and disposed of the Scripture so as it might be a most sufficient and absolutely perfect way and means of communicating ... that saving knowledge of God and his will which is needful that we may live unto him, and come unto the enjoyment of him in his glory.[39]

Simplest of all is Calvin, who asks, 'Is not all the doctrine of God contained in the Bible? What can a man say more?'[40]

These affirmations were not made in a vacuum. They stood over against competing views that denied the sufficiency of Scripture – like

---

37   The Second Book, Homily X: An information for them which take offence at certain places of the Holy Scripture, in *Certain Sermons or Homilies appointed to be read in Churches in the time of Queen Elizabeth* (London: SPCK, 1864), p 392; cf. also the First Book, Homily I:
      '[T]here is no truth nor doctrine necessary for our justification and everlasting salvation, but that is or may be drawn out of that fountain and well of truth... in holy Scripture is fully contained what we ought to do and what to eschew, what to believe, what to love, and what to look for at God's hands at length... We may learn also in these books to know God's will and pleasure, as much as for this present time is convenient for us to know' (pp 1-2).

38   John Owen [1616-1683], *The Works of John Owen*, edited by William H. Goold, sixteen volumes (Edinburgh: Banner of Truth, 1965-1968), 4: p 148.

39   *Works*, 4: p 187.

40   John Calvin, *Sermons on the Epistles to Timothy and Titus* (Edinburgh: Banner of Truth, 1983 [1579]), p 803.

that of the Quakers, for example.[41] These views provide the context for the following statement about how God leads us:

> He hath tied us to the standing rule of the word, forbidding us to give heed to any other voice or spirit, leading us another way ... Scripture-light is a safe and sure light, a pleasant and sufficient light.[42]

Along with the other statements just quoted, this also challenges such views as those presented in the book we have just considered. This is obviously a point of fundamental importance, for it goes to the heart of how we are to live before God. Accordingly, it needs to be emphasized that we are dealing here with one of the foundations of Evangelical spirituality: namely, that the Scriptures are entirely sufficient as a disclosure of God's will and ways, and of how we are to relate to him. No other 'words' are needed – everything we can know here and now about God is given to us in the Bible.

> It is a full and complete rule and measure, both of things to be believed and practiced; it will admit no addition, because it is defective in nothing ...[43]

This conviction about the sufficiency of Scripture goes hand-in-hand with our recognition of the supremacy of the Lord Jesus as Revealer. He is the pinnacle and climax of God's work of revelation: 'all the treasures of wisdom and knowledge' are present in him;[44] he is 'full of grace and truth'.[45] With him, the Father's full and final Word,[46] the revelation we are given in this life is complete:

> In the past God spoke to our ancestors through the prophets at many times and in various ways, but in these last days he has

---

[41] So Robert Barclay insists that 'the Scriptures are not sufficient, neither were ever appointed to be the adequate and only rule, nor yet can guide or direct a Christian in all those things that are needful for him to know' (*An Apology*: The Second Proposition: Of Immediate Revelation, §IX).

[42] Flavel, *Works*, 3: p 483. Flavel's discussion of 'False teachers ... pretending to extraordinary Revelation, visions, and voices from heaven' (3: p 481) is found in 3: pp 481-484.

[43] George Swinnock, *Works*, 2: p 438.

[44] Colossians 2:3.

[45] John 1:14, 17.

[46] John 1:1, 14.

spoken to us by his Son ... [47]

What we need now is not fresh revelation, but constantly-renewed insight into the significance of what has been revealed in him.

> In giving us His Son, His only Word (for He possesses no other), He spoke everything to us at once in this sole Word – and He has no more to say... Those who desire to ... receive some vision or revelation are guilty not only of foolish behavior but also of offending Him, by not fixing their eyes entirely on Christ ... God could reason as follows: If I have already told you all things in my Word, my Son, and if I have no other word, what answer of revelation can I now make that would surpass this? Fasten your eyes on Him alone because in Him I have spoken and revealed all and in Him you will discover even more than you ask for and desire.[48]

7.2.2. Our need for guidance

But are things really this simple? Does the Bible actually give us everything that we need? The view that we are considering insists that it doesn't, arguing that we need individualized words from God in addition to the Bible:

> I happily insist that so far as principles are concerned, the Bible says all that needs to be said or can be said. But the principles have to be applied before they can be lived out ... Our reverence for and faith in the Bible must not be allowed to blind us to the need for personal divine instruction *within* the principles of the Bible and yet beyond the details of what it explicitly says.[49]

> [W]e must certainly go beyond ... the words of the Bible to find out what God is speaking to us... They have to be *applied* to us as individuals and to our individualized circumstances, or they remain no part of our lives.[50]

---

[47] Hebrews 1:1-2.
[48] John of the Cross [1542-1591], *Selected Writings*, edited with an Introduction by Kieran Kavanaugh, O.C.D. (Classics of Western Spirituality; New York: Paulist Press, 1987), pp 128f.
[49] Willard, *Hearing God*, p 59.
[50] Willard, *Hearing God*, p 167 (his italics).

So the Bible is needed for teaching the general principles that apply to us all. But we will not know how to live in a way that pleases God unless we are given specific personalized applications of those principles.

This is by no means a new approach. It sets out the same argument that the Quaker theologian Robert Barclay used against his Puritan opponents and their teaching about the sufficiency of Scripture:

> That which is given to Christians for a rule and guide, must needs be so full, that it may clearly and distinctly guide and order them in all things and occurrences that may fall out.

> But in that there are many hundred of things, with a regard to their circumstances, particular Christians may be concerned in, for which there can be no particular rule had in the Scriptures.

> Therefore the Scriptures cannot be a rule to them.[51]

The directions for life that the Bible was said to be unable to give were, according to Barclay, given by the Spirit:

> the Spirit of God leadeth, instructeth, and teacheth every true Christian whatsoever is needful for him to know.[52]

This was basic to the Quakers' way of life. So we find William Penn saying that their

> main fundamental in religion, is this, 'That God, through Christ, hath placed a principle in every man to inform him of his duty, and to enable him to do it ...'[53]

This 'principle' is the Holy Spirit:

> we assert the holy spirit [sic] to be the first and general rule and guide of true Christians, as that by which God is worshipped, sin detected, conscience convicted, duty manifested ...[54]

Thus the Quakers looked to the Spirit within rather than to the Scriptures to teach them how to live.

---

[51] *An Apology*: The Third Proposition: Concerning the Scriptures, §III.

[52] *An Apology*: The Second Proposition: Of Immediate Revelation, §X.

[53] William Penn, *Primitive Christianity Revived in the Faith and Practice of the People called Quakers* [1696], *Works*, 3: p 473.

[54] William Penn, *A Testimony to the Truth of God as held by the People called Quakers* [1698], *Works*, 3: p 576f.

The essential point being made here is that there is much we need to know that the Bible doesn't tell us. So God needs to make specific to each one of us what he has said in the Bible to all of us in general. Unless he does so, we will not know how to live out in the specific circumstances of our daily lives the general principles the Bible teaches. It is precisely this kind of guidance that God is said to give us by the Spirit in the here and now. What are we to make of this view?

I think we need to respond in two ways. The first is to say that it underestimates the scope of the Bible. We are told that it gives us all we need for entering into God's salvation. Then it is useful not only for teaching us, but also for rebuking, correcting, and training us in righteousness. In fact, its revelation is so comprehensive that by it God's servant is 'thoroughly equipped for every good work'.[55] This certainly doesn't sound as though the Bible needs to be supplemented in order to teach us how to live!

Secondly, we should admit that the Bible doesn't address all of the circumstances that we face in daily life. There are many decisions we must make where the Bible has nothing specific to say. Furthermore, it is right that we rely upon the Spirit's help to make the right connections between the general principles of Scripture and the particular situations that confront us. But how does the Spirit give us this help? That is, how does God guide us? Our Evangelical forebears had a ready answer:

> In general, he guides and directs his people, by affording them, in answer to prayer, the light of his Holy Spirit, which enables them to understand and to love the Scriptures... By treasuring up the doctrines, precepts, promises, examples, and exhortations of Scripture, in their minds ... they grow into an habitual frame of spiritual wisdom, and acquire a gracious taste, which enables them to judge of right and wrong with a degree of readiness and certainty, as a musical ear judges of sounds.[56]

We will return to this vital issue later in this chapter. We will argue that when the apostles are teaching us how to live, we are not given any instruction to rely upon the whispered word. Instead, we are to rely upon the Spirit to teach us wisdom and give us insight. As a general rule, he doesn't give us more revelation, this time of a specific,

---

[55]   2 Timothy 3:15-17.
[56]   John Newton, *Works*, 1: p 330.

personalized kind. Instead, he gives us greater illumination. He teaches us how to use what has been revealed – how to make wise applications of what the Bible teaches.[57] So, against the views of Quakers ancient and modern, we need to insist that the Spirit's role in applying the Bible is about making us wise, not giving us whispers.

7.2.3. What should we expect?

Before we investigate this point further, we need to face an obvious objection: that this can't be the whole story! What about all the occasions in the Bible when God spoke to his servants – people like Moses and Samuel, as well as all those in the book of Acts? And what about the testimonies, given throughout church history and still today, that God guides his people by speaking to them? This is an important question, but we are not the first people to face it. So how have Christians before us dealt with this issue?

One useful discussion is by the Puritan William Bridge, who asks, 'But may not God speak by an immediate voice to a soul now?' His answer is as follows:

> What God may do is one thing; and what he doth in the way of a settled ordinance, wherein we are to wait on him and expect from him, is another thing... Thou hast the Scriptures, go search the Scriptures, wait thou upon God therein; for in them are the words of eternal life: they are a sure and safe light, more sure, safe and certain, than all Revelation, visions, dreams, or immediate voices... the safest, surest way, is to keep close to the written word of God, which is both the judge of all our doctrines, and the only rule of all our practices; and therefore above and beyond all impressions, whether with or without a word.[58]

---

[57]   Jonathan Edwards refers to the view of the Spirit's leading 'which consists not in teaching them God's statutes and precepts, that He has already given, but in giving them new precepts by immediate inward speech or suggestion', and protests that 'there is no such thing as any judgment or wisdom in the case. Whereas in that leading of the Spirit which is peculiar to God's children, is imparted that true wisdom and holy discretion so often spoken of in the Word of God; which is high above the other way, as the stars are higher than a glow worm'. (*The Religious Affections*, p 211).

[58]   William Bridge [1600-1670], *The Works of the Reverend William Bridge*, five volumes (Beaver Falls, PA: Soli Deo Gloria, 1989 [1657/1845]), 1: pp 422, 423, 427.

Bridge is making two essential points here. Yes, God might speak to us – but he has given no promise that he will do so. So any whispers – or intuitions, dreams, or visions – that God might give fall into the category of what Christians used to call 'uncovenanted blessings'. And not only has he made no promise to give such blessings, but he has given us no instruction to seek them. We thus have no basis – no 'settled ordinance' – for relying on such gifts. If and when they come, we will test them as we must, and welcome what is good and true.[59] But we will not base our lives on the assumption that God will give them. And (this is Bridge's second point) since we have God's sure and sufficient word in the Bible, why would we want any other words?

We find a very similar approach in the writings of Richard Baxter. Like Bridge, he agrees that God might well speak to people today:

> It is possible that God may make new Revelation to particular persons about their particular duties, events, or matters of fact, in subordination to the Scripture, either by inspiration, vision, or apparition, or voice; for he hath not told us that he will never do such a thing ...

However, he does not want anyone to rely on this kind of divine speaking, precisely because God has given no promise that he will do this:

> Though such revelation and prophecy be possible, there is no certainty of it in general, nor any probability of it to any one individual person, much less a promise. And therefore to expect it, or pray for it, is but a presumptuous testing of God.

Baxter's experience of the Quaker movement in particular leaves him with little confidence that this is the right way forward for Christian people:

> And all sober Christians should be the more cautious of being deceived by their own imaginations, because certain experience telleth us, that most in our age that have pretended to prophecy, or inspiration, or Revelation, have been melancholy, crack-brained persons, near to madness, who have proved deluded in the end.[60]

---

59   1 Thessalonians 5:20-22; 1 John 4:1-6.
60   Richard Baxter [1615-1691], quoted in Nuttall, *Holy Spirit*, pp 56f.

Indeed, his experience tells him that it is 'younger, weaker Christians' who are prone

> to take their own passionate imaginations for the workings of the Spirit. It is ordinary with them to say, this or that was set upon my heart, or spoken to me, as if it had been some divine inspiration, when it was nothing but the troubled workings of a weak, distempered brain; and it is their own fancy and heart that saith that to them, which they think the Spirit of God within them said.[61]

Our experience might well differ from Baxter's here, but this should not lead us to overlook the fundamental point he shares with Bridge: that we should not expect our lives to be directed by messages from the Spirit because God has given us no promise that he will give them. To seek to live this way thus involves some significant problems, as John Newton recognized:

> Upon the whole, though the Lord may give to some persons, upon some occasions, a hint or encouragement out of the common way; yet expressly to look for and seek his direction in such things ... is unscriptural and ensnaring.[62]

The approach we have been considering recognizes that God sometimes 'speaks' to people: he did so in the Bible, and it appears that he does so today. This 'speaking' takes various forms. It can be a strong hunch or intuition, a sudden flash of insight, a slowly-growing awareness or conviction, a gentle nudge or a powerful sense of compulsion, or even a voice. I know a number of people who have had intuitions that proved to be true. One was a lady who one night had a sudden and overwhelming sense that her husband was about to die. The next day he flew overseas to a business conference. While he was away, he experienced some unusual symptoms and sought medical assistance. Tests quickly established that he had inoperable cancer. He died just a few months later, while still in his thirties. To the best of my knowledge, this lady has never had another experience of this kind. I don't know of any way of explaining how this intuitive knowledge is possible—but since we clearly have this capacity, is there any reason why the God who built it into us should not use it for his purposes? But what was God doing in this case? What was this lady meant to do with this unsought intuition?

---

[61]   Baxter, *The Practical Works*, p 746.
[62]   John Newton, *Works*, 1: p 329.

If this was guidance, she needed more guidance to know how to take it—something we will return to below.

So while Bridge and Baxter do not exclude the possibility that God might give people direction in this way, they insist that we should not base our lives upon such 'words'. That is because we have no promise from God to give us whispers, and no instruction from God to expect them. Instead, we should find his guidance by a very different means. We will consider what that is once we have dealt with the next matter before us.

7.2.4. Building on the right foundation

There is another problem with the view that God guides us by speaking to us. This has to do with the foundations on which this view is based. Two kinds of difficulty emerge here. The first of these is the tendency to bypass the Bible at the critical point of the argument. This is seen especially in a reliance upon the analogy with human relationships:

> My strategy has been to take as a model the highest and best type of communication that I know of from human affairs and then place this model in the even brighter light of the person and teaching of Jesus Christ. In this way it has been possible to arrive at an ideal picture of what an intimate relationship with God is meant to be and also come to a clear vision of the kind of life where hearing God is not an uncommon occurrence.[63]

The problem with this approach is that it argues from what human relationships are to what relationship with God should be. Instead of allowing the Bible to define what our fellowship with God is like, this imposes a certain view of what it must be like:

> How could there be a personal relationship, a personal walk with God – or with anyone else – *without* individualized communication?[64]

The obvious response here is to pose this question: Why should we assume that our relationship with God – which is a unique privilege, and with a unique Person – will be just like our relationships with each other? Doesn't this assumption tend to reduce God to our level? – as we see in the staggering claim that our fellowship with God is 'the sort of

---

63   Willard, *Hearing God*, p 10.
64   Willard, *Hearing God*, p 22 (his italics).

relationship suited to friends who are mature personalities in a shared enterprise ...'!'[65]

The second difficulty with this view is the way it uses the Bible when it does bring it into play. I am referring to the tendency to argue from what people in the Bible did experience to what we should experience. It is pointed out that God spoke clearly and directly to people in the Bible – and the conclusion is then drawn that this pattern still applies:

> If there is a pattern in Scripture regarding whispers, it is that we serve a communicating God – a God of words... Throughout all of history, God has communicated, and he is still at it today. The issue isn't whether or not God is speaking; it's whether we will have ears to hear what he says.[66]

In the recital of Biblical evidence the events reported in the book of Acts usually feature prominently, as we find there numerous examples of people hearing from God. So in order to keep the discussion within reasonable bounds, we will limit ourselves to the Acts narrative. What are we to make of these stories?

7.2.5. Hearing all of the evidence

There are two points we must make about how the biblical evidence is being used here. The first is that we must take account of all that Acts says. That is, we must not only note when the Spirit speaks; we must also note when he doesn't. When we read the narrative from this perspective, the first thing we notice is how seldom God speaks directly to the people involved. Take Paul and his ministry, for example. According to Acts, he heard from God on eight occasions.[67] This sounds impressive, until we realize that these incidents were spread across some thirty years. It appears that even Paul heard God speaking to him only very occasionally. While we should not underestimate the importance of these eight occasions, neither should we overlook the fact that the vast majority of Paul's ministry apparently proceeded without such interventions by God. In fact, some of the most important and

---

[65] Willard, *Hearing God*, p 29.
[66] Hybels, *Whisper*, p 50.
[67] Acts 9:3-6; 13:2; 16:9-10; 18:9-10; 21:10-11; 22:17-21; 23:11; 27:23-24. This does not include the Spirit's interventions in 16:6-7, as Acts gives no indication as to how the Spirit's will was made known.

influential decisions made in these crucial years did not involve any special leading by the Spirit. Consider what happened at Antioch, for example, as described in Acts 11:19-26. While some of the refugees from persecution shared the gospel only with Jewish people, others took the decisive step of evangelizing Gentiles (11:20). The Lord blessed this initiative, and a great many people became believers (11:21). The result was a largely Gentile church. As they had done when many Samaritans believed,[68] the Jerusalem church sent someone to check on this new development. Barnabas was the person they chose for this very important role (11:22). When he met the church there, he regarded what had happened not as something irregular but as a clear sign of the grace of God (11:23). As the church continued to grow, Barnabas went to Tarsus to recruit Paul to help him with the work – and he agreed to Barnabas' request (11:25-26). All of these decisions were hugely influential: had any of them been other than they were, who knows how different the story of the early church would have been? Imagine what would have happened if Barnabas had chosen someone from the Jerusalem church instead of recruiting Paul—or what would have happened if Paul had refused, and stayed in Tarsus.

Despite the critical importance of these decisions, there is no indication of any intervention by God, any special guidance. All of them seem to have been made in the ordinary way that wise and godly people make decisions. So where was God in all of this? He was not in the foreground, speaking to the decision-makers, but in the background, superintending their choices. And because he is God, he works out his purpose just as effectively by the latter as he does by the former. When it comes to God's guidance, we should not be asking what he can do, for he is free to use whatever means he chooses. Instead, we should be asking what we should do – that is, how does God want us to make decisions?

7.2.6. Description or prescription?

This brings us to the second observation we must make about how those advocating this view of Christian living use the narrative of Acts. They tend to treat descriptions as prescriptions, taking accounts of what God did on some occasions as indications of his will for all occasions. But we find out how God wants us to live as Christians – including how

---

68   Acts 8:14.

he wants us to make decisions – not by noting what he did with this or that person, but by studying the teaching of Jesus and the apostles. And what do we learn from their teaching? Again, to keep our discussion within reasonable bounds we will limit ourselves to some of the most basic points that need to be made here.

We can begin with this question: Isn't the Holy Spirit meant to guide us into all the truth?[69] The answer we must give is, 'Yes, but ...' When Jesus promised that the Spirit of truth[70] would do this, he was speaking to his disciples.[71] His prayer for them was shortly to reveal that their message was to be the means by which the whole world would believe in him.[72] When there is only one bridge that gets us where we need to go, we have to be sure that it is strong enough to carry all the traffic! So how would the disciples' message be capable of carrying the world to Jesus? This is why Jesus made it clear that the Spirit was going to do a special work in them. He would remind them of all that Jesus had said to them and teach them what it meant.[73] He would bear testimony to Jesus in their testimony, which was to be based on their unique relationship with Jesus throughout his ministry.[74] The Spirit would speak to them about what was still to come[75] – that is, he would enable them to understand Jesus' death, resurrection, and return to the Father. In all of these ways, he was going to guide them into all the truth about Jesus.[76] By doing so, he would glorify Jesus.[77]

The result of this work of the Spirit in and with the disciples is our New Testament![78] He guided them into all the truth about Jesus as they taught and wrote what is in these twenty-seven books. And this is how and where he now does this work in our lives – he guides us with the

---

[69] John 16:13.
[70] John 14:17; 15:26.
[71] Robert Barclay takes what Jesus says here to be directly applicable to every believer: we are all meant to know the ministry of 'this inward and immediate guide, this Spirit that leads into all Truth'; and on the basis of 'these words of Christ, it will follow, that Christians are always to be led inwardly and immediately by the Spirit of God dwelling in them' (*An Apology*: The Second Proposition: Of Immediate Revelation, §X).
[72] John 17:20.
[73] John 14:26.
[74] John 15:26-27.
[75] John 16:13.
[76] John 16:13.
[77] John 16:14.
[78] On which see Peter Adam, *Written For Us*, Chapter 19.

truth into which he guided them, the truth written in the Bible. That is how verses like John 14:26 and 16:13 apply to us today. They refer not to 'the whispered promptings of God', but to what we learn by reading the New Testament in prayerful dependence upon the Spirit's tuition.[79] The Spirit of God works by and with the word of God when he teaches the people of God.

7.2.7. Led by the Spirit?

But is that all? Aren't we meant to be 'filled with the Spirit'? And won't this result in our being 'led by the Spirit'? As it happens, there is only one passage in the New Testament, in Ephesians 5:18, that tells us to be 'filled with the Spirit'. What does Paul mean by this? How does the Spirit fill us? And how does this bear upon the way we are to make decisions?

This passage in Ephesians clearly addresses these issues, because its primary theme is how we live as Christians.[80] When we look at what follows the exhortation to be filled with the Spirit, we discover that Spirit-filled living means encouraging and building up other believers (5:19), expressing joy and thanks to God (5:19-20), and humbly submitting to each other (5:21). When we look at what leads up to this exhortation, we find that Spirit-filled living also means being what we are now – what we are in Christ (5:8) – rather than continuing in what we used to be. So we will live as children of light who refuse to compromise with the darkness (5:8-11). And we will not be unwise or foolish because now we are wise (5:15, 17; cf. 4:17-18). So Paul expects that we will be able to understand the Lord's will and to find out what pleases him (5:10, 17). This is because we have been taught the truth that is in Jesus (4:21).

Paul had made this clear at the beginning of this letter, where he tells us what God's will and pleasure is. He states that with all wisdom, God has revealed the mystery of his will in the gospel (1:8-9). In his glorious grace, God saves us in accordance with his pleasure and will (1:4-7, 11). And by the Spirit of wisdom he enlightens us to understand the greatness of this salvation (1:17-19). How does he do this? Not by giving us whispers, but by enabling us to grasp the significance of what the gospel tells us. So how do we learn of the unrivalled greatness of

---

[79]   The quotation is from Hybels, *Whisper*, p 50.
[80]   Ephesians 5:8, 15.

God's power, for example? We do so by reflecting on the fact at the centre of the gospel – the fact that God raised Jesus from the dead and exalted him to heaven as Lord of all (1:19-23).

With all of this in view, what does being filled with the Spirit turn out to mean? It is all about living out the new life God has given us. In particular, it means living wisely as people who are instructed by the gospel. But is that all? Doesn't the Bible tell us to pray 'in the Spirit'[81] – and won't this mean being given directions by the Spirit? Indeed it will, for to pray in the Holy Spirit is to be moved and guided by the Holy Spirit. We pray by his *power* and according to his *direction*.

But what does this actually mean? How does the Spirit give us his guidance in our prayers? The best answer I know comes from John Piper:

> These two – the Spirit's power and direction – correspond to two ways that the Word of God functions in our prayer. The *power* of the Spirit is offered in the promises of God's Word, and we experience it by *faith* in the promise. The *direction* of the Spirit is embodied in the wisdom of God's Word, and we experience it by being *saturated* with that wisdom. So if we would 'pray in the Holy Spirit' we should ... pray the Word of God, trusting the promises and absorbing the wisdom.[82]

So in our praying we are meant to be guided by the Scriptures, for this is how the Spirit guides us. He instructs us in God's will as we learn the promises in Scripture, and imparts God's wisdom as we learn the precepts and patterns in Scripture. That is why praying in the Spirit is closely linked with taking the Spirit's sword, the word of God,[83] and with building ourselves up in our most holy faith.[84] As always, the Spirit and the word belong together.

We learn much the same from Paul's prayer in Colossians 1:9-14, to take just one more example. His primary request is for God to fill the readers with a knowledge of his will (1:9) so that they might please him in every way and grow in their knowledge of him (1:10). How does Paul expect God to do this? He indicates that they will come to know God's

---

[81] Ephesians 6:18; Jude 20.
[82] John Piper, *When I Don't Desire God*, p 167 (his italics).
[83] Ephesians 6:17.
[84] Jude 20.

will for their lives 'through all the wisdom and understanding that the Spirit gives' (1:9), How will the Spirit give this wisdom? By directing them again and again to the Jesus of the gospel, for 'all the treasures of wisdom and knowledge' are found in him (2:3). This is one aspect of the over-riding theme of this letter, that God's great purpose is both accomplished and revealed in the person and work of Jesus. For knowing God and his will, and for living as God's people, 'Christ is all' (3:11). So Paul expects that the readers of this letter will be taught by the Spirit as they keep focusing on the gospel, which tells us of the complete supremacy of Jesus' person and the complete sufficiency of his work.

7.2.8. Spirit-taught wisdom

So what have we learned about how the Spirit fills us and leads us? The Bible does not teach us to expect the Spirit to give us special words or whispers. Instead, in answer to our prayers,[85] he gives us wise insight into the implications and applications of the word of God.

> [T]he true way to honour the Holy Spirit as our guide is to honour the Holy Scriptures through which He guides us. The fundamental guidance which God gives to shape our lives ... is not a matter of inward promptings apart from the Word but of the pressure on our consciences of the portrayal of God's character and will in the Word, which the Spirit enlightens us to understand and apply to ourselves.[86]

As we keep feeding on the Scriptures, learning the truth that is in Jesus,[87] the Spirit goes on teaching us how to live a godly life in accordance with the will of God. This means making decisions that are wise because they are Scripture-nourished, God-focused, grace-centred, and Spirit-directed.

But aren't we meant to rely upon God to guide us through life? Indeed we are. The question is what this guidance is and how he gives it to us. The Bible does not indicate that God will make our decisions for us and then whisper to us, so that we can know what he has decided. It is not that he has our lives mapped out in great detail, and what we need is for him to reveal what is on this hidden blueprint. Although this

---

[85] James 1:5.
[86] J.I. Packer, *Knowing God* (London: Hodder & Stoughton, 1973), p 265.
[87] Ephesians 4:21.

outlook is sometimes found amongst Christians, the Bible does not teach it. Instead, the Bible makes it clear that God gives us the awesome responsibility of making real decisions. And it keeps pointing us to our need for the gift of wisdom so that the decisions we make will be good and God-honouring.

Consider what Paul prays for his churches. He asks God to give the Ephesians 'the Spirit of wisdom and revelation' so that they will 'know' the gospel truths that are especially important for them.[88] He prays for the Philippians to become increasingly insightful in their love and discerning in their choices, so that they will be pure and blameless on the Day of Christ.[89] He asks for the Spirit to give the Colossians wisdom and understanding so that they will live lives that are pleasing to God, lives that are governed by his will.[90] Why do his readers need this Spirit-given wisdom? So that they will know how to live godly lives. And how will this wisdom come to them? The Paul who prays like this for his churches also writes to them. What his letters contain is not merely human words, but words taught by the Spirit,[91] words that come from God and convey his will.[92] So Paul is confident that the Spirit will use his letters to the churches to answer his prayers for the churches. As believers read and ponder them, they will gain a clearer and deeper grasp of 'all the treasures of wisdom and knowledge' that are found in Christ,[93] treasures that are conveyed in the gospel,[94] the gospel that Paul expounds in his letters.

The letter of James points us in the same direction. James assures his readers that God will give them whatever wisdom they lack if they ask for it in faith.[95] But why would their lack of wisdom be a problem? We find the answer a little later in the letter where James indicates that heavenly wisdom shows itself in a life that is pure and good.[96] In other words, James believes that wisdom is the key to a life that pleases God. He also believes that his letter offers the readers the kind of wisdom

---

[88]   Ephesians 1:17-19.
[89]   Philippians 1:9-10.
[90]   Colossians 1:9-10.
[91]   1 Corinthians 2:13.
[92]   1 Corinthians 14:37; 1 Thessalonians 4:8.
[93]   Colossians 2:3.
[94]   Ephesians 3:8.
[95]   James 1:5-6.
[96]   James 3:13-17.

they need. That is why he takes such care to spell out what a godly life involves, and to warn against many kinds of ungodliness. So his readers should ask God for wisdom and study James' letter carefully.

There is obviously much more of the Bible that we could look at here. But these few examples will have to suffice. Our point is this: everyday life requires us to make all kinds of decisions, big and small. So that we will have the guidance we need, God gives us the gift of wisdom. He wants us to live as wise people who understand his will (Ephesians 5:15-17), as people who know how to please him (1 Thessalonians 4:1-2). This is one reason he gives us his Spirit, the teacher of heavenly wisdom. It is also why he gives us his word, the source of heavenly wisdom. So we are meant to pray, asking the Spirit to make us wise – and we are also meant to search the Scriptures, eager to imbibe their wisdom.

Are we meant to listen for the voice of God, as the mystics teach? Yes we are – but not in the way they mean. We hear him speaking not in Spirit-given whispers but in the Spirit-given Scriptures. This is what we mean by calling the Bible 'the word of God'. The Bible is God speaking to us: teaching us, correcting us, encouraging us, warning us, comforting us, guiding us, nourishing us. What he says in the Bible gives us everything we need to bring us into his salvation and to equip us for his service.[97] That is why we do not live our lives waiting for whispers from God.

But suppose he did speak to me, by giving me a powerful intuition, like the lady I referred to earlier in this chapter. What should I do with it? How should it shape my life or change my behaviour? It is obvious that such an experience would face me with an important decision. And like the other decisions I must make, I would need the gift of wisdom here too, so that I knew how to interpret what I had just experienced. But this wisdom could not take the form of another inner 'voice' – for I would need more guidance to know what to make of it! Instead, it is by the objective standard of the Bible that I must test and evaluate all of my subjective experiences. The wisdom we need for living rightly before God is given in the Spirit-taught words of the prophets and apostles.

We have been arguing that when it comes to guidance our focus should not be on what God might do, but on what we must do. God is

---

[97]   2 Timothy 3:15-17.

free to do whatever he chooses, but we are bound to do whatever he wants. How do we find out what that is? Not from anecdotes about what he has done, but from instruction about what we are to do. Anecdotes generally tell us what is possible, not what is required. At best, they remind us that God is immensely kind in his dealings with us. Isn't this what we learn from Numbers 22:28-30, for example? I doubt that anyone is going to argue that it is meant to teach us to expect messages from donkeys – or (if we contemporize the passage) from our cars! The same applies to stories about people who experience God's guidance through the 'still, small voice': they show us what God has chosen to give to some, not what he requires for all. We should not use them as lessons teaching us how to live the Christian life; for that we go to the teaching of Jesus and the apostles. And when we do, we discover that we are to rely upon the Spirit, not for whispers, but for wisdom. What he gives us is not new revelation but fresh illumination,[98] not additional words from God but greater insight into the word God has already spoken.

To conclude: if the Bible is a sufficient and reliable guide to true devotion, then the mystical approach to prayer as conversational dialogue involves some significant problems. This is also true of the mystic's tendency to distinguish different levels of prayer. That is the focus of our next chapter.

---

[98]   Ephesians 1:17-18.

8. The Way to Pray

In Chapter 7 we examined a prominent feature of the mystical approach to prayer: its view of prayer as a dialogue between two partners. We saw how this is part of a larger picture, according to which God is said to speak to us regularly so that we will know how he wants us to live with him and for him. We gave several reasons for distancing ourselves from this way of understanding the Christian life. Now we come to another questionable characteristic of the mystical path: its tendency to distinguish various levels of prayer.

8.1. Contemplation

It is common for mystics to regard spoken prayer – especially petition – as the lowest form of prayer. Its highest form is said to be contemplation, which is wordless:

> prayer is seen as becoming gradually less and less a matter of words or motions of the will and more and more a simple loving attention to God, until this too merges into a new realization or experience of the presence of God in the soul ... Herein is the beginning of the mystical life.[1]

It is important to recognize that 'contemplation' has a special meaning in this context. It does not refer to considering some aspect of God's truth, focusing on it, thinking it over, taking it in. That is, it is not being used as a synonym for 'meditation'. Rather, it stands for a way of praying that is regarded as the highest and purest form of prayer. We are told that this kind of prayer needs no words:

> The truest word of prayer is the interior and spiritual word, that word of the spirit which consists in the silent movements of the

---

[1]   David Knowles, *The Nature of Mysticism* (New York: Hawthorn, 1966), p 81. Simon Chan makes the point this way:
'The one who grows in prayer moves farther and farther away from self-interested prayers of petition to God-directed prayers of adoration and thanksgiving. Prayers become less vocal and more mental. Words and images become unnecessary as the soul draws deeper into the heart of prayer... The highest prayers are those in which God prays in us ...' (*Spiritual Theology: A Systematic Study of the Christian Life* (Downers Grove: IVP Academic, 1998), p 133).

soul's desires towards God.[2]

Another writer makes the point this way:

> Prayer is more than words, for it is mightiest when wordless. It is more than asking, for it reaches its highest glory when it adores and asks for nothing ... There are stages of prayer. In one stage we pray and ask him to help. There is a more wonderful way in which he prays and we assent, and his praying is ours ...[3]

A popular book on prayer commends this contemplative praying as follows:

> Contemplative Prayer immerses us into the silence of God... Contemplative Prayer is the one discipline that can free us from our addiction to words. Progress in intimacy with God means progress towards silence... Contemplative Prayer is not for the novice... [but] is for seasoned veterans in the life of faith.[4]

Indeed, some discussions insist that contemplation is a necessary means of Christian maturity:

> there is no way to genuine saintliness that does not include genuine contemplative, mystical prayer.[5]

This author goes even further, treating contemplation as central and foundational to authentic Christian living:

> Prayer – meditative and contemplative prayer – is in a vital sense that channel of grace that makes effective the other means of grace. It is a divinely appointed lubricant to allow and to cause believers to enjoy fellowship with their God and from this to gain the necessary illumination, inspiration, and insight to do his will.[6]

---

[2] James Hastings (ed), *The Christian Doctrine of Prayer* (Edinburgh: T&T Clark, 1915), p 444.

[3] Samuel Chadwick, *The Path of Prayer* (1931), quoted in Gillett, *Trust and Obey*, p 177.

[4] Richard J. Foster, *Prayer: Finding the Heart's True Home* (London: Hodder & Stoughton, 1992), pp 163, 164, 167. It is important to acknowledge that Foster calls the dismissal of petition as the lowest form of prayer 'a false spirituality' (p 189).

[5] Peter Toon, *The Art of Meditating on Scripture: Understanding Your Faith, Renewing Your Mind, Knowing Your God* (Grand Rapids: Zondervan, 1993), p 18.

[6] Toon, *The Art of Meditating*, p 59.

8.1.1. Mystical prayer

What precisely is meant by 'contemplative prayer'? Calling it 'the prayer of loving attention', the author we have just quoted says that it is usually seen as the bridge between meditative and affective prayer and the ever-enlarging possibilities of mystical prayer. Such contemplation is understood as a simple, loving gaze upon some divine object, whether of God himself or one of his perfections; on Christ or on one of his offices; or on some other Christian truth. The movement of the mind in search of truth has ceased. In its place is a simple intellectual gaze that is motivated by love.[7]

This is the goal and endpoint of a process that begins with vocal prayer:

> Vocal prayer acts as a stimulus to contemplation, in such a way that the words disappear little by little from the lips and the soul enters into ecstasy, becoming unconscious of the world.[8]

So, in short, contemplation is

> that experience of God in prayer where the mind is without images and concepts and the soul is still and tranquil.[9]

It is to rise above concepts, words, images and discursive thinking and to be united to the Lord in love and worship, adoration and purity.[10]

> [It is where] the Christian ... meets God directly, face to face, in an unmediated union of love. Since the deity is a mystery beyond words and understanding, it follows that in such contemplation the human mind has to rise above concepts, words, and images – above the level of discursive thinking – so as to apprehend God intuitively through simple 'gazing' or 'touching.' ... Its goal is 'pure prayer,' prayer that is not only morally pure and free from sinful thoughts but also intellectually pure and free from all thoughts... At the higher levels of contemplation, then, awareness of the subject-object differentiation recedes, and in its place there is only a sense of

---

[7] Toon, *The Art of Meditating*, p 87f.

[8] Isaac of Nineveh [d. c.700], in Bloesch, *Spirituality*, p 56.

[9] Toon, *The Art of Meditating*, p 153.

[10] Peter Toon, *Meditating Upon God's Word: Prelude to Prayer and Action* (London: DLT, 1988), p 96.

all-embracing unity.[11]

8.1.2. The 'Jesus Prayer'

Secondly, it is in this connection that some authors recommend the use of what the Orthodox strand of Christendom knows as the 'Jesus Prayer'. This consists of the words, 'Lord Jesus Christ, Son of God, have mercy on me, a sinner.' One writer on Christian prayer says that

> the Jesus Prayer is sometimes known as the prayer of the heart, the prayer of silence, or the unceasing prayer. It is meant to be repeated over and over again in order to bring the prayer-giver to deeper levels of communion with God... When I first heard about the Jesus Prayer I am afraid I dismissed it as a step too far into Eastern mysticism. Perhaps I was not ready for it, being long on impatience and short on penitence. But ... I gave the Jesus Prayer a serious try. The repetition seemed strange at first, but to cut a long story short, it worked.[12]

8.1.3. Holistic prayer?

Thirdly, it is quite common to meet the claim that a deeper experience of God requires a more holistic approach to prayer, in which not only the imagination and emotions but also the body are involved. This takes several forms. At one end of the spectrum we find this testimony concerning the daily use of the Jesus Prayer:

> I use the abbreviated version of this prayer [by which the author means the name, Jesus] as I turn from the busyness and attempt to enter the grand silence of God. As I breathe in, I whisper the beginning of the name: 'Je' and as I breathe out, I complete the name: 'sus'. Praying in this way, I find, brings me back to that still point where God is most easily met and where his voice is most clearly heard.[13]

---

[11] Kallistos Ware, "Ways of Prayer and Contemplation, I. Eastern" in Bernard McGinn and John Meyendorff, in collaboration with Jean Leclerq (eds), *Christian Spirituality: Origins to the Twelfth Century* (London: SCM, 1985), p 399 (his italics).

[12] Jonathan Aitken, *Prayers for People under Pressure* (London: Continuum, 2005), p 77. See also Joyce Huggett, *Finding God in the Fast Lane* (Guildford: Eagle, 1993), pp 61-63; Toon, *The Art of Meditating*, pp 146-54; Toon, *Meditating*, pp 93-97.

[13] Huggett, *Finding God*, p 62.

At the other end of the spectrum is the approach that looks to the body as our teacher in prayer:

> When the body teaches us to pray, our relationship to God is expanded and deepened... [and] many new prayer forms are open to us.[14]

Another writer gives the body a vital role as we seek to open ourselves to God:

> One of the quickest ways of stilling ourselves in the presence of God is to enlist the help of the body. The body can welcome God. Indeed, almost literally, our bodies can open up to God. Open hands illustrate this... Similarly, we can enlist other parts of our body as partners in prayer.[15]

8.2.   Silence and God

What are we to make of this approach to prayer? In the first place, what are we to say about the claim that wordless contemplation is the highest form of prayer? This is often connected with the idea of the 'silence of God'. So prayer is said to be 'dropping into the grand silence of God'.[16] This is why we are told that progress 'in intimacy with God is progress towards silence'.[17] One recent discussion of contemplation describes it as 'the deepest and highest form of prayer':

> Eventually, your thoughts fall away before the deep and profound silence that characterizes the presence of God... Eventually, your interest and focus in prayer will turn from your words ... to the silence that lies behind and beneath and before them.[18]

But it is difficult to see how these ideas could be derived from the Bible. From the beginning of the Bible to its end, the God of the Bible is a God of words, a speaker.[19] And it is only because he has given us his words that we can know him. But the Bible not only gives us words of revelation; it also gives us words of response to revelation. It not only has God addressing his people; it also shows his people addressing him

---

[14]   Jane E. Vennard, *Praying with Body and Soul* (Minneapolis: Augsburg, 1998), p 10.
[15]   Huggett, *Open to God*, p 38f. See also Foster, *Prayer*, pp 122-123.
[16]   Huggett, *Open to God*, p 32.
[17]   Foster, *Prayer*, p 164.
[18]   McColman, *The Big Book*, pp 215-216.
[19]   Genesis 1:3, 28-30; Revelation 21:3-8; 22:20.

in turn – the Psalms being the most obvious and extensive example. So the overwhelming thrust of Scripture has to do with the words that God both speaks and hears – his words that create relationship with him and our words that express this relationship.

Then what about silence? – what does the Bible have to say on this subject? One contemplative claims that

> the Bible contains numerous passages that encourage a spirituality grounded in silence, solitude, and stillness.[20]

This is a claim that it is very difficult to substantiate, for the Bible says very little about 'silence, solitude, and stillness.' It does make three important points about silence, however. The first is that there comes a time when silence in God's presence is appropriate.[21] But even here, this is interwoven with speaking to God and does not replace it:

> Be silent before me, you islands! Let the nations renew their strength! Let them come forward and speak ...[22]

Secondly, there is a time when silence in God's presence is improper. That is because it would represent a failure to respond rightly to his goodness:

> You turned my wailing into dancing ... that my heart may sing your praises and not be silent. LORD my God, I will praise you forever.[23]

Alternatively, my silence before God could represent a failure to repent of my sin:

> When I kept silent, my bones wasted away through my groaning all day long... Then I acknowledged my sin to you and did not cover up my iniquity.[24]

Or it could mean that I have failed to call upon God to deliver me:

> I was silent; I would not open my mouth ... Remove your scourge from me; I am overcome by the blow of your hand... Hear my prayer,

---

[20]   McColman, *The Big Book*, p 228.
[21]   See Habakkuk 2:20; Zephaniah 1:7.
[22]   Isaiah 41:1.
[23]   Psalm 30:11-12.
[24]   Psalm 32:3, 5.

LORD, listen to my cry for help; do not be deaf to my weeping.[25]

The third point the Bible makes concerns silence on God's part. This is anything but welcome, for it means a withholding of his saving activity. It is thus an expression of his judgment.[26] As a result, his people plead with him not to be silent:

O God, do not remain silent; do not turn a deaf ear, do not stand aloof, O God.[27]

So if the Bible is a sufficient and reliable guide to living with God, and thus to prayer in particular, we will not value silence – either God's or ours – above speaking. Does this mean that the Bible does not encourage the practice of contemplation?

Our conviction about the sufficiency of Scripture should lead us to be Bereans[28] here too, examining the Bible to see what it has to say on this subject. One who has done so is the Puritan theologian John Owen. His investigation leads him to a conclusion that is hard to gainsay:

for this contemplative prayer ... there is neither precept for it, nor direction about it, nor motive unto it, nor example of it, in the whole Scripture.[29]

In other words, the Bible gives not the merest hint of this practice.[30] As a result, it cannot have a necessary place in true devotion.[31] If the Bible does not teach it to us, then God does not require it of us. Calvin expresses what God does require here in this way:

---

[25]   Psalm 39:9-12.

[26]   Isaiah 42:14-16; 57:11; 62:1; 64:12; 65:6-7; Habakkuk 1:13.

[27]   Psalm 83:1; see also Psalms 28:1; 35:22; 109:1.

[28]   Acts 17:11.

[29]   *Works*, 4: p 337. Peter Toon misrepresents John Owen by claiming that he commended and practised contemplation (see *The Art of Meditating*, pp 113-125). In fact, as this quotation shows, his explicit rejection of it could not be clearer (see his whole discussion in *Works*, 4: pp 328-338).

[30]   It is very significant that when Joyce Huggett wanted to learn how to engage in contemplation, she did not turn to the Bible but relied entirely upon two books given to her by a friend (*Listening to God*, pp 38-42). As this was an important stage in her pilgrimage to know God more deeply, the fact that the Bible played no role in it is very revealing.

[31]   Convinced that Paul was a contemplative, Toon finds the practice reflected in passages (such as Romans 5:1-5; 8:14-17; Ephesians 3:14-21) that give no direct hint that they spring from this source or deal with this topic (see *The Art of Meditating*, pp 83-89).

only out of faith is God pleased to be called upon, and he expressly bids that prayers be conformed to the measure of his Word... faith grounded upon the Word is the mother of right prayer; hence, as soon as it is deflected from the Word, prayer must needs be corrupted.[32]

8.3. 'Deflected from the Word'?

But is contemplation prayer that has been 'deflected from the Word'? If it is, why is it given such an important role in the mystical approach to prayer? There are three principal reasons that emerge from these discussions.

8.3.1. The guidance of the Spirit

One is that the Holy Spirit is said to lead people to embrace contemplative prayer.[33] This claim is part of a bigger picture, in which God is seen as guiding people by speaking to them outside and apart from Scripture – the view that we examined in the previous chapter. What we said there applies here too. Since the Bible is entirely sufficient as our guide to true devotion, the Spirit will not lead people to adopt as vital and necessary something that the Bible never teaches. Conversely, what the Bible teaches must direct us in prayer – especially when those regarded as spiritual guides offer a different approach. So even though the Bible makes it clear that God is far above even our highest thoughts, it does not draw the conclusion that it is best to approach him in wordless contemplation. On the contrary, the Bible gives us words with which to address him – words that come from God himself. And if God has given us words and invited us to draw near to him, then surely it is not a deeper piety but a misguided super-spirituality that leads us to place a premium on wordlessness. The Bible's very different outlook is seen in Hosea 14:2: 'Take words with you and return to the LORD.'

8.3.2. The direction of Scripture

There is a second reason for giving prominence to contemplative prayer. This is the belief that the Bible does speak of it. At least, the well-known words of Psalm 46:10 – 'Be still, and know that I am God' – are often

---

32   *Institutes*, III.xx.27 (2: p 887).
33   See Joyce Huggett's account of how she came to adopt the practice (*Listening to God*, pp 38-44).

taken this way. The verse is generally understood to be saying, 'If you are still, then you will realize that God is God.' So stillness and silence are seen as the necessary prelude to recognizing the reality of God or experiencing the presence of God:

> Until our bodies, minds and spirits let go of the clutter we bring to our places of prayer, we automatically tune out the still, small voice of God. Until we come into stillness before God we do not detect either the fullness of his presence or the winsomeness of his voice.[34]

It is very doubtful that this verse should be understood along these lines, however. It is not saying that stillness (and the silence that goes with it) is a necessary condition for knowledge of God. In the context of the psalm as a whole, 'Be still' does not beckon us to the discipline of silence. It is a call to stop. For Israel, it is a call to cease frantic attempts to defend and secure their lives in turbulent times, when the 'nations are in uproar' and 'kingdoms fall' (v.6). For the nations, it is a call to stop waging war against God's city and his people. And 'know' does not mean something like 'be reminded' or 'discover', as though silence will restore our vision of God. Instead it means 'acknowledge'. We are being exhorted to admit that God is truly Lord and God, to exalt him by confessing that he is sovereign over the whole world (v.10). As the rest of the psalm shows, for Israel this will mean turning to him as 'its refuge and stronghold, its help and its haven'.[35] This much-quoted verse is thus misused when treated as a call to contemplative prayer.

8.3.3. The goal of contemplation

A third reason why contemplative prayer is advocated is that it is thought to involve union with God: 'the heart is bound in a union of love and contemplation to the Lord Jesus'.[36] This is referring to an altered state of consciousness in which the mind has passed beyond all words and concepts. This state is interpreted as loving union with God. There are difficulties at a number of levels here. For example, non-theistic exponents of the mystical path also refer to such a state,

---

[34] Huggett, *Listening to God*, p 55.
[35] John Goldingay, *Psalms, Volume 2: Psalms 42-89* (Baker Commentary on the Old Testament Wisdom and Psalms; Grand Rapids: Baker Academic, 2007), p 72.
[36] Toon, *The Art of Meditating*, p 147.

although they assign quite a different significance to it, of course.[37] More important for our purposes, however, are the ways in which this approach differs from what we find in the Bible. There are two particular areas of concern here, both related to the fundamental idea of loving union with God. The first is the notion that this union is achieved as the climax of a process which only some believers – the 'contemplatives' – seem able to sustain. But according to the Bible, union with God-in-Christ is not a distant goal; it is our starting-point:

> evangelical piety turns upside down the medieval paradigm of a pathway to God. There the journey of faith began with purgation, moved on to illumination, and finally, ended in unification, that is, union with God. In the evangelical understanding, we begin with union with Christ (the new birth) and move on through Word and Spirit to illumination and the process of sanctification until, at last, in heaven we see Christ face to face.[38]

This union is entered by faith in Christ in response to the gospel, and not by progress through a difficult mystical process. As a result, it is for every believer and not just for a select few. It is also the outcome of God's approach to us and not of ours to him:

> Love is not the upward ascent of our souls that sublimates us into union with the deity. Rather, love is the descent of God's royal grace that conquers our rebellion, atones for our guilt, and draws us into sonship.[39]

The second problematic aspect of this concept is the idea that we have to leave thought and words behind in order to encounter and express love. As we noted above, the Bible not only exhorts us to love God but also gives us the words with which we can express this love. In addition, it gives many examples of believers doing just this.[40] So in the Bible love is expressed by personal address and not just wordless adoration: 'I love

---

[37] 'This unmistakable experience has been achieved by the mystics of every religion; and when we read their statements, we know that all are speaking of the same thing'. (Underhill, *Practical Mysticism*, p 86.)

[38] Timothy George, "Introduction" in Timothy George & Alister McGrath (eds), *For All the Saints: Evangelical Theology and Christian Spirituality* (Louisville: WJK, 2003), pp 1-7 (at p 4).

[39] Edmund P. Clowney, *CM*: *Christian Meditation* (Nutley, NJ: Craig, 1979), p 47.

[40] This includes not only the Psalms, but many other passages – including those in the Gospels showing the Lord Jesus at prayer.

you, LORD ...'[41] In addition, we learn from the Bible that our highest calling as human beings is to love God with heart and soul and mind and strength.[42] I cannot do so in a thoroughgoing way by shutting down such a major aspect of myself as my mind – especially when this is meant to be renewed as I consecrate myself to God.[43] A wholehearted love for God, heartfelt devotion to him, must involve my mind along with all the other dimensions of my self. It is thus a false step to drive a wedge between love and words and concepts.

8.3.4. The Reformers on contemplation

There is another reason that contemplative prayer has not featured in Evangelical spirituality. Not only does the Bible not teach it, but the fact is that the Reformers knew it and rejected it. With his usual gusto, Martin Luther refers to his previous involvement in this practice and voices his firm rejection of it:

> Let him who wants to contemplate in the right way reflect on his Baptism; let him read his Bible, hear sermons, honour father and mother, and come to the aid of a brother in distress. But let him not shut himself up in a nook, as the sordid mob of monks and nuns is in the habit of doing, and there entertain himself with his devotions and thus suppose that he is sitting in God's bosom and has fellowship with God without Christ, without the Word, without the sacraments, etc... I certainly had to pay a high price before I was freed from this error, for it pleases reason and seems to be a worship of angels, as Paul calls it (Colossians 2:18)... beware of these snares of Satan, and set up a definition of the contemplative life different from the one they taught in the monasteries, namely, that it is the true contemplative life to hear and believe the spoken Word and to want to know nothing 'except Christ and Him crucified' (1 Corinthians 2:2). He alone, with his Word, is the profitable and salutary object of contemplation...[44]

---

[41] Psalm 18:1; cf. Nehemiah 1:5; Psalms 116:1; 119:47-48, 97, 113, 119, 127, 132, 159, 163, 167; 122:6.

[42] Deuteronomy 6:4-5; Mark 12:28-30.

[43] Romans 12:1-2.

[44] *Works*, 3: p 275f.

In other words, there is a right kind of contemplation – but it is not that of the mystics. What this is, we will consider in Chapter 11. Also worth noting are the wise counsels of Thomas Manton:

> Such ravishing experiences are not to be sought for, but referred to the good pleasure of God. We cannot pray for them in faith, having no promise of them, and we must not be too hasty to eat of the fruits of paradise before our time. It is enough for us to go to heaven in the usual roadway ... It is good to content ourselves with grace, and peace, and joy in the Holy Ghost, though we have not those transports and high ecstasies of love and affection. We must not tempt God with immodest requests and expectations, but sit down humbly and quietly, and if the master of the feast bid us to sit higher, and call us to a more choice dispensation, well and good.[45]

8.4.   Petition in prayer

As to whether petition is the lowest form of prayer, surely all we need to say is that no one could get that impression from the example and teaching of Jesus![46] Jesus' disciples asked him to teach them to pray[47] – and what was his response? He gave no instructions about any of the postures and practices that usually feature so large in mystical treatments of prayer. He said nothing about levels of prayer, and gave no guidance about how to move into the deeper regions of prayer. He certainly never counselled them to embrace silence as the highest form of prayer.[48] Instead he simply gave them some words – words with which to address God, and to petition him concerning our deepest commitments[49] and our most basic needs.[50] This must shape the whole way we understand and practise prayer:

> Many books on prayer exhort us to search for deeper experiences in

---

[45]   Thomas Manton [1620-1677], *The Complete Works of Thomas Manton*, twenty two volumes (Worthington: Maranatha, n.d.), 17: p 296f.

[46]   See Matthew 6:9-13; 9:38; 24:20; 26:39-41, 53; Luke 10:2, 21; 11:1-13; 18:1-14; 21:36; 22:31-32; 23:34, 46; John 11:41-42; 12:27-28; 14:13-14, 16; 15:7, 16; 16:23-24; 17:1-26.

[47]   Luke 11:1.

[48]   If Jesus is our Lord and Teacher (John 13:13-14) in the matter of prayer, we would never reach the conclusion that 'prayer without words is the best ...' (as claimed in C.S. Lewis, *Letters to Malcolm: Chiefly on Prayer* (London: Fontana, 1966), p 12).

[49]   Luke 11:2.

[50]   Luke 11:3-4.

prayer or more sophisticated modes of prayer ... The Bible invites us to find the model of prayer in the simple petitioning of a child before a father.[51]

As a teacher of prayer, Jesus displayed and encouraged straightforward confidence in the heavenly Father. He handed down nothing except simple words[52] – the same kind of words with which he addressed the Father. Yes, John Greenleaf Whittier's hymn tells us that 'Jesus knelt to share with Thee the silence of eternity, interpreted by love' – but the fact is that the Jesus of the Gospels spoke to his Father in prayer, and more often than not as a petitioner.[53] And he encouraged his disciples to pray with these well-known words:

> Ask and it will be given to you; seek and you will find; knock and the door will be opened to you. For everyone who asks receives; the one who seeks finds; and to the one who knocks, the door will be opened.[54]

All of this leads to an important conclusion about the nature of Christian prayer:

> Prayer is not the silencing of petition (as in mysticism) but the deepening of petition, the subordination of personal need to the glory of God and the advancement of his kingdom.[55]

In this connection, it is also worth bearing in mind another of Screwtape's observations:

> False spirituality is always to be encouraged. On the seemingly pious ground that 'praise and communion with God is the true prayer', humans can often be lured into direct disobedience to the Enemy, who (in His usual flat, commonplace, uninteresting way) has definitely told them to pray for their daily bread and the recovery of their sick.[56]

---

[51]   Tim Chester, *The Message of Prayer: Approaching the Throne of Grace* (Leicester: IVP, 2003), p 49.

[52]   Matthew 6:9-13.

[53]   Mark 14:35-39; Luke 10:21; 23:34, 46; John 11:41-42; 12:28; 17:1-26.

[54]   Matthew 7:7-8.

[55]   Bloesch, *Spirituality*, p 80.

[56]   Lewis, *Screwtape Letters*, p 137.

The point is not that petition is the whole of prayer – in his prayers Jesus both praised[57] and thanked[58] the Father – but that it is at the heart of prayer. In petition I express my total dependence on the Father who is both able, because of his unlimited power, and willing, because of his unlimited love, to do everything that is for our good. So petition is one of the most important ways in which I acknowledge who God is and recognize who I am in relation to him. Any move to treat petition as an inferior form of prayer thus amounts to a move away from the truth about God and the nature of our relationship to him.

8.5. Posture in prayer

Now we come to consider the role of the body in prayer. What are we to make of the views reported at the beginning of this chapter? Our starting-point must be the fact that the Bible is a sufficient guide to true devotion.[59] Accordingly, all teaching about devotional practices is subject to this yardstick: if the Bible does not teach it, then we are not bound to do it. On the other hand, if it is not at variance with what the Bible teaches, I am free to adopt the practice – as well as being free not to do so, of course. This applies to such things as my posture in prayer:

> It is of little importance whether you stand, kneel, or prostrate yourself; for the postures of the body are neither forbidden nor commanded as necessary. The same applies to other things: raising the head and the eyes heavenward, folding the hands, striking the breast.[60]

So this is an area in which I am free to use whatever postures and gestures seem best.

But if I am free in this matter, why am I being advised to adopt certain breathing techniques and body postures when I pray? Am I to take them up for the effect this will have on God or for the effect it will have on me? If it is the former – presumably in the belief that God is

---

[57]   Matthew 11:25.
[58]   John 11:41.
[59]   See Chapters 3 and 7.
[60]   Martin Luther, quoted in Brian G. Najapfour, "Martin Luther on Prayer and Reformation" in Joel R. Beeke and Brian G. Najapfour (eds), *Taking Hold of God: Reformed and Puritan Perspectives on Prayer* (Grand Rapids: Reformed Heritage, 2011), pp 1-26 (at p 16).

more likely to hear and answer prayer that involves all of me – then its practitioners simply need to be reminded of the gospel! We are justified by faith, not by intensity. This has direct implications for our praying, as Luther saw with great clarity:

> some fail disastrously in their prayer... because they will not believe that they are heard until they know, or imagine that they know, that they have prayed well and worthily. Thus they build on themselves... Only that prayer is acceptable which breathes a firm confidence and trust that it will be heard (no matter how small and unworthy it may be in itself) because of the reliable pledge and promise of God. Not your zeal but God's Word and promise render your prayer good. This faith, based on God's words, is also the true worship; without it all other worship is sheer deception and error.[61]

It is vital to recognize that our access to God depends entirely upon the merits of our Saviour – and in no way upon the merits of our approach to him. Again, Luther makes the point crystal clear:

> our prayer must not be based upon or depend upon our worthiness or that of our prayer, but on the unwavering truth of the divine promise. Whenever our prayer is founded on itself or something else, it is false and deceptive, even though it wrings your heart with its intense devotion or weeps sheer drops of blood ...[62]

As we have seen, Spurgeon makes the same point this way: 'Never make a Christ out of your faith ...'[63]

There is another possibility, however. I might do these things because they have a beneficial effect on me. But if they do, then why not do them simply for that reason? Why muddy the waters by linking them with prayer? It is obvious that people can follow such practices for the benefits they receive, even when they have a quite unorthodox view of God:

> I find that retiring to my room at a quiet hour, sitting in a modified lotus position and putting myself in the presence of God who is my Mother is the most relaxing and invigorating spiritual experience

---

[61] *Works*, 42: p 77.
[62] *Works*, 42: p 88f.
[63] Spurgeon, *All of Grace*, p 57.

that I know.[64]

The value of this custom is not the result of approaching God as Mother! Instead, it shows that we have much to gain by slowing down, relaxing tensed muscles, experiencing quietness, and so on – a point we will discuss again in Chapter 10.

8.6. Repetitive prayer

What about the use of the 'Jesus Prayer'? What should we make of this as an expression of Christian devotion? Try as I might, I cannot understand how constant repetition of these words can be regarded as Christian praying. In the first place, it is hard to see why the criticism of Matthew 6:7 should not apply in this instance.[65] In response to this, it has been argued that use of the Jesus Prayer is not mere repetition, but that it is like the constant refrain of the angelic hosts: 'Holy, holy, holy ...'[66] However, there is no real parallel here, for the seraphim are addressing each other,[67] and the living creatures are either doing likewise or addressing the elders.[68] The point is that both groups are making declarations about God; neither is addressing him in prayer.

Secondly, the use of Christian words does not justify the practice, but to my mind only makes it all the more unacceptable. It seems indefensible to me to use the name of Jesus as what is for all practical purposes a mantra.[69] It is no defence to say that

---

[64] Ailene Swidler, quoted in Peter F. Jensen, "Prayer in Reformed Perspective", *Reformed Theological Review* 44.3 (1985), pp 65-73 (at p 65).

[65] Richard Foster argues that this does not apply here, because Jesus was condemning the public praying of the Pharisees that was 'filled with vanity' (*Prayer*, p 135). There are two problems with this defence: (1) in Matthew 6:7 Jesus is speaking about the pagans, not the Pharisees, and (2) he obviously expects private prayer also to be free of this vain repetition, for this is the subject of the immediately preceding verse (Matthew 6:6).

[66] Toon, *The Art of Meditating*, p 147.

[67] Isaiah 6:3.

[68] Revelation 4:8-11.

[69] Kallistos Ware maintains that it is misleading to regard the Jesus Prayer as a Christian mantra: 'It is not simply a rhythmic incantation, but implies a specific personal relationship and a consciously held belief in the incarnation. The aim is not simply the suspension of all thought, but an encounter with Someone'. ("Ways of Prayer", p 403). His twofold 'not simply' more or less concedes that this Prayer is used as a rhythmic incantation that aims at the suspension of all thought. That is why I find it difficult to regard this as Christian praying.

rather than a vain repetition or a meaningless mantra, this is a meditation on Scripture; it is a telegram request to our Lord and Savior Jesus Christ.[70]

It is true that the words of this prayer can remind us of fundamental biblical themes – but telegrams are not sent repeatedly unless they are not delivered or not answered! To go on repeating the prayer suggests that the person using it has no confidence of being heard – despite Luke 18:13-14!

Thirdly, this constant repetition of a set of words has been justified on the grounds that

we do not aim to suspend all thought (as mantras are used in meditation in Eastern religions) but rather to encounter a Person ... within the context of a personal (covenant) relationship.[71]

However, it is very difficult to see how this repetition of what just becomes a formula can be a way of expressing a personal relationship. Why would anyone address another person – and particularly, such a great and gracious Person – in such a relentlessly repetitive way? Surely this is to forget all that we learned in Chapter 5: what the Bible tells us about how we enter and sustain personal relationship with God.

Finally, it is difficult to escape the conclusion that the reason for this repetition is that it has a desirable effect on the speaker. We are told that it is

the path into the deeper form of prayer that is contemplative and nondiscursive ... [in which] the heart is bound in a union of love and contemplation to the Lord Jesus.[72]

In practice, this appears to mean that constant repetition of the words induces a change of consciousness, and this is interpreted as loving union with God. This seems to be what Jonathan Aitken, the former

---

[70] Issler, *Wasting Time with God*, p 270. He also calls it an 'orienting prayer', adding: 'Repetition is the key to this orienting process. The verse must be repeated several times (e.g., begin with twenty times and increase the repetition to one hundred or more times a day)' (p 162). This gives the impression that it is more important that I feel 'oriented' than that I focus on the Lord Jesus.

[71] Toon, *The Art of Meditating*, p 147; cf. Simon Chan: 'The aim of praying the Jesus Prayer is not to induce a certain psychological state but to bring one closer to the person of Jesus' (*Spiritual Theology*, p 146).

[72] Toon, *The Art of Meditating*, p 147.

sceptic quoted at the beginning of this chapter, means by saying that this repetitive praying 'works'. What he experienced obviously left him wanting more. But presumably this is why Hindus, Buddhists, and others engage in the repetitive chanting that is a little too close for comfort to this use of the 'Jesus Prayer'. It appears that this has brought us again to where we were in Chapter 6, as we discussed the 'God-feeling' and all of the problems it raises.

Our discussion of the mystical approach to prayer cannot be concluded without a return to the fundamental point in the first section of this book: that true devotion is a spirituality of the gospel. This means that the gospel must shape everything about our approach to prayer – its character and its contents; its basis and its focus.

> The basis of prayer is the gospel... There is no 'advanced' teaching on prayer. There is no 'higher' spirituality. Prayer is continually rooted in the gospel. The basis of Christian prayer is the basis of Christian salvation. The access to God through the Son that we experience in prayer is a snapshot of the gospel.[73]

Here we find the chief problem with the mystical approach to prayer: that it is not the gospel that determines how we pray. Instead, the decisive factor shaping both the understanding and practice of prayer is the traditions of mysticism. Over the centuries these have tended to develop a life of their own. As a result, they are often appealed to in their own right, with no attempt to ensure that they are grounded in the Bible and shaped by the gospel. In the end, they fail this crucial test, and are therefore best left alone.

To conclude: if the Bible is a sufficient and reliable guide to true devotion, then the mystical approach to prayer involves some significant problems. This is also true of the mystic's concept of the inner journey. That is the focus of our next chapter.

---

[73]   Chester, *The Message of Prayer*, p 58.

9.   The Inward Journey

In his famed Confessions, Augustine recalls a significant moment in his journey towards conversion to Christ:

> Under your guidance I entered into the depths of my soul, and this I was able to do because your aid befriended me. I entered, and with the eye of my soul, such as it was, I saw the Light that never changes ...[1]

This experience exemplified what he regarded as the right approach to the discovery of truth – something that lies at the heart of true spirituality:

> Do not wander far and wide but return into yourself. Deep within man there dwells the truth.[2]

Around seven centuries later, we find much the same recommendation in the writings of Anselm, the Archbishop of Canterbury:

> Enter the inner chamber of your soul; shut out everything except God and that which can help you in seeking him, and when you have shut the door, seek him.[3]

What we meet in these words is one of the central features of classical mysticism – the conviction that God is to be encountered in the depths of the soul. The journey to him is inward.

9.1.   Across the centuries

It is not difficult to find this view expressed across the centuries, as the following examples demonstrate. We begin with the Dominican theologian Albertus Magnus:

> To mount to God means to enter into oneself. Whoever enters within and penetrates his own depths, goes beyond himself and in

---

[1] Augustine, *Confessions,* translated with an Introduction by R.S. Pine-Coffin (Harmondsworth: Penguin, 1961), VII.10 (p 146). He also says, referring to the ascension, 'He departed from our sight, so that we should turn to our hearts and find him there' (IV.12 [p 82]).

[2] Augustine, in Bloesch, *Spirituality,* p 49.

[3] Anselm [1033-1109], in Aitken, *Prayers,* p 110.

truth mounts to God.[4]

According to the German mystic Meister Eckhart, 'What is truthful cannot come from outside in; it must come from inside out ...'[5] Catherine of Siena voices the same approach: 'If thou wouldst arrive at a perfect knowledge of Me the Eternal truth, never go outside thyself'.[6] Julian of Norwich says simply, 'Man's soul is the true home of God'.[7] Johannes Tauler speaks of God's presence in the ground of the soul:

> If we become aware that we have strayed from God, then we should leave all things and go quickly to the Temple, which means to say that we should gather all our faculties in our inner Temple, in our deep ground. When we have fully withdrawn there, then we shall without doubt find God and know him again.[8]

The Anabaptist Hans Denck holds that 'God ... is in the deepest abyss within us and is waiting for us to return to Him'.[9] Teresa of Avila says that 'in the centre of the soul there is a mansion reserved for God Himself.' This mansion is 'the most heavenly part of the soul, which must be in the centre of the soul since God resides there'.[10] As a result of this view, she maintains that to 'seek God within ourselves avails far more than to look for Him among creatures'.[11] The Quaker William Penn says of their appeal to their contemporaries:

> we are incessant in our cries unto them, that they will turn their minds inward ... that they may hear his heavenly voice and knocks, and let him in, and be taught of him to know and do his will ...[12]

The theologian Schleiermacher testifies that

> as often as I turn my gaze inward upon my inmost self, I am at once

---

4   Albertus Magnus [1193-1280], in Bloesch, *Spirituality*, p 55.

5   Meister Eckhart [d. 1327], in Bloesch, *Spirituality*, p 68.

6   Catherine of Siena [1347-1380], in Bloesch, *Spirituality*, p 68.

7   Mother Julian of Norwich [1342-1416], *Revelation of Divine Love* (London: Hodder, 2009 [1393]), p 186.

8   Johannes Tauler [c.1300-1361], in Oliver Davies, *God Within: The Mystical Tradition of Northern Europe*, 2nd ed. (New York: New City, 2006), p 83.

9   Hans Denck [c.1500-1527], in Bloesch, *Spirituality*, p 53.

10   Teresa of Avila [1515-1582], *Interior Castle* (Alachua, FL: Bridge-Logos, 2008 [1577]), pp 194, 142.

11   *Castle*, p 75.

12   William Penn, "A Discourse of the General Rule of Faith and Practice and Judge of Controversy" [1673], *Works*, 2: p 25.

within the domain of eternity.[13]

A more contemporary classic makes the point this way:

> Deep within us all there is an amazing inner sanctuary of the soul, a holy place, a Divine Center, a speaking Voice, to which we may continuously return. Eternity is at our hearts ... calling us home unto Itself.

> How, then, shall we ... live the life of prayer without ceasing? By quiet, persistent practice in turning all of our being, day and night, in prayer and inward worship and surrender, toward him who calls in the deeps of our souls. Mental habits of inward orientation must be established... Begin now ... to offer your whole selves, utterly and in joyful abandon, in quiet, glad surrender to him who is within.[14]

Another contemporary work says that

> with our imagination we can come close to Christ at the core of our being and appreciate the reason why prayer, of necessity, is a journey inwards.[15]

Despite some important differences between them, the key idea common to all of these works is that God is to be encountered in the depths of the soul. We find him by turning inwards.

Perhaps the most celebrated presentation of this approach is Brother Lawrence's *The Practice of the Presence of God*.[16] The essence of his view emerges when he urges, 'Let us seek Him often by faith: He is within us; seek Him not elsewhere'.[17] He insists that God 'rests in the depth and center of his soul', that he is 'always in the depth or bottom of his soul'.[18] As a result, he says, 'I keep myself retired with Him in the depth or center of my soul as much as I can'.[19] He is not completely consistent in maintaining this inward focus, however, for he speaks of

---

13   Friedrich Schleiermacher [1768-1834], in Donald G. Bloesch, *The Crisis of Piety: Essays Toward a Theology of the Christian Life*, 2nd ed. (Colorado Springs: Helmers & Howard, 1988), p 88.

14   Thomas Kelly, *A Testament of Devotion* (New York: Harper & Row, 1941), pp 29, 291f.

15   Joyce Huggett, *Open to God*, p 37.

16   Brother Lawrence [1614-1691], *The Practice of the Presence of God* (Hendrickson Christian Classics; Peabody: Hendrickson, 2004).

17   *Practice*, p 64.

18   *Practice*, p 38; cf. pp 72, 73.

19   *Practice*, p 43.

lifting up the heart to God.[20] But this has to be seen as secondary, for his basic orientation is clearly inward, not upward: 'We must make our heart a spiritual temple, wherein to adore Him incessantly'.[21]

9.2. Where should we be looking?

What are we to make of this understanding of spirituality? The first thing we must say is that there is little support in Scripture for the idea that true devotion is essentially about the inward journey to meet God in the soul. To begin with, the Bible directs us to address God with our souls, not in our souls: 'Praise the LORD, my soul; all my inmost being, praise his holy name'.[22] What we see here, we see in the rest of Scripture: we do not seek the Lord or turn to him in our souls, but with our souls.[23] Likewise, we do not descend to him in our souls, but lift our souls to him.[24] The soul does not contain him but clings to him; it does not hold him but holds to him.[25]

Secondly, as we saw in Chapter 4, the Bible directs us to look upward and forward – faith is focused above to the reigning Jesus and ahead to the returning Jesus. This faith is expressed in our praying, in which we look both above and ahead. The German theologian Jürgen Moltmann makes an important observation about forward-looking prayer:

> Pray watchfully – that is only possible if we don't pray mystically with closed eyes, but pray messianically, with eyes open for God's future in the world... We don't watch just because of the dangers that threaten us. We are expecting the salvation of the world. We are watching for God's Advent.[26]

There is a clear contrast here with the mysticism which turns inwards to encounter God. Shaped by salvation-history, biblical faith is directed

---

[20] Practice, p 45; cf. pp 33, 38, 80.

[21] Practice, p 61.

[22] Psalm 103:1; cf. 1 Samuel 1:15; Psalms 42:4; 103:2, 22; 104:1, 35; 146:1.

[23] Deuteronomy 4:29; 30:10; 2 Kings 23:25; 2 Chronicles 6:38; 15:12.

[24] Psalms 25:1; 86:4; 143:8 (ESV).

[25] Deuteronomy 30:10; Joshua 22:5; 1 Kings 8:48; Psalm 63:8.

[26] Jürgen Moltmann, "Praying with Eyes Open" in Michael Welker & Cynthia A. Jarvis (eds), Loving God with our Minds: The Pastor as Theologian (Grand Rapids: Eerdmans, 2004), p 199.

ahead to what we hope for.[27] It involves waiting upon God, looking for him to bring to its glorious completion the salvation he has already established through the work of his Son.[28]

Biblical faith is also directed above, to what we do not see.[29] So our prayers are focused upwards, to heaven, not inwards to our souls. This is because the Bible makes it clear that the God to whom we pray is in heaven, not in the depths of our souls.[30] Even though there is a sense in which the Lord Jesus is in us,[31] we go to him in heaven, where he is seated at God's right hand.[32] Prayer is not communing with the God within us, but calling upon the God above us.

> Is there a constant trade driven betwixt God and thy soul – God sending down mercies, and thou sending up prayers? This is the daily exchange.[33]

Prayer means approaching the throne of grace[34] – one of the most common themes in studies of prayer that rely on the Bible.[35] Calvin's treatment of prayer serves as a good example.[36] He says that in prayer we enter 'the heavenly sanctuary': our prayers reach heaven.[37] We present them 'before his throne', the throne of grace which is established in heaven.[38] Prayer means lifting our thoughts and desires – our hearts – to God.[39] There are also many examples of this heavenly focus in Puritan discussions of prayer.

Saints in Scripture have looked upon the throne of grace as their

---

[27] Hebrews 11:1.

[28] See, for example, Psalms 119:81; 130:5-8; Romans 8:23-25; 1 Corinthians 1:7; Philippians 3:20-21; Hebrews 9:28.

[29] Hebrews 11:1.

[30] See, for example, 1 Kings 8:27-30; Psalms 18:3, 9, 16-17; 20:1, 6, 9; 33:13-22; 57:1-3; 80:14; 115:3; 123:1.

[31] John 14:20; 15:4; 17:23, 26; 2 Corinthians 13:5; Galatians 2:20; Ephesians 3:17.

[32] See, for example, Ephesians 1:20; Colossians 3:1; Hebrews 1:3; 1 Peter 3:22.

[33] George Swinnock, quoted in Yuille, *The Inner Sanctum*, p 70.

[34] Hebrews 4:16.

[35] John Bunyan [1628-1688], for example, wrote a study of Hebrews 4:16 entitled *The Saints' Privilege and Profit, or, The Throne of Grace*. This was published in 1692, after his death. It is available in John Bunyan, *Prayer* (Edinburgh: Banner of Truth, 1965), pp 63-172.

[36] Calvin, *Institutes*, III.xx (2: pp 850-920).

[37] *Institutes*, III.xx.2, 15, 20 (2: pp 851, 870, 878).

[38] *Institutes*, III.xx.5, 17, 40 (2: pp 855, 875, 903).

[39] *Institutes*, III.xx.5, 29, 50 (2: pp 854, 891, 917).

asylum and sanctuary and have come there for refuge and strength in their troubles and temptations.[40]

One defines private prayer as

the soul's colloquy with God, and secret prayer is a conference with God upon admission into the private chamber of heaven...[41]

In prayer, our gaze is directed upwards, not inwards – prayer's 'private chamber' is heaven, not my soul. Prayer is 'an errand to the throne of grace',[42] or 'heavenly commerce with God'.[43] To pray is 'to correspond with heaven'.[44] Or in the case of short, sharp prayers like Nehemiah's,[45] it means 'a darting unto the Throne of Grace'.[46]

9.3.   Seeking God in the soul?

The first point to make about the inward journey, therefore, is that the Bible does not teach or endorse it. This leads us to the second point we must make: seeking God in the soul is likely to lead us away from true devotion. There are two primary ways in which this happens. The first is that this approach cannot help but undermine the greatness of God. A God who is found within my soul is not the majestically great God we meet in the Bible. If even the highest heaven cannot contain him,[47] my soul certainly cannot do so! And if he fills heaven and earth,[48] then he cannot be confined within my soul. But is this what advocates of the inward journey mean? They may regard God as contained within the

---

[40] Vincent, *The Spirit of Prayer*, p 135.

[41] Samuel Lee [1627-1691], *Secret Prayer Successfully Managed*, in *The Puritans on Prayer*, p 245. In the same volume, this point is also made on pages 112, 146, 224, 237, 245, 261, 281.

[42] Matthew Henry, *Communion with God*, pp 10, 27.

[43] Anthony Burgess [d. 1664], in Joel R. Beeke, "Anthony Burgess on Christ's Prayer for Us" in Beeke and Najapfour (eds), *Taking Hold of God*, pp 83-108 (at p 98).

[44] Isaac Watts, *A Guide to Prayer*, p 169. Note also these words of E.M. Bounds: 'Prayer is an appeal from the lowness, from the emptiness from the need of earth, to the highness, the fullness, and to the all-sufficiency of heaven. Prayer turns the eye and the heart heavenward ...' *The Complete Works of E.M. Bounds on Prayer* (Grand Rapids: Baker, 1990 [1907-1931]), p 235.

[45] Nehemiah 2:4.

[46] John Downame [1571-1652], in Gordon S. Wakefield, *Puritan Devotion: Its Place in the Development of Christian Piety* (London: Epworth, 1957), p 68.

[47] 1 Kings 8:27.

[48] Jeremiah 23:24.

soul, but surely they do not believe that God is confined within it. Isn't it more likely that they are making the same point that David makes – that the God who is present in the heavens is also present in the depths?[49] There would be no difficulty if this is what they meant. But the problem becomes evident in these words of Brother Lawrence: 'He is within us; seek Him not elsewhere.' Note also the claim of the noted French mystic, Jeanne Guyon:

> The Lord is found *only* within your spirit, in the recesses of your being, in the Holy of Holies; this is where He dwells.[50]

If God is only to be sought within, this can only mean that he is present there in a way that is not true elsewhere. While his presence might not be limited to the soul, it must be focused there to a special degree. And this is where this teaching parts company with the Bible, for God's essential dwelling-place is heaven, not the human soul.[51] He is seated on his heavenly throne,[52] and it is from his heavenly sanctuary that he answers those who call upon him.[53] The God of the Bible is far above me – and that is why he is 'able to do immeasurably more than all we ask or imagine'.[54] The basic problem with the inward journey is that it diminishes God. The God within is far too small.

The second problem with this approach is that it compromises the otherness of God. The God of the Bible is the Holy One.[55] This is true only of him and of no other: '"To whom will you compare me? Or who is my equal?" says the Holy One'.[56] He is in a class of his own, without peer or parallel. There is no one beside him: 'I am God, and there is no other'.[57] And there is no one – either heavenly being or human being –

---

49 Psalm 139:8.

50 Jeanne Guyon [1648-1717], quoted in Richard J. Foster, *Sanctuary of the Soul: Journey into Meditative Prayer* (Downers Grove: IVP, 2011), p 72 (her italics).

51 Deuteronomy 26:15; 1 Kings 8:30, 39, 43, 49; 2 Chronicles 30:27; Psalm 33:13-14; Isaiah 33:5; 63:15; 66:1; Jeremiah 25:30; Micah 1:3.

52 Psalms 2:4; 11:4; 102:12, 19; 103:19; 113:5-6; 123:1; Isaiah 40:22.

53 1 Kings 8:30, 32, 34, 36, 39, 43, 45; Psalms 20:6; 102:1-2, 19-20.

54 Ephesians 3:20.

55 2 Kings 19:22; Job 6:10; Psalms 22:3; 71:22; 78:41; Isaiah 1:4; 5:19, 24; 10:20; 12:6; 17:7; 29:19, 23; 30:11, 12, 15; 31:1; 37:23; 40:25; 41:14, 16, 20; 43:3, 14, 15; 45:11; 47:4; 48:17; 49:7; 54:5; 55:5; 60:9, 14; Jeremiah 50:29; 51:5; Ezekiel 39:7; Hosea 11:9, 12; Habakkuk 1:12; 3:3.

56 Isaiah 40:25.

57 Isaiah 45:22; see also Deuteronomy 4:35, 39; 1 Kings 8:60; Isaiah 44:8; 45:5, 6, 4, 18; 46:9; Joel 2:27.

who is like him: 'I am God, and there is none like me'.[58] This is a God who is utterly unique. And in his uniqueness he is totally other – he is quite distinct, separate from all created beings. This is one reason for the Bible's horror of idolatry, when the glory of God is exchanged for images of created beings.[59] By representing God as a creature, the idolater denies the holy otherness of God, reducing him to the commonplace and containing him within the familiar. But idolatry is not the only way in which God's otherness is compromised. Every attempt to confine God or to limit him is a refusal to glory in his transcendence and to revere his holiness. And this is the danger we face by taking the inward journey to the God within.

9.3.1. God and my emotions

There is an inescapable problem in locating God in the depths of my soul. If God is within, it is all too easy to confuse what happens within me with the presence and activity of God. This can take one or both of two forms. The first has to do with my feelings. The problem here is that I will be inclined to read the changes in my mood as changes in God's presence with me or favour towards me. When I feel good, I will assume that I have God's blessing – but when I am down, I will feel that God has withdrawn from me. So when I am in a good mood, I can easily become far too sanguine about my spiritual condition. How else are we to explain Brother Lawrence's claim that 'he had always been governed by love, without selfish views'?[60] Clearly, this is a case where 1 John 1:10 needs to be heard: 'If we claim we have not sinned, we make him out to be a liar and his word is not in us.' And to believe that I have reached the point where I no longer break the two great commandments must surely serve as a reminder that 'the heart is deceitful above all things'![61]

To be misled like this by my feelings is such an obvious mistake that it is one of the most basic discipleship lessons we have to learn. As we saw in Chapter 4, we have to reach the point where we recognize that we live by faith and not by feel! This is because our moods and

---

[58] Isaiah 46:9; see also Exodus 8:10; 9:14; 15:11; Deuteronomy 33:26; 1 Samuel 2:2; 2 Samuel 7:22; 1 Kings 8:23; Psalms 71:19; 86:8-10; 113:5-6; Isaiah 40:18, 25; Jeremiah 10:6-16; Micah 7:18.

[59] Psalm 106:20; Jeremiah 2:11; Romans 1:23, 25.

[60] Practice, p 7.

[61] Jeremiah 17:9.

emotions are very changeable – and they vary according to such spiritually irrelevant things as the state of the weather, how much sleep we have had, the state of our digestion, and so on. This means that while we live with our feelings, we learn not to live by them. We have to recognize that God is not changeable in the way that our feelings are. Rather, he is stable and faithful: he 'does not change like shifting shadows'.[62] As a result, we can and should go to him whatever our mood – something that we learn from the Psalms in particular. God is above us and thus outside our changing emotions. By contrast, the God within is not only far too small; he is also far too familiar – and far too fickle!

This misuse of the feelings can take another form. This sees a conflict between certain good feelings and the God-feeling. As a result, it leads to the attempt to suppress the feelings that are thought to get in the way. So Brother Lawrence insists that in order to maintain the sense of God's presence it is necessary to

> control and master the senses, inasmuch as no soul which takes delight in earthly things can find full joy in the presence of God. To be with Him we must leave behind our animal nature.[63]

The first problem with this is one we discussed in Chapter 4, that it is a mistake to identify the presence of God with a particular feeling. There is also another problem here: this is a very different view of God from that which recognizes that he 'richly provides us with everything for our enjoyment'.[64] The Bible views such everyday pleasures as food and drink and satisfaction in our work as God's gifts.[65] But if our enjoyment of such gifts prevents us from finding 'full joy in the presence of God', then it makes little sense for God to give them to us! By giving us what is good, he would be withholding from us what is best: namely, joy in God himself. Yet part of our joy in God stems from the fact that he is so lavish in his giving – by relishing the gifts, we rejoice in their Giver: 'the enjoying of him in all we have'.[66] If the heavens declare the glory of God,[67] then we do no wrong by delighting in them. The only way our enjoyment of God's gifts would threaten our joy in God is if we

---

[62] James 1:17.
[63] *Practice*, p 85.
[64] 1 Timothy 6:17.
[65] Ecclesiastes 2:24-25; 3:12-13; 5:18-19; 9:7.
[66] Matthew Henry, *Communion with God*, p 47.
[67] Psalm 19:1.

separated the gift from the Giver, failing to thank him for all that we receive at his hands.

> God, the Lord, created all creatures and all temporal things for our need, not for us to cling to with our love, but that we might seek and know God in temporal creatures and cling to the Creator with our love and hearts, that is, the creatures are only the footprints of God, signs of God that are to lead us to God. Thus, we are not to cling to them.[68]

9.3.2. God and my will

There is a second form of this confusion between God and my soul, which has to do with my will rather than my emotions. Consider the following claim by Brother Lawrence:

> I have no will but that of God ... to which I am so resigned, that I would not take up a straw from the ground against His order, or from any other motive but purely that of love to Him.[69]

A similar view is found in Teresa of Avila, who speaks of 'the true union of our will with the will of God':

> With the help of God's grace, true union can always be attained by forcing ourselves to renounce our own will and being obedient to the will of God in all things...[70]

What are we to make of this identification of the human will with God's will? Despite the acknowledgement of God's grace, this surely goes far beyond anything a sinner should claim in this life. In effect, this is to put myself in the position that is occupied only by the angels![71] But I am never justified in seeing myself this way: 'If we claim to be without sin, we deceive ourselves and the truth is not in us'.[72] The fact is that all too often we prefer our will to God's – and do we ever act purely out of love for him? How, then, is it possible to reach the point where I am convinced that I am being 'obedient to the will of God in all things' – that 'I have no will but that of God'? This fusion of the human will with

---

[68] Johann Arndt [1555-1621], *True Christianity*, translation and introduction by Peter Erb (Classics of Western Spirituality; New York: Paulist, 1979), p 97.

[69] *Practice*, p 31.

[70] *Interior Castle*, pp 103, 99.

[71] See Psalm 103:20-21.

[72] 1 John 1:8.

God's amounts to a confusion of the human soul with God. I can only think that God's will has become mine because I am confusing my will with his. And this merging can happen only because when I regard God as being within me rather than above me, I no longer make proper allowance for the fundamental distinction between us. It seems that when I concentrate on looking in rather than looking up I lose the capacity to see clearly.

That this is not a merely theoretical danger is evidenced by Teresa of Avila's claim, 'There is nothing in me that is not God: my 'me' is God'.[73] Or consider these words from an anonymous English mystic late in the fourteenth century:

> you have become one with God, united in spirit, love and harmony of will... you, or anyone else who perfectly contemplates, may truly be called 'a god' in this unity ...'[74]

Similar thoughts are found in another English mystic of the same period:

> How we should rejoice that God dwells in our soul! And yet how much more that our souls dwell in God! Our soul is made to be God's dwelling-place; and the soul's dwelling-place is God ... I could see no difference between God and our own being: it seemed to be all God.[75]

This has gone much further than putting myself in the position occupied only by the angels! It seems that G.K. Chesterton was not completely overstating the case when he observed,

> That Jones shall worship the god within him turns out ultimately to mean that Jones shall worship Jones.[76]

A different version of the same problem surfaces in some claims made by George Fox, the founder of the Quakers:

> I knew nothing but pureness, and innocency, and righteousness, being renewed up into the image of God by Christ Jesus, so that I say I was come up to the state of Adam which he was in before he fell. [T]hey asked me whether I was sanctified. 'Sanctified? yes,' for I

---

73 Quoted in Bloesch, *The Struggle of Prayer*, p 104.
74 *The Cloud of Unknowing* (London: Hodder, 2009), p 82.
75 Julian of Norwich, *Revelation of Divine Love*, pp 150-1.
76 G.K. Chesterton [1874-1936], *Orthodoxy* (Mineola, NY: Dover, 2004 [1908]), p 68.

was in the paradise of God. They said, had I no sin? 'Sin?' said I, 'Christ my Saviour hath taken away my sin, and in him there is no sin'.[77]

Here this merging of the self with the Christ within has led to claims that are plainly excluded by the Bible: 'If we claim to be without sin ...'[78]

9.4.   The location of revelation

This brings us to a third point we must make about the inward journey. We have seen that the Bible does not teach or endorse it, and we have argued that seeking God in the soul might well lead us away from true devotion. Now we note that this approach locates revelation in the wrong place. For the Bible, our knowledge of God is based on his self-revelation. We can know him only because he has made himself known. And according to the Bible, God's revelation of himself is objective and historical. It has been given in the public domain, because God makes himself known in his words and works, and these reach their climax in his Son:

> In the past God spoke to our ancestors through the prophets at many times and in various ways, but in these last days he has spoken to us by his Son, whom he appointed heir of all things, and through whom also he made the universe. The Son is the radiance of God's glory and the exact representation of his being, sustaining all things by his powerful word. After he had provided purification for sins, he sat down at the right hand of the Majesty in heaven... This salvation, which was first announced by the Lord, was confirmed to us by those who heard him... Remember your leaders, who spoke the word of God to you.[79]

And this revelation, given through prophets and apostles and supremely in the Son, is now lodged in the public domain, because it is recorded in

---

[77]   George Fox, The Journal, in *Quaker Spirituality*, pp 68, 72. Cf. William Penn's summary of the Quaker approach:
'...we have urged the necessity of a perfect freedom from sin, and a thorough sanctification in body, soul, and spirit, whilst on this side of the grave, by the operation of the holy and perfect Spirit of our Lord Jesus Christ, according to the testimony of holy Scripture ...' (*Works*, 3: p 521).

[78]   1 John 1:8.

[79]   Hebrews 1:1-3; 2:3; 13:7.

the Bible.[80] As a result, faith not only looks upwards and forwards, it also looks outwards. It is directed to the reigning and returning Lord, and also to the self-revealing Lord. So I do not seek him in the ground of my soul but in the gospel of his Son.

To conclude: if the Bible is a sufficient and reliable guide to true devotion, then the mystic's inward journey to encounter God in the soul has some significant problems.

---

[80]   On all of this see Peter Adam, *Written For Us: Receiving God's Words in the Bible* (Nottingham: IVP, 2008).

10.   Mystics and Reformers

In our review of the mystical pathway in the last four chapters, we have often quoted Luther and Calvin in support of our criticisms. This is therefore a convenient point at which to consider something we passed over in Chapter 1. We noted then that some recent advocates of the mystical way claim that Evangelical piety has been impoverished as the result of an unfortunate legacy of the Reformation. They believe that the rich heritage of spirituality in the Catholic tradition has been kept from us because the Reformers went too far in their anti-Roman polemic.

> The Reformers and we their evangelical descendants, acting in reaction to medieval Rome, threw out a great deal of spiritual wisdom, insight, and important practices ... God was leading me to honor what was true in my own tradition while welcoming back authentic Christian insights and practices from the older tradition...[1]

They welcome the signs of much greater openness to this spirituality, and want to encourage more Evangelicals to display and thus to benefit from this openness. What are we to make of this approach? Did the Reformers go too far – and do we need a change of course here as a result?

If you have stayed with me to this point, you may be wondering what happened to the openness I claimed I was going to display (Chapter 1). Can it be right to sweep aside the testimony of thoughtful people – including professional theologians – who have found a new lease of spiritual life as a result of the ideas and practices I have been critiquing? In Chapter 1 we noted the testimony of Bruce Demarest:

> I found it exhilarating to enter into the Christ-centered experiences of church fathers, desert mothers, ancient martyrs, scholastics, and responsible Christian mystics through the centuries... Discovering these perspectives and practices of an older Christian spirituality has led me into the most transforming time of my four decades as a Christian.[2]

Why can't we just accept this testimony and rejoice with its author? Surely the proof of the pudding is in the eating!

---

[1]   Demarest, *Satisfy Your Soul*, p 29.
[2]   Demarest, *Satisfy Your Soul*, pp 34-35.

10.1. Arguments from experience

I am not suggesting that Demarest and others have not experienced something that has proved very beneficial. But I do want to make three points about the testimonies we find in their books.

10.1.1. Biblical testimony

The first is that there are strong biblical reasons for being cautious about the way we argue from experience. Look at the way Paul did – and did not – do so in a very striking passage: 2 Corinthians 12:1-10. He insists that he is not going to make any claims on the basis of remarkable experiences of God. This is not because he hasn't had any such experiences (vv. 1-7a). Rather, he refrains from speaking of them 'so no one will think more of me than is warranted by what I do or say' (v. 6). That is, his relationship to the church in Corinth is to be based on his public life and teaching, not his private experiences. He takes exactly the same approach to his own ministry as he later took to Timothy's, when he urged him to 'watch your life and doctrine closely'.[3] The only experiences he is prepared to make public voluntarily are those which demonstrate his weakness, not his greatness – because his inability highlights the Lord's power, and his handicaps highlight the Lord's grace.[4] I think this means that Christian authors should be reticent about revealing their experiences, and Christian readers should be hesitant about envying them.[5]

---

[3]   1 Timothy 4:16.

[4]   2 Corinthians 12:8-10.

[5]   Note the sensible comments of Dallas Willard, "Spiritual Formation in Christ is for the Whole Life and the Whole Person" in Timothy George & Alister McGrath (eds), *For All the Saints: Evangelical Theology and Christian Spirituality* (Louisville: WJK, 2003), pp 39-53 (at pp 52-53):
'I am one who has had glorious experiences, and who owes much to them. They have a special role in the spiritual life. I don't talk about the ones I have had, because I think they are between me and the Lord, and in any case they are to be known by their effects... We should expect many profound, key moments. I don't want to miss a one of them... I hope your life is full of "Whoopee!" moments. We should all have them, but they will not transform us. What transforms us is the will to obey Jesus Christ from a life that is one with his resurrected reality day by day, learning obedience by inward transformation.'
Note, too, Graeme Goldsworthy's important observations about the dangers of arguing from the experience and example of others (*Prayer*, pp 10-14).

More significantly, does arguing from experience tell us any more than that God is remarkably generous to his children? If so-and-so has had a certain experience, there is no reason to assume that I either will or should have it – unless God has promised it to us, or has commanded us to do whatever it is. If the experience is not the subject of either God's promises or his commands, then it belongs in the category of 'uncovenanted blessings', as Christians of previous times called them. The wise words of Oswald Chambers are worth noting in this regard:

> If we try to re-introduce the rare moments of inspiration, it is a sign that it is not God we want... Never live for the rare moments, they are surprises. God will give us touches of inspiration when He sees we are not in any danger of being led away by them. We must never make our moments of inspiration our standard; our standard is our duty.[6]

We can state the basic issue as follows. We need to distinguish between the faithfulness and the freedom of God. Where he has given a promise, his nature as an entirely faithful God means that he is 'bound' to keep that promise – and this entitles us to ask him to keep it, confident that he will do so. However, where he has not given a promise, he is free to do whatever he decides, whenever he likes, however he chooses, for whomever he wants. There may be no biblical reason why I should not ask him to do for me what he has done for someone else, but I have no biblical warrant for believing that he will do so.

So the question I need to ask about the experiences of other Christians is this: Is this something God has promised or commanded? If not, then there is no reason to expect that I will or should have the same experience.[7]

10.1.2. Interpretations of human experience

There is a second point I wish to make about testimonies like those of Demarest. I think that there is another way of thinking about their experiences, in addition to the meaning they see in them. One of the crucial issues in all of this is the fact that people of other religions (or

---

6   Oswald Chambers, *My Utmost for His Highest* (London: Marshall, Morgan & Scott, 1927), p 122.

7   There is a helpful discussion of these matters in Graham Cole, "Experiencing the Lord: Rhetoric and Reality" in B.G. Webb (ed), *Spirit of the Living God, Part Two* (Explorations 6) (Homebush West: Lancer, 1992), pp 49-70.

none) have similar experiences when they use some of the mystical practices we have considered. Thus, although God can obviously use them as a means of giving blessing to his children, there is nothing intrinsically Christian about these practices or the experiences they generate. It may therefore be more sensible to interpret them as *human* experiences, rather than specifically 'spiritual' ones. That is, what we are dealing with is the fact that the human psyche works in certain ways. It is only natural that those who have the experiences in question interpret them in line with their worldview – so what we think the experience means is a product not just of the experience itself, but of the interpretive framework we bring to the experience.

Let me explain what I mean by drawing attention to a revealing comment from Bruce Demarest:

> I admit I was a typical product of evangelical academic culture... I'd been 'saved' and that was that. Now it was up to me to work hard as a Christian, to succeed in higher education, and to prove myself to the watching world. My experience was not entirely foreign to that described by Robert A. Johnson, the Episcopal therapist and author, who wrote of 'the standard American way of life, with the goals, the excessive work schedule, the constant feeling of pressure and deadlines, money to be made and people to be impressed.' With this mind-set, I could feel satisfied at the end of a day if I had completed my ministry assignments, even if time alone with the Lord was squeezed out by the clock.[8]

In the light of this description of his way of life, is it out of the question to see the renewed vitality to which he testifies as the result, not of a particular way of being Christian, but of taking time out (a six-week retreat), slowing down, making room for quietness and having time to think? In other words, is he getting the benefit of living in a way that is more in tune with how we are made? Is his new freshness and joy in the faith actually the way his mind and body are saying, 'Thanks for giving us a break, and taking things at a pace we can handle'? This explanation does not exclude the one he gives himself: namely, that what he has experienced is an expression of God's goodness and a closer relationship with him. We do not have to choose between these interpretations, because God often chooses to use 'ordinary' means in

---

[8]   Demarest, *Satisfy Your Soul*, p 25.

doing his work – and what is more likely than that the one who designed our nature should make use of it?

10.1.3. The testimony of the Reformers

The third and most important point I want to make about the testimonies of writers such as Demarest is that we must take more seriously than they do the testimonies of the Reformers. Unless we do so, we are unlikely to understand why they did what they did in the area of spirituality. So, what do they have to say about these matters?

The best way in to this aspect of their teaching is to note what they say about the piety on which they had been reared. Their comments make it clear that they regarded this piety as something deeply flawed. Calvin says simply, 'I had all my life long been in ignorance and error'.[9] But this did not apply only to him; it was true also for his contemporaries:

> impiety so stalked abroad that almost no doctrine of religion was pure from admixture, no ceremony free from error, no part, however minute, of divine worship untarnished by superstition.[10]

Luther speaks about his past in similarly bleak terms:

> For more than twenty years I was a pious monk, read mass daily, and so weakened myself with fasting and praying that I would not have been long for this life if I had continued... I must now condemn it as sin committed in idolatry and unbelief ...[11]

Because of the errors they now saw in it, they believed that it was necessary to repudiate their former piety in decisive terms:

> Acknowledging, then, the evil that we formerly committed while thinking we were doing good, let us learn to regret our past and to ask our gracious God to save us from ever falling again into such

---

[9] John Calvin and Jacopo Sadoleto, *A Reformation Debate: Sadoleto's Letter to the Genevans and Calvin's Reply*, edited, with an introduction, by John C. Olin (Grand Rapids: Baker, 1966), p 88.

[10] *A Reformation Debate*, p 75. Speaking of the pre-Reformation situation, Calvin also says that 'every place was filled with pernicious errors, falsehoods, and superstition' (p 82). He describes Catholic churches thus: 'In them Christ lies hidden, half buried, the gospel overthrown, piety scattered, the worship of God nearly wiped out' (*Institutes*, IV.ii.12 [2: p 1053]).

[11] *Works*, 24: pp 227-228; cf. 24: pp 23-24.

depths of abomination.[12]

It is important to emphasize that the Reformers are not looking on from afar at something they do not really understand, and which they therefore reject out of ignorance and prejudice. Instead, they are speaking about their own past. They are not condemning others so much as bearing witness to God's grace in setting them free.

The next thing we need to note is that the Reformers did not regard these errors as peripheral or unimportant. On the contrary, they viewed their past as something enslaving, from which God in his mercy has rescued them. Calvin puts it like this:

> We have been delivered from the wretched bondage of the papacy... Therefore, let us acknowledge God's love for us, since God has delivered us from our former yoke and bondage.[13]

Luther's background was different from Calvin's in many ways, but he too testifies to what he views as a deliverance:

> I lived for more than fifteen years in pure idolatry and blasphemy, in unbelief in God and false trust in the dead saints whom I invoked and in my masses and monastic life... But now God has mercifully liberated me from this and given me to see that this is pure perversion and godlessness ...[14]

One of the most common ways they spoke of this past was as a great and terrible darkness. So Calvin observes, 'We remember with amazement how deep was the whirlpool of ignorance and how horrible the darkness of errors in the papacy'.[15] Luther too speaks of this darkness: 'Under the papacy ... there was a great darkness that completely blacked out the light of Christian teaching'.[16] But they rejoiced that God was now powerfully at work, dispelling this darkness by the light of the gospel. So Calvin urges:

---

[12]   John Calvin, *Sermons on the Book of Micah* (Phillipsburg, NJ: P&R, 2003), p 39.

[13]   *Micah*, pp 416, 417.

[14]   Luther, *Works*, 51: p 345.

[15]   *Concerning Scandals* (Grand Rapids: Eerdmans, 1978 [1550]), p 83. Note also his reference to 'the dense darkness of the papacy' (*Scandals*, p 82), and to the time 'when divine truth lay buried under this vast and dense cloud of darkness' (*The Necessity of Reforming the Church* (Dallas: Protestant Heritage, 1995 [1544]), p 38). There are many similar statements, for example, in his *Timothy and Titus* (pp 78, 85, 274, 284).

[16]   *Works*, 21: p 181.

let us acknowledge our former poverty which existed before our Lord illumined us with the knowledge of his Gospel.[17]

This was the essential problem about their past: it lacked the gospel. So when the Reformers refer to the present, to the Reformation itself, they speak of the re-emergence of the gospel. Calvin characterizes his generation as the time of 'the renascent gospel', when 'the gospel has begun to be revived'.[18] Speaking of the contrast with 'the time of our ignorance', he says that

> God has worked in us a particular grace when He withdrew us from the shadows of error where we were, and gave us His Gospel to lead us into view of salvation.[19]

Luther says simply that 'the light of the Gospel has been restored'.[20]

The Reformers believed that what they were doing was contending for the gospel. They were not anti-Catholic but pro-gospel. It is vital that we see this point, lest we make the serious mistake of assuming that the right way of following them is to be anti-Catholic. We will follow them only by being as earnestly committed to the gospel as they were. What they objected to about Rome was what they regarded as its denial of the gospel:

> all Popish rituals represent a rejection of the Lord Jesus Christ, of the cleansing that he purchased through his death and resurrection, and also of the grace offered to us in the gospel.[21]

And the stiff opposition they faced from Rome was not seen as directed against them so much as against the gospel: 'the unyielding Papists ... corrupted, perverted and falsified the truth of the gospel'.[22] So they saw a simple choice facing the people of their day. Those who embraced the

---

[17]   *Micah*, 39; cf. *Scandals*, p 58: 'the torch of the gospel has been brought in'; *Timothy and Titus*, p.1223: 'the preaching of the Gospel is as a lamp to give us light, that we may know the things that were hidden from us before'. He says that 'God raised up Luther and others, who held forth a torch to light us into the way of salvation' (*Necessity*, p 13).

[18]   *Scandals*, pp 79, 57. He also refers to this as a time in which 'God has planted the doctrine of the gospel ... [and] the gospel began to spring up' (p 64).

[19]   Calvin, *The Deity of Christ*, p 277.

[20]   *Works*, 8: p 181; cf. 3: p 275; 6: p 148; 13: p 42; 17: p 271: 'before the Gospel was revealed'; 47: p 52: 'all the good which the dear gospel has again restored and established'.

[21]   John Calvin, *Sermons on Galatians* (Edinburgh: Banner of Truth, 1997 [1563]), p 396.

[22]   Calvin, *Galatians*, p 148.

Reformation 'renounced the Pope and ... came over to the side of the gospel'.[23] For many today, that choice will mean turning away from defective forms of Protestantism.

10.2. The choices we face

We need to acknowledge that it is very hard for us to handle such strong statements as those we have been considering. There are two reasons for this. The first is that our ecclesiastical context is strongly ecumenical – people of other denominations are to be seen as no less Christian than we are. The second is that our social and cultural context places us under great pressure to be 'tolerant'. In practice, this means to be accepting of all religious opinions – except those of the 'fundamentalists', of course! This is especially true of spirituality, where there is a strong tendency to regard all approaches as valid. Yet if we do not hear what the Reformers are saying about their own experience, and especially the dramatic contrast between their Catholic past and their gospel-centred present, we will not understand the rest of their teaching. And in view of all that they say about this, it should be clear that any reclaiming of this piety on our part would be a very serious step. It would amount to saying that the Reformers were wrong to reject it. But if they were wrong here, they were very wrong indeed, for (as we have just seen) they believed that nothing less than the gospel was at stake.

10.2.1. Spiritual 'Classics'

This is something that generally needs to be taken more seriously by studies of Christian spirituality that profess to be Evangelical. This applies especially to discussions which treat as 'spiritual classics' works which the Reformers criticised. Consider, for example, what Luther says about the writings of Pseudo-Dionysius:

> he is downright dangerous, for he is more of a Platonist than a Christian. So if I had my way, no believing soul would give the least attention to these books. So far, indeed, from learning Christ in them, you will lose even what you already know of him. I speak from experience.[24]

---

[23] Calvin, *Scandals*, p 35.
[24] *Works*, 36: p 109; see also *Works*, 54: p 112.

It is difficult to think of a more complete rejection – and one that is based on first-hand experience. Yet we find a modern discussion of spirituality commending these same works in very strong terms, claiming that they provide

> one of the clearest expressions of how to begin, understand and grow in our life with God.[25]

If this assessment is right, then Luther is very wide of the mark! Not only so, but he is steering believers away from works that will benefit them greatly. However, to read these works in the light of the gospel is to discover that Luther had good reason to warn us against them. They do not deserve to be treated as spiritual classics.

10.2.2. Icons

The concern we are expressing applies also to those works which regard as live options, or even as necessary features of authentic spirituality, practices which the Reformers excluded. Take the use of icons, for example. On the one hand, we find this recommendation of their use:

> As we lovingly behold the icon, we seek to pass beyond the image in wood or paint to the person of Jesus himself, and from the person of Jesus into the very presence of the triune God.[26]

On the other hand, we have Calvin stating what he regards as a fundamental biblical principle:

> every statue man erects, or every image he paints to represent God, simply displeases God as something dishonourable to his majesty.[27]

He also refers specifically to icons in this connection. He notes the tendency of 'Greek Christians' to 'wantonly indulge in pictures', and then adds:

---

[25]   Richard J. Foster and Gayle D. Beebe, *Longing for God: Seven Paths of Christian Devotion* (London: Hodder & Stoughton, 2009), p 227.

[26]   Foster, *Sanctuary of the Soul*, p 39.

[27]   Calvin, *Institutes*, I.xi.2 (1: p 101). Calvin's whole discussion of images (I.xi-xii [1: pp 99-120]) should be read. Also worth reading is the debate between Dr Harding and Bishop John Jewel over the adoration of images (*The Works of John Jewel*, four volumes (The Parker Society; Cambridge: CUP, 1847), 2: pp 644-668), which Jewel concludes by stating, 'Neither doth God throughout all his holy scriptures any where condemn image-breakers; but expressly and every where he condemneth image-worshippers and image-makers' (2: p 668).

But the Lord forbids not only that a likeness be erected to him by a maker of statues but that one be fashioned by any craftsman whatever, because he is thus represented falsely and with an insult to his majesty.[28]

The second Helvetic Confession, in the fourth chapter entitled, 'Of Idols or Images of God, of Christ, and of Saints', says plainly, 'We ... reject not only the idols of the Gentiles, but also the images of Christians.' It then adds:

For although Christ took upon Him man's nature, yet He did not ... take it that He might set forth a pattern for carvers and painters... He promises that 'He would by His Spirit be present with us for ever';[29] who would then believe that the shadow or picture of His body in any way benefits the godly?[30]

So, again, we are faced with a choice: do we go with the modern discussion of spirituality that commends this practice, or do we follow the Reformers who excluded it?[31]

I have been arguing that we must take seriously what the Reformers say about their experience of piety. This has been in response to testimonies of a new spiritual vitality gained through exposure to Catholic devotion – testimonies that claim the Reformers went too far when they excluded these riches. My point is that we are not in a position to determine the validity of this claim unless we hear what the Reformers say about their own experience. Our survey of their testimony has shown that they view the gospel as the criterion of authentic spirituality. This is why they did not regard the writings and practices of the mystics as a treasure to be preserved and passed on.

---

[28] *Institutes*, I.xi.4 (1: p 104f). Note also his question, 'Did they not suppose the power and grace of God attached to pictures and statues, would they flee to them when they are desirous to pray?' (*Necessity*, p 44).

[29] John 16:7; 2 Corinthians 5:5.

[30] The Second Helvetic Confession (1566), in *Reformed Confessions of the 16th and 17th Centuries in English Translation*, compiled with Introductions by James T. Dennison, Jr., two volumes (Grand Rapids: Reformation Heritage, 2010), 2: p 815.

[31] Foster claims that the 'seventh ecumenical council of 787 ... settled the matter for the Christian community by affirming the use of icons' (*Sanctuary*, p 39). Calvin's analysis of the council's discussions (*Institutes*, I.xi.14-16 [1: pp 114-116]) shows that the matter is (or ought to be) anything but settled!

10.3.   The testimony of Luther

We have just considered what Luther says about such writings as those of Pseudo-Dionysius. It is clear that he is not reacting suspiciously against something that is new to him. Instead, he is warning about the dangers of ideas and practices that were very familiar to him. He is not neglecting treasures he has failed to recognize but rejecting errors he knows only too well. It is difficult to miss the pathos in his blunt, 'I speak from experience.' When viewed from the perspective of the gospel – that is, 'learning Christ' and knowing God – Luther believes that he experienced significant harm rather than any benefit through his exposure to such writers. His testimony should surely be taken seriously by those who are just becoming acquainted with this literature.

Luther sought to replace the mystical disciplines with a piety of great simplicity. This was not because he was unable to restrain his anti-Roman zeal. It was because he regarded the mystical way as insufficiently grounded in and expressive of the gospel.

> Formerly – before God revealed the light of the Gospel – much was written and said about the contemplative and active life ... and in the monasteries and convents monks and nuns who, on the whole, were very pious eagerly strove to have visions and Revelation presented to them. Consequently, some even noted down all their dreams. Evidently they all waited for extraordinary illuminations without external means. What else is this than a desire to ascend into heaven without ladders? Consequently, these monks and nuns were very frequently deceived by delusions of the devil...[32]

> The speculation [i.e., contemplation] by which Christ is grasped is ... a theological, faithful, and divine consideration of the serpent hanging from the pole, that is, of Christ hanging on the cross for my sins, your sins, and for the sins of the entire world (John 3:14-15).[33]

> [I]t is certain that he who bypasses the Person of Christ never finds the true God; for since God is fully in Christ, where He places Himself for us, no effort to deal with God without and apart from Christ on the strength of human thoughts and devotion will be successful. Whoever would travel the right road and not go astray

---

[32]   *Works*, 3: p 275f.

[33]   *Works*, 26: p 287.

with his faith, let him begin where God says and where He wants to be found. Otherwise he will surely miss the goal, and all that he believes and does will prove vain.[34]

It is clear from such comments that Luther's rejection of the mystical way stems from his conviction that it represents a false alternative to the gospel. His zeal for Christ and the gospel is what motivates his desire to exclude it. We see this from another angle when he is defending himself against the accusation that he rejects 'all the holy teachers of the church.'

I do not reject them. But everyone, indeed, knows that at times they have erred, as men will; therefore, I am ready to trust them only when they give evidence for their opinions from Scripture, which has never erred... Scripture alone is the true lord and master of all writings and doctrine on earth.[35]

So Luther gives this counsel about 'the pope and his followers' who 'preach human doctrine':

In brief, reject whoever does not preach the gospel to you and do not listen to him... beware of everything that is told you that does not agree with the gospel; do not put any trust in it ...[36]

10.4.   The testimony of Calvin

What we have seen in Luther we also see in Calvin. Note, for example, what he says about our union with God-in-Christ:

whenever Paul joins us to God through Christ and faith in Him, there is an implied contrast, which shuts up every other approach and excludes all other ways of union.[37]

This contrast is between the way of the gospel (Christ and faith in him) and all of the other ways in which people sought to achieve union with God – most likely a reference to the mystical practices of Calvin's own day. Elsewhere he makes the same point in this way:

---

[34]   *Works*, 24: p 23.
[35]   *Works*, 32: p 11f.
[36]   *Works*, 52: p 69f.
[37]   Calvin, *The Epistles of Paul the Apostle to the Galatians, Ephesians, Philippians and Colossians* (Calvin's New Testament Commentaries; Grand Rapids: Eerdmans, 1965 [1556]), p 164.

since our Lord Jesus Christ offers and puts himself forward to be the way to lead us to God his Father, we must not go bustling up and down. If we wish to seek any other way we shall only go astray and prove ourselves bunglers... all they that think they will obtain favour at God's hand by any other means only run astray, and have shut themselves out of the door already. And therefore there is now no excuse, but we must in all simplicity keep to the way which the gospel shows us, the way by which we come to God, that is to say, in the name of our Lord Jesus Christ, without adding any other creature as we see the whole world doing.[38]

As is the case with Luther, it is the gospel that drives Calvin's concerns about our practice of piety. That is why he too insists that it must be 'conformable to God's Word'.[39] He asks the fundamental question as to what should determine our spirituality: 'What ... must be our rule by which to know God?' His answer is very clear:

To allow ourselves to be taught by his Word, and to be so discreet as to receive whatever it contains without contradicting, and not to presume to add anything at all to it.[40]

In another context, he expands on what this means:

when it is a matter of worshiping God, we are not to give any attention whatever to our imagination. But we are to follow in all simplicity what he has ordained by his Word, without adding anything to it at all... we should know that it is unnecessary to parade our 'good intentions' as a cover-up for what we have invented, indeed; but on the contrary we should know that the principal service which God requires is obedience.[41]

---

[38] Calvin, *Ephesians*, pp 282, 286.

[39] *Ephesians*, p 286.

[40] *Ephesians*, p 180.

[41] John Calvin, *John Calvin's Sermons on the Ten Commandments*, edited and translated by Benjamin W. Farley (Grand Rapids: Baker, 1980), pp 66, 67. There is a marked contrast between this rejection of imagination and the prominent place given to it in some modern discussions of spirituality: see, for example, Joyce Huggett, *Open to God*, pp 53-66; Peter Toon, *Meditating upon God's Word*, pp 39-41; Peter Toon, *Meditating as a Christian* (London: Collins, 1991), pp 117-125. Also worth noting is Richard Sibbes' extended discussion of the imagination, and his insistence that 'fancy must yield to faith, and faith to divine revelation' (*Works*, 1: pp 178-191 (the quotation is on p 185)).

It is not enough that particular ideas and practices have a long heritage in the church; what matters is that they be in line with the gospel. Nor is it enough to mean well in our devotional practices; it is our solemn responsibility to God 'to serve him as he commands and to find nothing good save what he approves'.[42]

For both Calvin and Luther, then, spirituality must be governed by the gospel – it too has to pass the test of *solus Christus* (Christ alone), *sola gratia* (grace alone), *sola fide* (faith alone), and *sola Scriptura* (Scripture alone).

10.5. The goal of the Reformers

All of this introduces us to a point of fundamental importance about the agenda of Luther and the other Reformers. It was clear to them that they were engaged in something much more radical and far-reaching than simply the removal of some religious abuses:

> the Reformation which Luther initiated was also intended to be a Reformation of spirituality ... Luther and the evangelical movement proposed to change the actual pattern of Christian living ... [He] set about to install a new piety, that is, a new way of living and practicing the Christian religion.[43]

At its simplest level, this involved Luther in aiming 'to return to the people the right way of praying'.[44] This reflects his negative judgment of the praying he had been accustomed to: 'It would be better not to pray at all than to pray like the priests and monks'.[45] But his reform agenda went much further than this, as we see, for example, in what he says about the 'kingdom of grace' and 'the Christian way of life'. He states the essence of this kingdom thus:

> we must become righteous, alive, and saved without any of our deserving through God's pure grace in Christ, which is given us as a gift. Beyond that, there is no other walk or way ... that might help us.[46]

---

[42]   Calvin, *Ten Commandments*, p 249.

[43]   Scott Hendrix, "Martin Luther's Reformation of Spirituality", *Lutheran Quarterly* 13 (1999), pp 249-70 (at pp 250, 252).

[44]   *Luther's Spirituality*, edited and translated by Philip D.W. Krey and Peter D.S. Krey (Classics of Western Spirituality; New York: Paulist, 2007), p 202.

[45]   *Luther's Spirituality*, p 211.

[46]   *Luther's Spirituality*, p 147.

This has serious implications for the monasteries and convents and their focus on 'works and merits' instead of the Christian way of life:

> to consider theirs a way of life better than the ordinary Christian way of life is wrong and denies and curses Christ. They should serve and enhance the Christian way of life ... [which] should hover over everything like heaven over the earth, for it is Christ's own way of life and God's own work. Now, because they do not want to do this, like the stiff-necked Jerusalem they have to be torn apart and torn down.[47]

Dissolution was the only alternative to major reform: 'If they would preserve their monasteries and convents', they should be 'simply Christian schools as they were originally founded'.[48] Luther's vision in all of this was that 'citizens, farmers, shoemakers, tailors, clerks, knights, masters, servants' should live a life based on God's grace in the gospel.[49]

10.6. The 'simplicity of the gospel'

This far-reaching agenda was true of Calvin as well as Luther. One of the ways in which this becomes evident is in his references to the 'simplicity of the gospel'. These are generally contrasted with practices Calvin regards as originating from perverse human religiosity rather than God's word. So, preaching on Micah 1:5-10, he says that we should not be astonished

> to discover that God both rejects and condemns all forms of worship invented by humankind. For the only thing that pleases God is our obedience ... For we all possess the seed of idolatry in our nature... And unless God draws us to himself and guides us according to the doctrines of his Word, we will continue to invent evil superstitions. We know all this from experience. And what a confusion exists in the papacy! But we should find none of this strange. For even today, if there were no idolatry in the world, just as soon as we should turn from the purity of God's Law and his Gospel, immediately we would see the world become corrupt and infected with idolatries ...[50]

---

[47] *Luther's Spirituality*, pp 133f.
[48] *Luther's Spirituality*, p 133.
[49] *Luther's Spirituality*, p 132.
[50] Calvin, *Micah*, pp 37-38.

He then exhorts his hearers,

> let us acknowledge our former poverty which existed before our
> Lord illumined us with the knowledge of his Gospel...
> Acknowledging, then, the evil that we formerly committed while
> thinking we were doing good, let us learn to regret our past and to
> ask our gracious God to save us from ever falling again into such
> depths of abomination... let us continue to be faithful and chaste
> toward God ... This faithfulness can occur wherever we are bound to
> the simplicity of his Word.[51]

Later, expounding Micah 6:12-16, he says that

> those who worship God in accordance with their fantasy, as in the
> papacy, dishonour and blaspheme God rather than worship God... If
> we would worship God as we should, then this passage forces us to
> expend the effort to ground ourselves in the pure simplicity that God
> has set forth in his Word... For if we hope to worship God in the
> manner that is acceptable to him, then we must divest ourselves of all
> silly superstitions and frivolous inventions, renounce all idolatry in
> order to worship God in spirit and in truth (as God commands us),
> and cling to the simplicity that we observe in his Word.[52]

We find the same point being made when Calvin expounds Titus 1:14:

> So then the simplicity of our faith is this, that we cast away all
> inventions of men, and cleave fast to that that God teacheth us, and
> is contained in his word, and put nothing to it ... Will we then hold
> fast this simplicity? Then we must cast away whatsoever men bring
> of their own, to blend it with the word of God.[53]

It is clear that the 'simplicity of the gospel' means a new piety that is
profoundly different from the piety in which Calvin and his hearers

---

[51]   *Micah*, pp 39-40 (footnote omitted).
[52]   *Micah*, pp 362, 363, 364 (footnote omitted).
[53]   Calvin, *Timothy and Titus*, p 1119. In this work we find many references to this
simplicity: 'the [pure] simplicity of the word [of God]' (pp 352, 799, 809, 813), 'the
simplicity that is contained in holy writ' (p 345) or 'the [pure] simplicity of [the
doctrine which is contained in] the holy Scripture' (pp 723, 800, 1121), 'the simplicity
of our faith' (pp 1118, 1119), 'the simple doctrine of the gospel' (p 1118), and especially
'the [pure] simplicity of the gospel' (pp 14, 17, 20, 42, 651, 653, 656, 657, 658, 681,
775, 802, 805, 812, 967, 969). (I have updated the spelling in all quotations from this
work.) This is not the only place that Calvin uses this language, of course: see, for
example, his *Galatians*, pp 44, 56, 69, 121, 147, 206, 299, 388, 496, 500, 508, 659.

were reared. It generates a simplicity of heart that forms the core of 'pure religion', and that stands over against the superstition of merely human religion.[54] Commenting on Isaiah 29:13, Calvin says that God

> reproves their superstitious and idolatrous practices... We may easily conclude from this what value ought to be set on that worship which Papists think that they render to God, when they worship God by useless ringing of bells, mumbling, wax candles, incense, splendid dresses, and a thousand trifles of the same sort ... when God is worshipped by inventions of men, he condemns this 'fear' as superstitious, though men endeavour to cloak it under a plausible pretence of religion, devotion, or reverence... But it is the will of the Lord, that our 'fear,' and the reverence with which we worship him, shall be regulated by the rule of his word; and he demands nothing so much as simple obedience, by which we shall conform ourselves and all our actions to the rule of the word ...[55]

Because this man-made religion is so corrupted, nothing less than reformation was required:

> We know there is nothing in Papistry but is marred and mangled. And therefore it was requisite for us to make a great change... as religion is corrupted and evil ordered, and men have blended their own inventions with it: all that must be cut off, we must come back to the pure and simple religion of God ...[56]

---

[54] *Timothy and Titus*, p 395; cf. pp 16, 392, 394. Elsewhere he asserts that 'all that the Papists refer to as the service of God is nothing more than a labyrinth, or an abyss, of superstitions which they have forged in their own heads' (*Galatians*, p 654).

[55] John Calvin, *Commentary on the Book of the Prophet Isaiah*, two volumes (Grand Rapids: Baker, 1981), 1: pp 323, 324, 325. This is very similar to Luther: '...we should learn that God is not pleased with self-chosen works and that no way of worship should be prescribed to Him according to our judgment... He must remain the Teacher and Guide. But the perversity of human nature is so great that we neglect what God commands and choose what He has not prescribed. But they say: "We are doing this with good zeal and purpose." For this is the source of all superstitions and heresies, and from it have come the monks ...' (*Works*, 7: p 355; cf. 2: pp 354-355; 25: p 158f).

[56] *Timothy and Titus*, p 679. Luther makes similar observations when speaking about his work: 'I have worked for the eradication of dangerous abuses and superstitions and the liberation of holy Christendom in its entirety from so many endless, innumerable, un-Christian, and damnable tyrannical diminutions [of the gospel], burdens, and blasphemies' (*Works*, 48: p 197).

Calvin insists that reformation involves the stripping away of their previous devotion:

> we must realize that we cannot become Christians until God has purged us of all idolatry and superstition. For though we regard them with the highest sanctity and devotion, God has to destroy them and remove them from our midst.[57]

Indeed, he believes that nothing less than their loyalty to Christ is at stake if they turn back to the piety of their past.

> As Saint Paul says: 'I have betrothed you to Jesus Christ' [2 Corinthians 11:2-3]... 'Take heed,' he warns, 'lest you, like Eve, who was seduced by Satan, also become seduced by Satan's cunning. And how might that happen? By turning aside from the simplicity of the Gospel... The moment you relinquish the simplicity of the Gospel, the Devil has seduced you!'[58]

For Calvin, true devotion requires spiritual chastity, as we saw in Chapter 3. It is in essence a spirituality of the gospel.

We have been listening to the testimonies of the Reformers as they speak about their experience of Catholic piety and the impact the gospel made in their lives. What they say makes it very difficult to accept the claim that they were being over-zealous when they rejected the piety of their past, including the teachings of celebrated mystics. Those who want to undo this legacy of the Reformation and to give an honoured place to ideas and practices the Reformers excluded face an important challenge. They will need to show how their approach meets the test of spiritual chastity – how it is true to the word of God and in line with the gospel of Christ. It should be clear by now that this is what governed the approach of the Reformers. And here at least, we should be their followers.

But it is critical to grasp what this means. Why did they reject the piety on which they were reared? It was not because it was Catholic. It was because it was not true to the gospel and the Bible. This is where the Reformers should be followed: in their resolute determination to be loyal to God's grace and truth. So we will follow them, not by opposing Catholicism as such, but by distancing ourselves from anything and

---

[57] *Micah*, p 306.
[58] *Micah*, p 40.

everything (no matter how pious and devout) that does not square with the gospel. In practice, for most of us, this will mean rejecting erroneous forms of Protestant spirituality. Our essential commitment is not to any 'ism' but to the Lord and his word.

PART III: THE WAY AHEAD

If the mystical way is not the right way forward, what is? What will a spirituality of the gospel look like in practice? What should I be doing to express true devotion? If you have turned to this last section of the book expecting to be given lots of specific instructions, I am going to disappoint you. This is not because I don't believe in being practical. Rather, it is because I don't believe in trying to make you like me. My views about what to do would inevitably reflect my personality, my circumstances, my current devotional practices, and so on – including my many flaws and limitations. What you need to do is to determine before God what you need to do! Let me explain what I mean.

This has to be what *you* need to do. Only you know how things stand with you – that is, where you are in your life with God. So only you know where changes are needed as you seek to grow stronger, deeper, and truer as a Christian. This is one of the ways you can use this book: each time it uncovers a new way forward or shows you that you have a problem, you can write down your resolution about the changes you plan to make. This will give you something specific to bring to God in prayer, as you ask him for help to make the changes that are needed.

And your decisions must be about what you need to *do*. Can I tell you about one of my great breakthrough-moments? It was at a stage in my Christian life where I was especially conscious of being way below where I should be. I made lots of resolutions about how I was going to make major changes. I set off in new directions and with fresh resolve many times – only to fail dismally again and again. The breakthrough I needed came in a very surprising way. I heard someone quote one of Chairman Mao's slogans (borrowed – I later discovered – from the Chinese philosopher, Lao Tze): 'The journey of a thousand miles begins with a single step.' This hit me like the proverbial baseball-bat! I realized that I had been attempting to make the spiritual journey of a thousand miles in one gigantic bound. At that moment, what I needed to do was obvious. Moving forward was about taking achievable steps, first one, and then another – and bit by bit, I would make progress. And bit by bit, I did. (By now, I've travelled at least a dozen of that thousand miles!) Why have I told you this story? Because I suspect that I am not the only person who took a long time to discover the principle of 'progress through achievable steps'. If you have been compiling a list of resolutions about changes you plan to make, perhaps you need to go through it, applying this reality-test to each item on your list: Is this an achievable step – or an impossibly huge leap? If you are only spending five minutes a day in prayer, there is little point in resolving to spend an hour a day, starting from tomorrow! But there is something to be said for planning to spend ten minutes a day from tomorrow onwards – and then after a week or two, going to fifteen minutes a day.

If this final section of the book is not intended to tell you what you should be doing, what is it for? Its purpose is to give proper attention to two important areas of true devotion. The first is a specific practice that seems to have dropped out of Evangelical piety. Here our aim is twofold – we want to get a clear understanding of what it is, and then to consider how its reintroduction would help us. That is what Chapter 11 seeks to do. The second area is totally different from the first. In fact, it is not really an aspect of Christian spirituality at all. As the title of Chapter 12 indicates, it is at the heart of all true devotion. It is like the hub at the centre of the wheel, binding all the spokes of our devotional attitudes and practices together. As a result, it has emerged at various points in the previous two sections of the book. Yet we have not so far given it the focused treatment it needs and deserves. That is what Chapter 12 will do. The final chapter draws a few conclusions from what the book has attempted to do.

II. The Missing Link?

When I was converted, I was given quite a good grounding in the basics of the Christian life. This included a strong emphasis on the importance of the daily 'Quiet Time', which had two ingredients: Bible-reading and prayer. I was given material that helped me to start reading the Bible systematically and thoughtfully. I was also given a clear framework that taught me how to pray. But I had the impression that the two activities were not closely connected. So I often found that after I had read and analysed the Bible passage for that day, I closed the Bible and then started working out what to pray about.

It was only many years later that I found out that somewhere along the way a third component of the Quiet Time had been lost. I discovered that for a long time after the Reformation, Evangelical piety included a practice that was regarded as the indispensable link between Bible reading and prayer. This missing link is the practice of meditation.[1] This was so important to the Puritans, for example, that many of them wrote detailed accounts of what it is and how to do it.[2] (We will refer to some of these guidebooks during the course of this chapter.) The Puritans saw meditation as an indispensable element of true devotion:

It is not more impossible to live without an heart than to be devout without meditation.[3]

They usually thrive best who meditate most. Meditation is a soul-fattening duty; it is a grace-strengthening duty; it is a duty-crowning

---

[1] Consider J.C. Ryle, for example. When he speaks of the 'private means of grace' he means 'private prayer, private reading of the Scriptures, and private meditation and self-examination' (*Holiness*, p 92).

[2] Probably the most famous of these is Richard Baxter's *The Saints' Everlasting Rest* (1656). On this whole subject, see Joel R. Beeke, "The Puritan Practice of Meditation" in Joseph A. Pipa, Jr & J. Andrew Wortman (eds.), *Reformed Spirituality: Communing with Our Glorious God* (Taylors, SC: Southern Presbyterian, 2003), pp 73-100, and in the same work, "Appendix I: Bibliography on the Puritan Practice of Meditation", pp 175-179. This material is now available in Joel R. Beeke, *Puritan Reformed Spirituality* (Grand Rapids: Reformation Heritage, 2004), pp 73-100, 449-451.

[3] Joseph Hall [1574-1656], *The Art of Divine Meditation* (1606), in Frank L. Huntley, *Bishop Joseph Hall and Protestant Meditation in Seventeenth-Century England: A Study, with the Texts of The Art of Divine Meditation (1606) and Occasional Meditations (1633)* (Binghamton: Center for Medieval and Early Renaissance Studies, 1981), p 108.

duty... You may read much and hear much, yet without meditation you will never be excellent ... Christians.[4]

What makes meditation so important is the simple fact that it means paying proper attention to God:

Solemnly set yourselves at chosen times to think on God. Meditation is of itself a distinct duty, and must have a considerable time allowed it among the other exercises of the Christian life... Is it reasonable that he who is our life and our all, should never be thought on, but now and then, as it were by chance, and on the by?[5]

So it is important in its own right – but it is important also because of the way it adds value to other essential elements of true devotion. Thus, despite the very high value they put on preaching, one Puritan treatise on meditation maintains,

It is better to hear one Sermon only and meditate on that, then [sic] to hear two Sermons and meditate on neither.[6]

Similar views are expressed about the relative importance of Bible reading and meditation:

One chapter ... read with understanding, and meditated with application, will better feed and comfort thy soul than five read or run over without marking their scope or sense, or making any use thereof ...[7]

---

[4]   Thomas Brooks, *Works*, 1: p 291. Cf. Edmund Calamy, *The Art of Divine Meditation, or, A Discourse of the Nature, Necessity, and Excellency thereof with Motives to and Rules for the Better Performance of that Most Important Christian Duty: In Several Sermons on Genesis 24:63* (London: Thomas Parkhurst, 1680), p 82: 'meditation is the life and soul of Christianity; it is that which makes you improve all the truths of the Christian religion, (you are but the skeletons of Christians without meditation) it is as necessary as your daily bread'.

[5]   John Howe [1630-1705], *The Works of the Rev. John Howe* (London: William Ball, 1838), p 404.

[6]   Thomas White [1628-1698], *A Method and Instructions for the Art of Divine Meditation with Instances of the Several Kinds of Solemn Meditation* (London: Thomas Parkhurst, 1672), p 17. Cf. Thomas Watson [c.1620-1686], *Select Works* (Ligonier, PA: Soli Deo Gloria, 1990 [1657]), p 255: 'better meditate on one sermon than hear five'; Calamy, *Art*, p 31: 'one sermon well digested, well meditated upon, is better than *twenty* sermons without meditation' [his italics].

[7]   Lewis Bayly [1565-1631], *The Practice of Piety, Directing a Christian how to walk that he may please God*, 71st edition (Perth: R. Morison, 1792 [1611]), p 95.

Clearly, these are people who regarded meditation as having great worth. We need to discover why that is.

11.1.   Meditation

So what is meditation? What does the Bible teach us about this? And what can we learn from Evangelicals of the past – how did they understand and practise meditation?[8] The place to begin is to note the distinction that was made between this kind of meditation and the contemplation that played a role in Catholic piety. So Luther urged his hearers:

> set up a definition of the contemplative life different from the one they taught in the monasteries, namely, that it is the true contemplative life to hear and believe the spoken Word and to want to know nothing 'except Christ and Him crucified' (1 Corinthians 2:2). He alone, with his Word, is the profitable and salutary object of contemplation...[9]

It was to be the Bible and not Catholic tradition that determined the subject and style of the believer's meditation. What we need to discuss now is what that meant in practice. But first we need to make another distinction.

11.1.1.   Biblical meditation

It is important to recognize that a biblical understanding of meditation has very little in common with a widespread modern view. Influenced by eastern mysticism, this regards meditation as the process of emptying the mind. In the Bible, however, it is a way of focusing the mind. We see this in the way 'meditate' is used in parallel with such words as 'consider' and 'remember'.[10] One of the Hebrew words for meditation is also translated as 'consider' and 'muse'; the other is also

---

[8]   In addition to the study by Beeke, the following treatments of this theme are worth consulting: Edmund P. Clowney, *CM*: *Christian Meditation* (Nutley NJ: Craig, 1979); Edmond Smith, *A Tree by a Stream: Unlock the Secrets of Active Meditation* (Fearn: Christian Focus, 1995); Peter Toon, *From Mind to Heart: Christian Meditation Today* (Grand Rapids: Baker, 1987).

[9]   Luther, *Works*, 3: p 275f.

[10]   Psalms 77:11-12; 119:15; 143:5.

translated as 'ponder' and 'think'.[11] So meditation is a way of using the mind: 'a serious and solemn thinking upon God'.[12] J.I. Packer thus defines it this way:

> Meditation is the activity of calling to mind, and thinking over, and dwelling on, and applying to oneself, the various things one knows about the works and ways and purposes and promises of God. It is an activity of holy thought, consciously performed in the presence of God, under the eye of God, by the help of God, as a means of communion with God. Its purpose is to clear one's mental and spiritual vision of God, and to let His truth make its full and proper impact on one's mind and heart.[13]

If meditation is an 'activity of holy thought', what kind of thinking does it involve? How do I use my mind when I am meditating? The simplest answer is that meditation is 'a dwelling, a musing, an abiding upon the things we know of God'.[14] It means focusing on the truth, staying with it until it registers as it should. This includes enabling us to see clearly:

> serious meditation represents every thing in its native colour; it shews an evil in sin, and a lustre in grace. By holy thoughts the head grows clearer ...[15]

11.1.2. Preaching to myself

But perhaps the most helpful answer is another given by the Puritans: meditation takes the form of preaching to myself.

> Puritan meditation on Scripture was modelled on the Puritan sermon; in meditation the Puritan would seek to search and challenge his heart, stir his affections to hate sin and love righteousness, and encourage himself with God's promises, just as Puritan preachers would do from the pulpit.[16]

---

[11]   See Judges 5:10; Psalms 63:6; 77:3, 6, 12; 143:5; Isaiah 33:18.

[12]   Watson, *Works*, p 200. Cf. 'Meditation is that duty or exercise of religion whereby the mind is applied to the serious and solemn contemplation of spiritual things ... it is the flower and height of consecrated reason' (Thomas Manton, *Works*, 17: p 270).

[13]   J.I. Packer, *Knowing God* (London: Hodder, 1973), p 20.

[14]   Calamy, *Art*, p 148; cf. pp 23, 61, 99.

[15]   Watson, *Works*, p 576.

[16]   J.I. Packer, *A Quest for Godliness: The Puritan Vision of the Christian Life* (Wheaton: Crossway, 1990), p 24.

It is not difficult to see how the Puritans got this from the Bible. The Old Testament uses the word for 'muttering' to refer to meditation – a muttering that takes two forms. One is seen in Joshua 1:8, which connects repeating the words of Scripture with reflecting on them: 'Keep this Book of the Law always on your lips; meditate on it day and night ...' As we meditate on God's words, we mutter them to ourselves. We are saying them to savour them, and repeating them so we remember them. The other kind of muttering is the conversation I have with myself while I am meditating. We see examples of this self-talk, this preaching to myself, in the Psalms. Psalm 42 is an obvious one, with its repeated refrain,

> Why, my soul, are you downcast? Why so disturbed within me? Put your hope in God, for I will yet praise him ...

This is how the writers of the Psalms preach to the congregation that consists of their soul – reminding, exhorting, encouraging.[7] Perhaps the clearest statement of this understanding of meditation (which he also calls 'contemplation') is found in Richard Baxter:

> contemplation is like preaching, where the mere explaining of truths and duties is seldom attended with such success as the lively application of them to the conscience ... By soliloquy, or a pleading the case with thyself, thou must in thy meditation quicken thy own heart. Enter into a serious debate with it. Plead with it in the most moving and affecting language, and urge it with the most powerful and weighty arguments. It is what holy men of God have practised in all ages... This soliloquy ... is a preaching to one's self ... Therefore the very same method which a minister should use in his preaching to others, every Christian should endeavour after in speaking to himself.[18]

Another way of making this point is to insist that

> *meditation must be particular and applicative*; for *generals* will not work at all ... if ever you would get good by the practice of *meditation*, you must come down to *particulars* ... Therefore the greatest part of meditation is *application* ...[19]

---

[7] Psalms 57:8-10; 62:5-7; 103:1-5; 104:1, 35; 116:7-9; 146:1-2.

[18] *Everlasting Rest*, p 271. Cf. Manton, *Works*, 17: pp 268, 305, 310-314.

[19] Calamy, *Art*, p 108 [his italics].

Meditation thus involves me in appropriating God's truth in specific and personal ways:

> Let thy resolutions be not only against thy sin, but against the means, occasions, and temptations to it ...[20]

For the Puritans, this self-directed preaching also means quizzing myself:

> To meditation join examination. When you have been meditating on any spiritual subject, put a query to thy soul ...[21]

This self-examination can be very beneficial – or it can be a recipe for unhealthy navel-gazing and self-absorption. There is a way of ensuring that it remains healthy and enables me to keep growing. This means asking myself about the extent to which I have grasped and responded to the message of the Bible passage I am considering. In other words, rather than attempting a general kind of self-analysis, I examine myself in relation to something specific that the Bible is saying. This helps to focus both my repentance for my sins and my resolutions about being more faithful – and my prayers that God will forgive me and make me true.

11.2.   The focus of meditation

Now that we have a good idea of what meditation is, we need to consider its focus and its aims. So what is the focus of meditation – what do we meditate about?

11.2.1.   The words of God

The Bible points us in three directions here. The most frequent subject of meditation is the words of God. This applies especially to his 'instruction'. (This is the best translation of the Hebrew word that our Bibles generally translate as 'law'. This conventional translation is a bit misleading, for it makes us focus solely on God's commandments – but his 'instruction', given to the people of Israel at Mount Sinai, also involves promises, encouragements and warnings, motivations and examples, and so on.) So Joshua was told:

---

[20]   White, *Method*, p 55.
[21]   Watson, *Works*, p 268.

Keep this Book of the Law always on your lips; meditate on it day and night, so that you may be careful to do everything written in it.[22]

The 'Book of the Law' contains all that Moses had told the people[23] – all the words God gave him at Mount Sinai, which he expounded again forty years later on the eastern side of the Jordan River.[24] It thus contains all that God had taught his people – all of his instruction. Meditating on God's instruction is not something that only Joshua should do: we learn from the Psalms that such meditation is the path of blessing for all of God's people:

Blessed is the one ... whose delight is in the law of the LORD, and who meditates on his law day and night.[25]

In Psalm 119 we have the words of a devout Israelite who does just this:

Oh, how I love your law! I meditate on it all day long.[26]

He tells us that he meditates on God's decrees (vv.23, 48), precepts (vv.15, 78), and statutes (vv.95, 99), as well as on his promises (v.148). In all of this he is a model for God's people, who are meant to consider, to reflect on, God's words.[27] But what would this be like in practice? How, for example, would I meditate on God's promises? In addition to meditating upon specific promises, I can also consider

the *freeness* of the promises, the *fullness* of the promises, the *infallibleness* of the promises; there is no condition a child of God can be in, but there is some promise or other to comfort him; the *universality* of the tender of the promises, thy *interest* in the promises, whether the promises of the gospel belong to thee or no ...[28]

11.2.2. The works of God

A second focus of meditation in the Bible is the works of God:

I will remember the deeds of the LORD ... I will consider all your

---

[22] Joshua 1:8.
[23] Joshua 1:7.
[24] See Exodus 24:3-4; 25:1–31:18; Leviticus 1:1–7:38; 11:1–23:44; 25:1–27:34; Deuteronomy 1:1–32:47.
[25] Psalm 1:1-2.
[26] Psalm 119:97.
[27] Note Jeremiah 2:31; Mark 4:24; Luke 2:17-19.
[28] Calamy, *Art*, p 139 (his italics).

works and meditate on all your mighty deeds.[29]

These works, these mighty deeds, are what God does as Saviour of his people:

> You are the God who performs miracles; you display your power among the peoples. With your mighty arm you redeemed your people ...[30]

We will give an example of how we do this later in this chapter, when we meditate our way through Psalm 77. But we are also to meditate on the mighty deeds God does as Creator and Ruler of the cosmos.

> How many are your works, LORD! In wisdom you made them all; the earth is full of your creatures... May the glory of the LORD endure forever; may the LORD rejoice in his works ... May my meditation be pleasing to him, as I rejoice in the LORD.[31]

Amongst other things, this helps to restore our perspective – it reminds us not only that God is great but also that we are not: 'When I consider your heavens ... what is mankind ...?'[32] So we meditate on God's word and on God's work – and thus also on God's world.

11.2.3. The worth of God

Meditating on God's words and works brings us to reflect on his worth, his excellencies as Creator, Ruler, and Redeemer. The Psalms provide us with several examples. In Psalm 145, there is a direct connection between focusing on God's mighty acts, his works, and recognizing his majesty, his worth (vv.4-5). In Psalm 48, what God has said and done concerning Jerusalem leads the sons of Korah to ponder his love: 'Within your temple, O God, we meditate on your unfailing love' (v.9). We see something similar in Psalm 19, which David refers to as the meditation of his heart (v.14). This begins by celebrating the glory of God as seen in the creation, the work of his hands (vv.1-6). It then considers some of the ways the words of God reflect his glory (vv.7-11). But where we see the glory of God most fully is in the person and work of the Lord Jesus. So our meditation is to focus especially upon him. We

---

[29]   Psalm 77:11-12. See also 1 Samuel 12:24; Psalms 107:43; 111:2-4, 9; 119:27; 143:5; 145:5; Isaiah 41:18-20.
[30]   Psalm 77:14-15.
[31]   Psalm 104:24, 31, 34.
[32]   Psalm 8:3-4.

are to consider him as the great Apostle and High Priest; we are to fix our eyes on him as the pioneer and perfecter of faith; we are to consider him who endured such opposition from sinners.[33] And we are to weigh all things in the light of the surpassing worth of knowing Christ Jesus as our Lord.[34]

11.2.4. *God in all things*

If we are to meditate on the words and works and worth of God, this means that the Bible will be our focus and guide. This is because the Bible gives us God's words. We look to the Bible also to learn what God has done to save his people. It also tells us of God's worth – the Bible teaches us what God is like and how we should respond to him and to all that he has said and done. And it is from the Bible that we learn how to see and to read what God is doing now. This concerns what he does in both creation and providence – what he does as Maker and Sustainer of the cosmos, and what he does as Ruler and Judge of human life. The Puritans linked both of these dimensions of God's work to their practice of meditation, rightly recognizing that there are countless elements of the natural world and of daily experience that can provide the occasion for fruitful meditation.[35] Their approach is summed up in this rule: 'A christian should labour to see all things in God, and God in all things'.[36] So meditation can focus anywhere, even on the insect – 'Go to the ant, you sluggard; consider its ways and be wise!'[37] – or the ravens and the wild flowers.[38] Yet the Puritans also recognized that we will be unable to do this unless we read these works of God in the light of his word.

If you would meditate on God in reference to his works, be sure of

---

[33]   Hebrews 3:1; 12:2-3.

[34]   Philippians 3:7-8.

[35]   Notable examples are, "Husbandry Spiritualized: The Heavenly Use of Earthly Things", and, "Navigation Spiritualized: A New Compass for Seamen", in John Flavel, *Works*, 5: pp 3-205; 5: pp 206-293. See also Baxter, *Everlasting Rest*, pp 307-308; William Bridge [1600-1670], *The Works of the Rev. William Bridge*, five volumes (Beaver Falls: Soli Deo Gloria, 1989), 3: pp 128-129; Calamy, *Art*, pp 7-9, 14-17; Calvin, *Institutes*, I.v.1-3; I.xiv.20-22; I.xvii.6-11 (1: pp 51-55, 179-182, 218-225); Manton, *Works*, 17: pp 339-348; Nathanael Ranew [1602-1678], *Solitude Improved by Divine Meditation* (Morgan, PA: Soli Deo Gloria, 1995 [1670]), pp 124-126, 173-176; George Swinnock, *Works*, 2: pp 416-424, 462-470; Watson, *Works*, pp 234-238.

[36]   William Bates [1625-1699], in W. Farmer (ed), *The Whole Works of the Rev. W. Bates*, four volumes (Harrisonburg: Sprinkle, 1990), 3: p 117. Cf. Manton, *Works*, 6: p 139.

[37]   Proverbs 6:6.

[38]   Luke 12:24, 27.

this, that you never go to read God's work but by God's candle. The work of God is a great book, but the work of God cannot be read but by God's word; God hath a candle of his own to read his work by.[39]

The Bible not only tells us where and how God is at work; it also interprets his work, so that we know the meaning of what he does.

There is another sense in which the Bible is our guide. It not only supplies the material for our meditation, but also sets its limits:

The secret things belong to the LORD our God, but the things revealed belong to us ...[40]

So Thomas Manton urges,

Do not pry further than God hath revealed; your thoughts must still be bounded by the word.[41]

Meditation is not speculation – what the Bible does not disclose, we do not pry into; we reflect only on what is revealed. This is the path of humility:

My heart is not proud, LORD, my eyes are not haughty; I do not concern myself with great matters or things too wonderful for me.[42]

It is also the path of safety, for it is all too easy for sinners to become 'puffed up with idle notions by their unspiritual mind'.[43]

In seeking to know the secrets and mysteries of God and godliness, you must not pry into them further than God hath revealed; for if you wade therein further than you have sure footing in his holy word, you will presently lose yourself, and be swallowed up in a maze and whirlpool of errors and heresies.[44]

No matter what my theme or focus, therefore, the surest path to follow is to meditate on the Bible and according to the Bible. I need to use the

---

[39] Bridge, *Works*, 3: p 142.
[40] Deuteronomy 29:29.
[41] Manton, *Works*, 17: p 278. Cf. Bridge, *Works*, 3: p 154: 'Be sure of this, that nothing fall within the compass of your meditation, but what falls within the compass of the Scripture'; Swinnock, *Works*, 2: p 435: 'Where Scripture hath not a tongue to speak, I must not have an ear to hear'.
[42] Psalm 131:1.
[43] Colossians 2:18.
[44] Henry Scudder [c.1590-c.1659], *The Christian's Daily Walk, in Holy Security and Peace* (Harrisonburg: Sprinkle, 1984 [1635]), p 105.

Bible as both the meat which nourishes me and the map which guides me.

11.3.   The aim of meditation

Why do I do this? Why do I reflect on the words of God – and thus on his works and his worth? What is the aim of meditation? We find the first part of our answer in what Paul urged Timothy to do: 'Reflect on what I am saying, for the Lord will give you insight ...'[45] This makes it clear that two things happen simultaneously: Timothy meditates on what Paul has said, and God illuminates Timothy as to Paul's meaning. These go together: meditation is not an alternative to God's work of illumination – the vital word in this verse is 'for', not 'or'! Timothy does not work it out by himself – and God does not give him understanding without his efforts. So these are two sides of the same coin: the means God will use to give me insight into the meaning of the text is my meditation – and the goal of my meditation is the insight that God gives. And such insight is the first step in the process by which God's word grips and shapes and changes me, taking root in me and bearing the fruit of deeper love for God, loyalty to God, and likeness to God.

11.3.1.   Grasping the meaning

The Puritans were careful to distinguish meditating upon a subject from studying it.[46] This is right enough – but what we have just seen tells us that while the two can be distinguished, they cannot be divorced. Consider what I do when I read a passage of Scripture. My initial aim is to grasp the point the passage is making. So I do not begin with meditation; I begin with exegesis. As I read the passage, I analyse the words so that I understand what it is saying. But then I seek to grasp what the passage is doing with what it is saying – why does it say what it says? As I pursue this question, exegesis leads to meditation and meditation flows out of exegesis. This is the kind of meditating that Timothy was to do, as he sought to draw Paul's meaning out of Paul's words. Meditation begins by reflecting on what the passage is saying.

---

[45]   2 Timothy 2:7
[46]   See, for example, Manton, *Works*, 6: p 140; 17: pp 268-269; Ranew, *Solitude*, pp 23-24; Watson, *Works*, p 203; White, *Method*, pp 14-16.

Converse with the word of God. Read his descriptions of himself; and do not content yourselves to have the words and expressions before your eyes, or in your mouths, that represent to you his nature and attributes; but make your pauses, and consider the things themselves signified by them ...[47]

Our aim is to get from the words to the meanings – not to go behind or beyond the words, but to go more deeply into them. We want to make sure that we see what the text is saying about its subject.

What then? What is meditation seeking to do? Once I have grasped the point of the passage, my meditation aims at ensuring that this sinks in, that I absorb what the passage teaches. Why is this important? Because it is only if the truth penetrates that it will go to work in me. It is meant to grow me in godliness:

Meditation waters and cherishes the plants of heavenly graces. It helps them to root deeper, shoot higher, and grow stronger. Such Christians as meditate most will grow most, be growing to the end.[48]

11.3.2. Nourished by God's word

One of the most common ways of thinking about this is to compare meditating to digesting food. This metaphor has been used independently by many writers over the centuries. We can see the point in these examples from, respectively, the twelfth, seventeenth (twice) and eighteenth centuries:[49]

O Christian soul ... arouse your mind, remember your resurrection, contemplate your redemption and liberation. Consider anew where and what the strength of your salvation is, spend time in meditating upon this strength, delight in reflecting upon it. Shake off your disinclination, constrain yourself, strive with your mind towards this end. Taste the goodness of your Redeemer, be aflame with love for your Saviour, chew his words as a honeycomb, suck out their

---

[47] John Howe, *Works*, p 403.
[48] Ranew, *Solitude*, p ix ff.
[49] In addition to the examples cited, this metaphor is also to be found in such places as Richard Baxter, *The Saints' Everlasting Rest* (Marshallton: NFCE, n.d. [1656]), pp 241, 242; Calamy, *Art*, pp 24, 31, 59, 75, 84, 105, 116; Manton, *Works*, 17: pp 273, 287, 302; Ranew, *Solitude*, pp ix, 110, 254; Scudder, *Daily Walk*, p 108; Swinnock, *Works*, 2: pp 425, 427; Watson, *Works*, pp 198, 202, 239.

flavour, which is sweeter than honey, swallow their health-giving sweetness. Chew by thinking, suck by understanding, swallow by loving and rejoicing. Rejoice in chewing, be glad in sucking, delight in swallowing.[50]

[H]earing the word is like ingestion, and when we meditate upon the word that is digestion; and this digestion of the word by meditation produceth warm affections, zealous resolutions, and holy actions...[51]

Our diligent and frequent reading [sc., of the Bible] ... must be attended with our holy meditations. We feed on what we read, but we digest only what we meditate of. What is in our Bible is God's, but that which is in our hearts is our own.[52]

[Y]ou hear the Word of God. This is good. But it is not enough that your ears hear it. Do you let it penetrate inwardly into your heart and allow the heavenly food to be digested there, so that you get the benefit of its vitality and power ...?[53]

Thinking of meditation this way emphasizes that God's word nourishes us, growing us in godliness. The truth needs to sink into me so that it does what it is meant to do.

The promises of the gospel do not convey comfort to us, as they are recorded in the word merely but as they are applied by meditation ... one promise that is ruminated upon, and digested by meditation, conveys more comfort than a bundle of promises in the head, that are not meditated upon, which we did not consider.[54]

11.3.3. Retaining God's truth

So, through meditation God's truth sinks in – and I meditate also so that it stays in. As we have seen, this is one reason why we 'mutter' God's words – we repeat them so that we remember them.

Without meditation the truths of God will not stay with us; the heart

---

[50]   Anselm of Canterbury [1033-1109], quoted in Toon, *Meditating*, p 3.

[51]   Bates, *Works*, 3: p 131.

[52]   Joseph Hall, *The Devout Soul, or Rules of Heavenly Devotion* (1643), in *Works* (Oxford: OUP, 1863), 6: p 527.

[53]   Philip Jakob Spener [1635-1705], *Pia Desideria*, translated, edited, and with an Introduction by T.G. Tappert (Philadelphia: Fortress, 1964 [1675]), p 66.

[54]   Bates, *Works*, 3: p 134.

is hard, and the memory slippery, and without meditation all is lost...'[55]

The obvious reason we do not want to lose what we learn from Scripture is that it is meant to go to work in us: 'humbly accept the word planted in you, which can save you'.[56] It is through meditation that the contents of the Bible penetrate deeply into my heart and take possession of me, shaping and directing my life. The 'main end of meditation ... [is] the affecting of our heart, and reforming of our lives ...'[57] So the aim of this self-talk, this preaching to myself, is to ensure that the truth of the text goes in deep enough to lodge in my memory, so that it is not quickly forgotten; deep enough to grip me, stirring my emotions in an appropriate way, so that my response to God is heartfelt; and deep enough to challenge me to become a doer of the Word in quite specific ways.

11.4.   A right response

This brings us to another fundamental reason why God's word needs to sink in and stay in. It is only when this happens that I respond to his word as I should. Meditation aims at right response to God's word of truth. There are four things we need to say about the character of this response.

11.4.1.   The response of faith

The first is that right response is the response of faith. Meditation is of vital importance here, for it is a faith-growing and faith-strengthening practice.

> Meditate upon the truth of God, if you would be supported in believing... Say then to your souls, Surely it cannot be but God must be true; that which God hath promised must come to pass... If this be the great attribute that will support our faith, the power of God, then it presseth you to meditate often upon the power of God. The life of faith and confidence lies in it.[58]

---

[55]   Watson, *Works*, p 238. Cf. Bridge, *Works*, 3: p 131: '*Meditatio firmat memoriam.* Meditation strengthens memory ...'; Ranew, *Solitude*, p 68: 'Such as meditate most, will have the surest memory for things heavenly'.

[56]   James 1:21.

[57]   White, *Method*, p 45; cf. pp 13, 83.

[58]   Manton, *Works*, 14: pp 370, 371, 374.

Faith gains life and strength through meditation on God's promises: 'God's promises are the best nourishment for faith'.[59]

> The promises must be pondered, prayed often over, as those which are for the wounded, weary, and heavy laden, to produce faith; not only to feed it, but ... to begin, and to build it up. Never leave pondering the promises, God's love, and Christ's fullness offered in them, until pondering comes to hope, hope to thirsting, thirsting to highest prizing, prizing to selling all, and buying the pearl, till thou comest to renouncing thy own righteousness, thou cast thyself upon God in Christ, by the promise first rested on ...[60]

Likewise, faith is nourished by meditating on God's works. We see an example in Psalm 143, where David is struggling, crushed by fierce opposition (vv.3-4). So he turns his mind to God's great deeds: 'I meditate on all your works and consider what your hands have done' (v.5). This leads him to turn to God in prayer (vv.6-7), as one who trusts him wholeheartedly (vv.8-9). Thirdly, faith gains life and strength through meditation upon God's character as infinitely great and gracious:

> Meditation upon the grace of God, and upon his power, is the most eminent supporter of our faith in all our temptations.[61]

When I focus on the words and works and worth of God, taking time to grasp and absorb them, then my faith grows – but it will struggle to grow unless it is fed like this.

11.4.2. A heartfelt response

A second characteristic of right response is that it is a heartfelt response. This follows from our understanding of what faith is:

> faith is not simple assent of the mind to what we are taught, but also we must bring the heart and the affections. For not only by mouth or by imagination must we accept what is said to us, but it must be impressed upon the heart ... Faith, then, is from the heart where it has its root and is not knowledge pure and simple. For if we were

---

[59]   Willem Teellinck [1579-1629], *The Path of True Godliness* (Classics of Reformed Spirituality; Grand Rapids: Baker Academic, 2003), p 119. Cf. Manton, *Works*, 6: p 141: 'Faith is lean unless it be fed with meditation on the promises'.

[60]   Ranew, *Solitude*, p 274.

[61]   Bates, *Works*, 3: p 132.

only convinced that the Gospel is a reasonable doctrine and meanwhile we did not at all relish it ... would that be obedience?[62]

The Puritans were thus clear that one of the primary objects of meditation is to get the truth 'from thy head to thy heart'.[63] It concerns 'the raising of the heart to holy affections'.[64] What does this mean? How are these 'holy affections' expressed? What is a 'heartfelt' response? The two most important qualities of this response are depth and warmth. A heartfelt response is one that is not shallow and superficial, but deep and genuine. It represents the real me, engaging and expressing my most deep-seated convictions and commitments. This is the only legitimate response to God's word of truth, which is to be believed with the heart and obeyed from the heart.[65] This reflects the fact that the gospel is not

> apprehended by the understanding and memory alone, as other disciplines are, but it is received only when it possesses the whole soul, and finds a seat and resting place in the inmost affection of the heart.[66]

Secondly, a heartfelt response is warm. For the Puritans, this is one of the principal effects of meditation, which is 'a heart warming work'.[67]

> Meditation is a great heart warmer; it renews and increases spiritual heats, drives away dullness and dead-heartedness, brings a new life, strength, and vigour into the spirit, when it faints and flags.[68]

In this connection, a common Puritan metaphor likens meditation to kindling or maintaining a fire. So meditation is 'the bellows of the affections'; it 'inflames the affections'; it 'keeps alive the fire on the

---

[62] Calvin, *The Deity of Christ*, p 292f.

[63] John Downame [1571-1652], quoted in Charles E. Hambrick-Stowe, *The Practice of Piety: Puritan Devotional Disciplines in Seventeenth-Century New England* (Chapel Hill: University of North Carolina, 1982), p 163. Cf. Watson, *Works*, p 255: 'reading may bring a truth into the head, meditation brings it into the heart'.

[64] Watson, *Works*, pp 200f. Cf. White, *Method*, pp 13, 45, 83.

[65] See, for example, Romans 6:17; 10:9-10.

[66] Calvin, *Institutes*, III.vi.4 (1: p 688). Cf. Swinnock, *Works*, 2: p 426: 'Whilst they [sc., our meditations] swim in the mind, as light things floating on the waters, they are unprofitable; but when they sink down into the affections, as heavy and weighty things, making suitable and real impressions there, then they attain their end'.

[67] Bridge, *Works*, 3: p 131. Cf. Ranew, *Solitude*, p 2; Swinnock, *Works*, 2: p 425.

[68] Ranew, *Solitude*, p 73.

altar, and helps to make it burn'.[69] Richard Sibbes makes the point this way:

> A man is the most miserable creature under heaven if he have not interest in Christ; he is a lost creature. Let us dwell upon the meditation and consideration of this till we feel our hearts warmed. If one pass through the sunshine, it doth not much heat; but if the sun beat upon a thing, there will be a reflection of heat. So let us stay upon this consideration of the infinite love and mercy of Christ to us wretches, and this warming the heart, it will transform us to the likeness of Christ ...[70]

Calvin also speaks of meditation in these terms:

> believers know by use and experience that ardor burns low unless they supply new fuel. Accordingly, among our prayers, meditation both on God's nature and on his Word is by no means superfluous.[71]

Meditation thus helps us to heed the exhortation: 'Never be lacking in zeal, but keep your spiritual fervour ...'[72] It is by warming my heart that it leads me into fervent prayer to God and zealous activity for God.

Another way of thinking about this is that meditation enables me to savour the truth as I should.

> Every divine truth hath a sweetness and a savour in it, and our souls are to relish it. If there be not relish in the palate, the relish in meat is to no purpose... If we have not a relish of divine truths, undoubtedly we know them not as we should.[73]

By meditating on the truths of Scripture, I get to 'taste' them. I do not simply swallow them, but chew on them until their flavour registers on my spiritual palate. In other words, meditation prevents the truth from being no more than ideas I quickly process and lodge in my mind. As I reflect on it, the truth makes it mark on me so that I take hold of it and respond to it in the appropriate way. It is only when grace becomes amazing yet again,

---

[69] Watson, *Works*, p 256; Bates, *Works*, 3: p 130; Ranew, *Solitude*, p 72. Cf. Calamy, *Art*, pp 26, 28, 105, 107, 144; Charnock, *Works*, 5: p.380; Manton, *Works*, 6: p 140; White, *Method*, pp 25, 29, 31, 44, 51.

[70] Sibbes, *Works*, 4: p 520.

[71] *Institutes*, III.xx.13 (2: p 867).

[72] Romans 12:11.

[73] Sibbes, *Works*, 4: pp 344-345.

when its sound is sweet, that it has registered in me as it ought to – and that I will then serve and pray as a grace-saved wretch should.

11.4.3. An obedient response

The third thing we need to say about right response is that it is an obedient response. So while my meditation aims to warm my heart, this is not for the purpose of private ecstasy, but for public obedience.

> The Christian must not only pray his good thoughts, but practise them; he must not lock them up in his mind, but lay them out in his life.[74]

This is what God tells Joshua about the meditation he must do:

> Keep this Book of the Law always on your lips; meditate on it day and night, so that you may be careful to do everything written in it.[75]

Meditation aims at obedience – it is 'the womb of my actions'.[76] I meditate on God's word so that I will put it into practice. This also applies to that form of meditation in which I am quizzing myself; 'I have considered my ways and have turned my steps to your statutes'.[77] We learn from James 1:22-25 that we must not merely read or hear the word, but must do what it says. So whether it issues in godly living is the crucial test meditation must meet. This faces the person who meditates with an important question:

> Has it transported him for a moment into a spiritual ecstasy that vanishes when everyday life returns, or has it lodged the Word of God so securely and deeply in his heart that it holds and fortifies him, impelling him to active love, to obedience, to good works?[78]

By meditating on God's truth, I come to see how it bears upon my life day by day – but I am unlikely to grasp its implications unless I take the time I need. And if I do not see how it applies to my life, I will not be taking hold of it and obeying it as I should.

11.4.4. A prayerful response

Fourthly, right response is a prayerful response. Meditation is intended to lead me into prayer – as one Puritan commented, it is 'the mother of

---

[74]   Swinnock, *Works*, 2: p 427f.
[75]   Joshua 1:8.
[76]   Swinnock, *Works*, 2: p 471.
[77]   Psalm 119:59.
[78]   Dietrich Bonhoeffer, *Life Together* (London: SCM, 1954), p 67.

prayer'.[79] As we have just seen, David gives us an example. He meditates upon God's works[80] and turns to him in prayer.[81] The two fit naturally together:

> Meditation is the best beginning of prayer, and prayer is the best conclusion of meditation.[82]

We see them linked again in Psalm 104, where the writer's meditation about God and his world (vv.2-23) leads him to speak to God in prayer (vv.24-30). The same is true in Psalm 19 – meditation upon God's world (vv.1-6) and God's words (vv.7-10) issues in prayer (vv.11-14). So just as Bible study rightly done shades into meditation, meditation leads almost imperceptibly into prayer. Consider this testimony from George Müller:

> my practice had been ... to give myself to prayer, after having dressed in the morning. Now I saw, that the most important thing I had to do was to give myself to the reading of the Word of God and to meditation on it, that thus my heart might be comforted, encouraged, warned, reproved, instructed; and that thus, whilst meditating, my heart might be brought into an experimental communion with the Lord ... The result I have found to be almost invariably ... that though I did not, as it were, give myself to prayer, but to meditation yet it turned almost immediately more or less into prayer.[83]

So meditation builds a bridge between my reading (or hearing) of the Bible and my praying.

> Meditation is a middle sort of duty between the word and prayer, and hath respect to both. The word feedeth meditation, and meditation feedeth prayer; we must hear that we be not erroneous, and meditate that we be not barren. These duties must always go hand in hand; meditation must follow hearing and precede prayer.[84]

> Meditation stands between the two ordinances of reading and praying, as the grand improver of the former, and the high

---

[79] Bridge, *Works*, 3: p 132. Cf. Bayly, *The Practice of Piety*, p 94: 'as faith is the soul, so reading and meditating of the word of God are the parents of prayer'.

[80] Psalm 143:5.

[81] Psalm 143:6-7.

[82] Swinnock, *Works*, 1: p 112. Cf. Calamy, *Art*, p 4.

[83] George Müller [1805-1898], quoted in Gillett, *Trust and Obey*, pp 136f (italics original).

[84] Manton, *Works*, 17: p 272. Cf. *Works*, 6: p 142: 'what we take in by the word we digest by meditation, and let out by prayer. These three duties help one another'.

quickener of the latter, to furnish the mind with choice materials for prayer, and to fill the heart with holy fervency in it.[85]

All three belong together, with each having its rightful impact upon the other two:

> In all your settled meditation, begin with reading or hearing. Go on with meditation; end in prayer... If you do read and not meditate, then you will want good affections. If you do meditate and not read or hear, you will want good judgment ... If you do read, or hear, or meditate, and not pray, you will want the blessing of the Lord upon both. Read or hear first; then meditate; and then pray upon both.[86]

11.5. *Meditation in practice*

Meditation is thus a response to reading the Bible – or to hearing it read or preached. It concentrates on a particular passage of Scripture, and processes it in a way that fuels my prayers. How does it do this? – how does meditation work? What do I actually do to meditate? Some answers to this question are very complex, and make meditation quite difficult. But I want to introduce you to a simple approach that is quite easy to learn. In a nutshell, it means questioning the text. This is not the questioning of the sceptic, who is determined not to believe. It is more like the questioning of the barrister, who is trying to get at the truth. I use questions to probe the text, to make sure it tells me what it wants to say. My questions slow me down, so that I have time to see what is there. They make me grapple with the text, until I see what it is doing with what it is saying. They enable me to appropriate the text and apply it to myself.

So let me show you how I meditate. I am not claiming that this is the only way to do it, or even necessarily the best way. But I do want you to see how simple and effective this approach is, so that you will be encouraged to 'have a go'. The passage I have chosen for this purpose is Psalm 77 – one of the psalms that speaks about meditating. I briefly set out the results of this meditation in Chapter 5; now I will show you how we got there. You will find it helpful to read the psalm at this point, before we engage with what it says. If you were reading the passage in order to meditate on it, this is where you would come to God, asking him to

---

[85]   Ranew, *Solitude*, p viii.
[86]   Bates, *Works*, 3: p 154.

enlighten your understandings, to quicken your devotion, to warm your affections, and so to bless that hour unto you, that by the meditation of holy things you may be made more holy ...[87]

11.5.1. *Interrogating the passage*

Now we are ready to begin our meditation – but where do we start? One obvious starting-place is to ask why Asaph wrote this psalm. The answer isn't obvious, is it? It isn't a psalm of praise, for it isn't directly extolling God's greatness or goodness. Nor is it a prayer, either thanking God or making requests of him. Instead, at least to begin with, it is all about Asaph himself. In the first six verses, 'I' is used twelve times, and 'my' is used five times. It is a kind of testimony, in which Asaph tells us about his experience in a particular situation. Yet he obviously thought that we could learn something from what happened – which is why this snapshot from his life has been preserved. So what did he experience – and how can we benefit from it?

Where does Asaph begin? He reports that he was in a bad way – he was in distress and unable to be comforted (v.2); he was groaning in his anguish (verse 3); he was too troubled to speak (v.4). And how did he respond to this pain? It brought him to God (v.1). Would it have affected me that way? I'm not sure that it would. When I am in pain, I have noticed that I am more likely to turn away from God than to turn to him. But Asaph didn't wait until he was calm and able to offer carefully-composed prayers; he cried out to God while his emotions were still raw. Could it be that this is an important part of what faith means – to come to God even though I'm in a mess, confident that I will still be welcome and heard? Does it mean that I can come as I am, not as I think I ought to be? Does trusting God mean that I am willing to be completely open and honest with him? It seems as though I've got something to learn here, for there are plenty of places in the Bible where other people do what Asaph has done. The most striking and memorable example is the Lord Jesus and his praying in the Garden of Gethsemane.[88] He prayed in terrible anguish and with complete honesty – and in doing so, gave us an example to follow.[89]

---

[87] Calamy, *Art*, p 172.

[88] Mark 14:32-42.

[89] Hebrews 5:7.

Why is Asaph in pain? And what happens when he brings his pain to God? I find the answer in verses 7-9, where Asaph turns his emotions into questions. Whatever is going wrong – and he never really tells us what that is – it is making him feel rejected and unloved. So what does he do? He puts his doubts and fears into words. Before God, he questions God. And his questions are not slight or incidental; they go to the heart of what God is like – is he really a God of unfailing love, of mercy and compassion? If I was in Asaph's shoes, would I have done what he does? Would I have questioned God like this? I'm not sure that I would have done so, because it feels improper to put God on the spot like this. Then why does Asaph feel free to do this? Again, could it be that this is how faith deals with doubt – not suppressing questions, but facing them with God? After all, the only alternative is to face them without him – and that is no way for a believer to operate. So here too I have something to learn from Asaph.

What happens now? How does Asaph find an answer to his questions? He sets himself to meditate on what God has done (vv.10-12). He puts his mind to work, remembering and considering God's mighty deeds. In this way, he turns from his questions to his convictions. And what happens when he does so? It has an immediate effect – now he is no longer asking questions about God, but speaking words of praise to God (vv.13-15). His focus shifts dramatically from 'I' (vv.1-6, 10-12) to 'he' (vv.7-9) to 'you' (vv.13-20). God is no longer a problem to be solved; instead, Asaph is celebrating his ways (vv.13-14).

Then what is all this about writhing waters and convulsing depths (v.16)? Why does Asaph start describing a thunderstorm (vv.17-18)? Why does he take us to the seaside (v.19)? Has he given us any clues as to what he means? I can see two. The first is in verses 13-15, where Asaph turns from the present to the past – from what God does to what God did: 'you redeemed your people' (v.15). He is no longer thinking of God's deeds in general (his 'ways', v.13), but of one particular sovereign and saving work. And this leads me to the second clue: Asaph names certain people. Those whom God redeemed were 'the descendants of Jacob and Joseph' (v.15) – that is, the people of Israel. And then at the end of the psalm, he refers to Moses and Aaron (v.20). These four names show us where we are in the story of God's saving work. We are back in Egypt, when God sent Moses and Aaron to the Pharaoh,[90] and

---

[90]   Exodus 6:28–7:6.

when he rescued the Israelites from their slavery.[91] Asaph takes us back to the great exodus, when God saved his people by leading them through the waters. That is what he is describing, in vivid poetry (vv.16-19) and in more direct statements (vv.15, 20).

This gives me two questions to answer: why does Asaph do this – and why doesn't he do anything else? What makes the exodus so important? And why does Asaph stop writing when we go back there? After all, he has asked some very pressing questions (vv.7-9) – so how can he bring his psalm to an end without answering them? Let us start with the first question: when Asaph is in pain – and pain that is severe enough to make him question God's love – why does he go back to Egypt and the exodus? We don't get a direct answer in the psalm, but we do get some clues. By the time we get to verse 15, it is clear that Asaph is not really thinking of God's works in a general way, but of the exodus in particular. And although all of God's works point in this direction, it is the exodus in particular that brings him to recognize and celebrate God's holiness, his greatness, and his miracle-working power (vv.13-14). And it is from this great work in particular that he finds reassurance about God's unfailing love and faithfulness to his promises (v.8). That is the most obvious answer to our second question. It is when he remembers the exodus that Asaph's doubts are resolved.

The psalm reveals that Asaph was in great pain and distress (vv.1-4) – and this gave him some troubling questions about what this might mean (vv.7-9). So why does he stop in mid-air, leaving his questions unanswered? Could it be that he has now received as much of an answer as he needs? So he ends the psalm where he does, not because he knows what the answer is, but because he now knows what it isn't! God has not rejected Asaph or withdrawn his favour; his unfailing love has not vanished, and his promise has not failed; he has not forgotten to be merciful or withheld his compassion. The God of the exodus is not a God whose people have an easy time in life – but he is a God who never fails them or abandons them. He is not a God whose people face no threats or suffer no pain – but he is a God who delivers them and delights in them. Going back to the exodus reminds Asaph that his confidence in God is well-founded. He is not believing fairy-stories or whistling in the dark when he trusts that God is both mighty and merciful, both great and good.

---

[91] Exodus 13:11–15:27.

11.5.2. *What Asaph teaches me*

Why do we have this testimony in our Bible? We have it because Asaph (and others after him) thought we could learn something important from it. And what is that – what does it teach me? It shows me how to deal well with times when I feel bad. When he was in great distress, Asaph did something crucial. He did not deny his feelings or try to suppress them, as though he should not have been feeling that way. Instead, he went to God with them. Then he took two very important steps. First, he focused his feelings – he turned his emotions into questions. That is, he put his fears and doubts into words. That was important, because it meant that he faced his torments – he recognized what he was dealing with. But to stop there would have meant staying trapped in his pain. So then came the really decisive step, when he focused his mind. He began to meditate, and this took him from his questions to his convictions. When he is in pain, and when his pain gives him doubts, he goes back to Egypt. Why does he do this? It is because that is the great landmark that enables him to find his way when he feels lost, the great lighthouse that lights up the darkness. This is the point at which the people of Israel saw most clearly and fully what God is like. This was the greatest foundation for their trust in him. That is why they go back again and again to the exodus.[92] It seems clear that Asaph had been doing so. Unless his meditations took him back there on good days, it is most unlikely that he would have been able to consider these mighty works of God when he was in great distress.

11.5.3. *Doing what Asaph did*

So how do I benefit from Asaph's testimony? What has he taught me to do? First of all, when I am hurting, I come to God and cry out for his help. I don't wait until I am in a fit state to present myself before him – as though that is ever the case! – but I come as I am. Even though I am in a mess, I will be welcome and my prayer will be heard. When mercy and help is what I need, the throne of grace is where I need to be.[93] And when I am hurting, like Asaph I can give voice to my doubts and fears. I don't need to suppress them, but I can face them with God.

---

[92] See, for example, Deuteronomy 7:7-9; Joshua 24:5-7, 16-17; 1 Kings 8:50-53; 1 Chronicles 17:20-22; Psalms 78:41-54; 105:1-7, 23-45; 106:7-12; 136:1-4, 10-16; Isaiah 43:1-7, 16-21.

[93] Hebrews 4:16.

But the most important way in which I can learn from Asaph is to keep returning to the great landmark, the great lighthouse – to that sovereign and saving work of God in which he shows most clearly and fully what he is like, and in which we have the strongest foundation for trusting him. I need to keep meditating on the mighty deed in which God redeemed his people. For Asaph, this was the exodus; for us, it is a much greater work than that – the death and resurrection of the Lord Jesus. This is where I see how deep and strong God's love is.[94] And this is where I see the greatest display of his sovereign power[95] – and of his wisdom, his wrath against sin, his faithfulness to his promises and his people, and so much else besides.

The way I am meant to deal with my hurts and my doubts is to be Christ-centred and Easter-focused, to take myself often to Jesus and his death and resurrection. Do I do this? As often as I should? Do I need to go there more regularly, so that I will be sure to do so when times are tough? Yes, I do. In fact, I think I need to begin each day there – so from now on, I am going to start each day by thanking God for loving and saving me in Jesus' death and resurrection.

That completes my meditation on Psalm 77. As we worked our way through it, I hope you noticed two things. The first is this: If that is what meditation is, then you have actually done some already! I would be very surprised if that were not so – even if you haven't meditated often or at length. But as you have been reading your Bible, or hearing people expound it, on at least some occasions you have found yourself thinking more deeply than usual about the ways it applies to you. I want to encourage you to be more focused and purposeful about this, so that you do it regularly and not just once in a while. This brings me to the second thing I hope you noticed – that my meditation did not involve anything very complicated, and nor did it require me to learn difficult new skills. In essence, the kind of meditating I want to encourage you to take up is very simple. (It can be made very complex, as some of the guides by Puritans and others reveal. But I think the simple approach I am recommending gives us everything we really need.)

---

94   Romans 5:8; Galatians 2:20; Ephesians 5:1-2; 1 John 4:9-10.
95   1 Corinthians 1:22-24; Ephesians 1:19-23.

11.6. Principles and techniques

There are really only three things I need to say about this approach. In the first place, it means slowing down sufficiently to notice what is there, to see what is going on in the Bible passage I am reading.

11.6.1. Slowing down

The way I slow myself down is to ask lots of questions. Never underestimate the importance of the humble question!

> I keep six honest serving-men; (They taught me all I knew)
> Their names are What and Where and When and How and Why
> and Who.[96]

If you do not find it easy to think of good questions, perhaps you could make a start by using these:

> What does the passage tell me about the person and purposes and promises of God?
> What does it tell me about God's great salvation?
> What does it tell me about loving and serving God?
> What does it tell me about loving and serving my neighbour?
> Does it give me any encouragements?
> Does it give me any warnings?

As you get used to quizzing the Bible like this, you will gradually get better at coming up with questions of your own.

Another helpful way of slowing myself down is to write down my questions and the answers I come up with. This is especially useful when I am just starting out as a meditator. Over time, as my mind gets used to functioning in the right way, writing will probably become less important – although it can be very useful to keep a record of what I am learning from the Bible.

11.6.2. Taking it personally

The second thing I need to say about the meditating we have just been doing is that it means personalizing what I learn. That is, I appropriate for myself and apply to myself what the Bible passage is saying and doing. As I take hold of the text like this, I find that I now have plenty of ways into prayer, as I thank God for his truth and ask him to let it have

---

[96] Rudyard Kipling, *Just So Stories* (London: Minster Classics, 1968), p 47.

its intended impact in my life. Again, at least in the early stages I will find it helpful to write down the main things I discover about the personal implications of each passage. This will help me to be clear and specific about what the Bible is saying to me; it will also give me a record of what God has been teaching me. And what I have written will shape my prayers.

11.6.3. *Being realistic*

The third point I want to make is this: it might be a good idea to begin meditating on a verse or two rather than a whole passage. Although not everyone is built this way, you will probably find that this will make it easier for you to get the hang of meditating. It will have the added advantage of helping you to remember and recall Bible verses – thus moving you in the direction of Psalm 119:11.

Why have we devoted a whole chapter to this? I am suggesting that recapturing this practice is an important part of the way ahead, in our quest for true devotion. I think the Puritans and others were right to build this bridge that gets us from the Bible to prayer. I also think that it can give those attracted to the mystical way at least some of what they are seeking. Let me explain what I mean. If their knowledge of God had not seemed to be too abstract and impersonal – little more than understanding and accepting certain propositions about him – would those who have recently found help in the mystical tradition have been looking for this help in the first place? You might remember the testimony of Bruce Demarest that we quoted in Chapter 1: he says that he had 'substituted knowledge of the Bible for knowing how to interact with God Himself ...'[97] It is not difficult to see how meditation would have made quite a difference at this point of need. Likewise, if the Bible had been more than a book to be analysed – that is, if the word of God had really seemed to be God speaking! – would we feel any need to listen for God's voice as we pray? The reason I think meditating upon Scripture will make a significant difference here and in other areas where the mystical way is appealing is that it enhances the relational character of my 'Quiet Time'. It enables me to appropriate and absorb what the Bible says in a manner that makes it more personal and me more prayerful. It becomes more personal in that it leads me to a heartfelt response to what the Bible teaches me. It makes me more

---

[97]   *Satisfy Your Soul*, p 25.

prayerful by giving me lots of reasons for turning to God with thanksgiving and requests.

I believe, in short, that we would be a lot further along the path to true devotion if we were able to reclaim this missing part of our Evangelical heritage. However, we could only do so and receive the benefits involved if we were prepared to devote enough time to it – and there's the rub! In a world of instant dial-up and instant noodles, there is no such thing as instant piety.

12. At the heart of it all

This is a good point at which to remind ourselves of what this book is about. We have been seeking to discover what spirituality is like when it is shaped and directed by the Bible. Does this mean that the Bible is all about spirituality? In a way, it is, for everything in the Bible bears upon and applies to our life with God. But the subject of the Bible – its centre and focus – is not our life with God. What that subject is has become clearer and clearer as we have gone to the Bible again and again. By the time we completed the first section of the book it was clear that our piety is how we respond to the subject of the Bible: the Lord Jesus Christ. True devotion – a spirituality that is shaped and directed by the Bible – is focused and grounded upon Jesus Christ, for he is the centre and the meaning of all of the Scriptures.[1]

> Is he not the subject of the whole Scripture, and, like a golden ore, runs through every vein in the mine? He is the centre wherein all the lines of Scripture meet; we can open no part of it but something of Christ strikes upon our minds ...[2]

12.1. *Making it clear*

This has three consequences of particular importance for what we are doing in this book. The first is that Jesus Christ is not only the centre and subject of the New Testament, for the Old Testament too is all about him:

> The knowledge of Jesus Christ is the very marrow and kernel of all the scriptures; the scope and centre of all divine Revelation: both Testaments meet in Christ.[3]

It is true that he is the focus of the Old Testament in a different way than he is the focus of the New Testament. Yet the Lord himself is clear: the Scriptures 'testify about me'; Moses 'wrote about me'.[4] It is not that he is mentioned or even just hinted at occasionally, for all of the Old

---

[1]   Luke 24:27, 44-47; John 1:45; 5:39, 46; 2 Corinthians 1:20; 1 Peter 1:10-12.
[2]   Stephen Charnock, *Works*, 4: p 97.
[3]   John Flavel, *Works*, 1: p 34.
[4]   John 5:39, 46.

Testament Scriptures speak about him.[5] The Old Testament has a number of ways of bearing witness to him – but he is the message in all of its media:

> None else was the centre of the prophecies, the subject of the promises, the truth of the types ...[6]

If we focus on the promises, for example, the New Testament is clear: 'no matter how many promises God has made, they are 'Yes' in Christ'.[7]

> The promise is but the casket, and Christ the jewel in it; the promise but the field, and Christ the pearl hid in it ...[8]

Since Jesus Christ is the centre and subject of the Old Testament as well as the New Testament, I should learn true devotion from the Old Testament and not just from the New Testament. All of my meditation on all of Scripture should lead me to him. And my need and desire to know him should lead me to the Scriptures:

> Let the word of God be familiar to you. What is to be known of Christ is here to be learned ... Those that are strangers to the Scripture will be strangers to Christ. You may as well see without light as know Christ without the knowledge of the Scripture.[9]

There is thus a close bond between the Lord and the word – and no matter what part of the Bible we focus on, he is at the heart of it all.

But isn't our piety meant to be a response to the gospel? Isn't that why the first section of the book concerns 'the spirituality of the gospel'? And didn't we discover there that the Bible is all about the gospel? 'Yes' is the answer to all of these questions – but what is the subject of the gospel? Again, our study of the Bible has made the answer clear: 'Jesus Christ in all his glories is the great and eminent subject of the gospel'.[10]

> Christ is both the matter and the author of the gospel ... in the dispensation of the gospel, Christ is both the sermon and

---

5   Luke 24:27, 44-45.
6   Charnock, *Works*, 5: p 176.
7   2 Corinthians 1:20.
8   Thomas Goodwin [1600-1679], *The Works of Thomas Goodwin*, twelve volumes (Edinburgh: James Nichol, 1862), 4: p 14.
9   David Clarkson, *Works*, 1: p 262.
10   Goodwin, *Works*, 4: p 263.

the preacher ...[11]

Because he is both the proclaimer and the proclaimed, a spirituality of the gospel has the Lord Jesus as its basis and focus. This is the second consequence of what we have learned about the subject-matter of the Bible. Whatever aspect of gospel-spirituality we consider, it all rests on him and revolves around him. He is at the heart of it all.

This leads us to a third consequence: because Jesus Christ is the centre of the Bible and the gospel, he is the heart and focus of all we have to say to the church and to the world.

> Christ Jesus the Lord, is the sum and centre of all divine revealed truth; neither is any thing to be preached unto men, as an object of their faith, or necessary element of their salvation, which doth not, some way or other, either meet in him, or refer unto him.[12]

In the end, he is our only message: we proclaim him.[13]

Each of these three consequences is important, and deserves to be considered in detail. But that would require another book! All that we have space for here is to concentrate on one of these consequences and look at its chief implications. The best way of doing this is to focus on one dimension of the spirituality of the gospel: the fact that it is a responsive spirituality.

12.2. A responsive spirituality

In Chapter 3 we saw that everything about true devotion stems from the fact that it is a response to the gospel. But since Jesus Christ is the subject of the gospel, responding to the gospel means engaging with him. Why is this? What makes him the focus of the gospel and thus the key to true devotion, the centre of biblical piety? The answer is obvious: nothing less can do justice to who he is and what he has done! If Jesus Christ is indeed God's Son[14] and our Lord,[15] the Messiah of Israel[16] and

---

[11]   Edward Reynolds [1593-1676], *The Whole Works of the Right Rev. Edward Reynolds*, six volumes (Pittsburgh: Soli Deo Gloria, 1993), 2: p 226.

[12]   Reynolds, *Works*, 2: p 5.

[13]   See 1 Corinthians 1:23; 2 Corinthians 4:5; Philippians 1:15-18; Colossians 1:28.

[14]   See, for example, Acts 9:20; Romans 1:3-4, 9; 5:10; 8:3, 32; 2 Corinthians 1:19; Galatians 1:16; 2:20; 4:4, 6; Colossians 1:13; 1 Thessalonians 1:10; Hebrews 1:2, 8; 3:6; 5:5, 8; 6:6; 7:3.

the Saviour of the world,[17] the last Adam, God's firstborn and image,[18] the Root and Offspring of David,[19] the head of the church, his body,[20] the Word of God and the Lamb of God,[21] our great High Priest and sacrifice,[22] the First and the Last, the Beginning and the End,[23] our life, our hope, our peace[24] – and so much else besides – then we simply cannot be other than Christ-centred, Christ-serving, Christ-savouring people.

The glory of his person and work is supreme and unsurpassable. So the heavenly beings who ceaselessly confess the worthiness of the Lord God[25] also celebrate the worthiness of the slain Lamb.[26] Millions of angels extol his worth,[27] and the whole creation will praise him.[28] The reason John heard and saw these things[29] was that we too should be counted among these worshippers, extolling the unrivalled and inexhaustible glories of Jesus.

There is nothing in him but what is excellent ... nothing in him deficient, distasteful, imperfect ... nothing in Christ but what is worthy of all love, all delight, all admiration, everlasting praises of saints and angels... All excellencies that are in the creatures are eminently to be found in Christ... All these excellencies are in him in a more excellent manner: perfectly, without any shadow of imperfection; infinitely, without any bounds or limits; unchangeably and eternally, they ebb not, they wane not, they are always there in

---

[15] See, for example, Acts 2:36; 10:36; 15:11; 16:31; 20:21; 22:8-10; Romans 1:4, 7; 4:25; 5:1, 11, 21; 6:23; 7:25; 8:39; 10:9, 12-13; 14:8-9, 14; 15:6, 30; 16:18.

[16] See, for example, Luke 2:11; Acts 2:36; 3:20; 5:42; 9:22; 17:3; 18:5; Romans 9:5; 1 John 2:22.

[17] Luke 2:11; John 4:42; Acts 5:31; 13:23; Ephesians 5:23; Philippians 3:20; 2 Timothy 1:10; Titus 1:4; 2:13; 3:6; 2 Peter 1:1, 11; 2:20; 3:2, 18; 1 John 4:14.

[18] 1 Corinthians 15:45-48; Colossians 1:15, 18; Hebrews 1:6; Revelation 1:5; 2 Corinthians 4:4; Colossians 1:15.

[19] Revelation 22:16; cf. Matthew 1:1; 9:27; 15:22; 20:30-31; 21:9; Acts 13:22-23; Romans 1:3; 2 Timothy 2:8.

[20] Ephesians 1:22; 4:15; 5:23; Colossians 1:18; 2:10, 19.

[21] John 1:1, 14, 28, 36; Revelation 19:13.

[22] Hebrews 2:17; 3:1; 4:14; 5:5, 10; 6:20; 7:23-28; 8:1-2; 9:11-14, 24-28; 10:5-14, 19; 13:11-12.

[23] Revelation 22:13.

[24] Colossians 3:4; 1 Timothy 1:1; Ephesians 2:14.

[25] Revelation 4:9-11.

[26] Revelation 5:8-10.

[27] Revelation 5:11-12.

[28] Revelation 5:13.

[29] Revelation 22:8.

the full, they alter not, they decay not... Not only all that are in the creatures, but innumerable more excellencies than are in all the creatures together, are in Christ alone. Not only the creatures' fullness, but the fullness of the Godhead dwells in him ...'[30]

Praising this supremely worthy Lord and Saviour with humble gratitude and wondering joy is one of the most fundamental elements of true devotion.

One of the chief marks of responsive spirituality is that it is a spirituality of grace – and the core of the spirituality of grace is both knowing[31] and growing in[32] the grace of the Lord Jesus. In this grace we are immeasurably enriched by his 'boundless riches':[33] 'Christ is a rich storehouse, and in him we have all'.[34] Because of who he is and what he has done, these riches are unsurpassable:

Whatsoever favours we have by Christ, they are choice ones. They are the best of every thing... The riches of grace we have by him are the only lasting and durable riches. Take any thing that you can, if we have it by Christ, it is of the best. All worldly excellencies and honours are but mere shadows to the high excellencies and honour we have in Christ. No joy, no comfort, no peace, no riches, no inheritance to be compared with the joy, peace, and inheritance which we have in Christ. Whatsoever we have by him, we have it in a glorious manner... There is abundance of grace, and excellency, and sufficiency in Christ.... as there is variety of excellency, so is there sufficiency and fullness in Christ. What he did, he did to the full. He is a Saviour, and he filleth up that name to the full. His pardon for sin is a full pardon; his merits for us are full merits; his satisfaction to divine justice a full satisfaction; his redemption of our souls and bodies a full redemption.[35]

To have this Saviour is to have everything that God has to give us[36] – but to have everything without him is, in the end, to have nothing.

---

[30]   Clarkson, *Works*, 1: p 257f.
[31]   2 Corinthians 8:9.
[32]   2 Peter 3:18.
[33]   Ephesians 3:8.
[34]   Sibbes, *Works*, 4: p 344.
[35]   Sibbes, *Works*, 2: pp 447-448.
[36]   Romans 8:32.

Get this Christ, and you get all; miss him, and you miss all... Nothing can make that man miserable that hath this rich Christ; nothing can make that man happy that wants this rich Christ... Hadst thou all the power of the world, without an interest in Christ, thou wouldst be but weak ... Hadst thou all the wit and learning in the world, without an interest in Christ, thou wilt be but a fool. Hadst thou all the honours in the world, yet without an interest in Christ, thou wouldst be but base. Hadst thou all the wealth in the world, yet without an interest in Christ, thou wouldst be but a beggar ...[37]

The riches of Christ are infinite: we will never exhaust them, not even by untold ages of eager seeking and joyful finding. This is the glorious prospect that beckons us in the age to come. And no matter how much progress we make in this life, we have barely begun:

The knowledge of Christ is profound and large ... Ah, the best of us are yet but upon the borders of this vast continent![38]

This is true especially of his love for us, which 'surpasses knowledge',[39] that is, it far outstrips our capacity to grasp it:

God's free grace and Christ's love ... [is like] a mighty sea, so deep, as it wants a bottom; so as though the thoughts of men and angels shall be diving into it to all eternity, they shall not come to ground. Of the length and breadth also, that it know no shore, that though they shall be sailing over it with that small compass of their capacities for ever, yet they shall never come to land ...[40]

As we discovered in Chapter 3, our responsive spirituality is also a spirituality of faith – and the core of the spirituality of faith is focusing on the Lord Jesus and trusting in him. Although this seems obvious, it still needs to be said, as one of the easiest mistakes to fall into is so to emphasize faith that we end up relying on it. But faith does not focus on itself – it does not put its confidence in faith:

it is not *thy hold* of Christ that saves thee – it is Christ; it is not *thy joy* in Christ that saves thee – it is Christ; it is not even faith in

---

[37] Thomas Brooks, *Works*, 3: pp 202-203.
[38] Flavel, *Works*, 1: p 36.
[39] Ephesians 3:19.
[40] Goodwin, *Works*, 4: p 236.

Christ, though that is the instrument – it is Christ's blood and merits; therefore, look not to thy hope, but to Christ, the source of thy hope; look not to thy faith, but to Christ, the author and finisher of thy faith ... it is not prayer, it is not faith, it not [sic] our doings, it is not our feelings upon which we must rest, but upon Christ, and on Christ alone. We are apt to think that we are not in a right state, that we do not feel enough, instead of remembering that our business is not with self, but Christ. Let me beseech thee, look only to Christ; never expect deliverance ... from any means of any kind apart from Christ; keep thine eye simply on Him; let His death, His agonies, His groans, His sufferings, His merits, His glories, His intercession, be fresh upon thy mind; when thou wakest in the morning look for Him; when thou liest down at night look for Him.[41]

It is true that faith is essential, and that without it we do not have true devotion. But it is necessary only as an instrument, a means: it is how we appropriate what is offered in the gospel:

faith ... is the hand of the soul, to lay hold of all the graces, excellencies, and high perfections of Christ.[42]

As the empty hand that receives the proffered gift, faith does not focus on itself. Instead, its focus is the Giver and his gifts. And what do we receive from him? From one perspective, we are given many gifts: all the dimensions of a comprehensive salvation. Yet his essential gift is himself: what we receive through a believing response to the gospel is the Lord Jesus Christ.[43] In all the riches of grace that come to us by faith, he is the greatest treasure – and it is their connection with him that makes all the rest so precious. At the heart of God's surpassing grace is his indescribable gift.[44] To have him is to have more than enough; it is to be made rich beyond measure.

God send me no more, for my part of paradise, but Christ: and surely I were rich enough, and as well heavened as the best of them,

---

[41]   C.H. Spurgeon, quoted in Iain Murray, *The Forgotten Spurgeon*, 2nd edition (Edinburgh: Banner of Truth, 1973), p 42 (italics original).

[42]   Sibbes, *Works*, 5: p 362.

[43]   Colossians 2:6.

[44]   2 Corinthians 9:14-15.

if Christ were my heaven.[45]

This is not just pious exaggeration, for the New Testament makes it clear that the heart of our destiny is to be with the Lord Jesus.[46]

It is heaven to be with Christ, it is his presence that makes heaven glorious, it is his presence enjoyed that makes heaven happy ...[47]

12.3. Christ-centred spirituality

This is only one of the host of ways in which the New Testament leads us to be Christ-centred. No matter where we begin, we are quickly drawn to him – as our brief return to the spiritualities of grace and faith has shown. When it comes to New Testament spirituality, he is at the heart of it all.

This was the most important thing we learned in Chapter 2 about the spirituality of the gospel. It is so important that we need to look at it again before we come to the end of the chapter. The most useful way of doing this is to focus on a suitable passage. There are many we could explore, but I have chosen Philippians 3 to guide us. Here we meet two strikingly different Pauls, one on each side of the dramatic day when Jesus Christ intervened in his life and took hold of him (v.13). Paul BC had an impressive array of assets (vv.5-6). These were significant advantages and achievements that he relied on to secure his position before God. But once the Lord Jesus had him in his grip Paul realized two things about belonging to God. The first was that all of his assets were worth nothing at all, and the second was that Jesus Christ was all that he needed. So he wrote off all that he had relied on, and entered 'Christ' on the credit side of the ledger (v.7). Paul AD has gone even further in this direction. He has written off absolutely everything, because he now knows that nothing that he has or does has any value for securing his place with God (v.8). There is still only one item in the assets register: 'the surpassing worth of knowing Christ Jesus my Lord' (v.8). In comparison with him, everything else counts as garbage (v.8). So to lose everything while gaining Christ is to end up massively in

---

[45]   Samuel Rutherford, in Smith (ed), *Gleanings*, p 117.

[46]   John 14:3; 17:24; 2 Corinthians 5:8; Philippians 1:23; 1 Thessalonians 4:17; 5:10.

[47]   Clarkson, *Works*, I: p 333.

credit. When it comes to knowing God, Jesus Christ alone suffices. He is all that matters.

Why has Paul given the Philippians this lesson in spiritual accounting? He wants to steer them away from pinning their hopes on anyone or anything except the Lord Jesus. Instead, he wants them to count knowing him as of supreme value, worth more than anything and everything:

> A man's heart is not sincere to Christ unless he doth prefer him before all the world... This is the true knowledge of Christ, to know him, and prize him, and embrace him as our Lord and Saviour, and prefer him above all things; to prize him more than all my goods, more than all my friends, yea, more than myself.[48]

There is a real danger that they will fail at this point, because they are coming under pressure to rely on their religious activities to secure their position before God (vv.2-3). But if we trust what we do for God instead of what he has done for us we will become enemies of Christ's cross (v.18). That was true of many in Paul's day (v.18) – and it can all too easily become true of us. How can we avoid falling into this trap? We do so by recognizing the absolute supremacy of the Lord Jesus, and by thus esteeming him above all else.

So far we have seen that Jesus Christ determines Paul's past and Paul's present. As to the past, he says simply, 'Christ Jesus took hold of me' (v.13). This had a very dramatic impact: it led to his complete about-face in regard to his personal 'assets':

> But whatever things were gain to me, those things I have counted as loss for the sake of Christ. (v.7, NASB)

His present is all about 'the surpassing worth of knowing Christ Jesus my Lord' (v.8). This has enabled him to see that everything that could be regarded as an 'asset' has no value at all. In comparison with Christ, it counts as garbage (v.8). What matters is being united to Christ – being 'found in him' (v.9), and sharing in both his sufferings and the power of his resurrection (v.10). Now we need to note that for Paul, Jesus Christ also determines the future. His destiny – the 'prize' he will win in the heavenly kingdom – is all about Jesus Christ (v.14). He is eagerly anticipating the return of Jesus Christ as Lord and Saviour (v.20). On

---

[48] Manton, *Works*, 20: pp 19, 22.

that great day, he will exercise his sovereignty by resurrecting and transforming all those who belong to him (v.21). So whether Paul is thinking of his past, his present, or his future, Jesus Christ is the key.

It is not only in this passage that Paul displays this outlook, of course. The 'surpassing worth' of the Lord Jesus is fundamental to his whole worldview and is thus frequently on view in his letters. In them, he speaks of Jesus' supreme and unsurpassable status in a number of quite striking ways. We have room to consider only four of these superlatives here.

12.3.1. The fullness of God

First, Jesus Christ is completely full of God. Paul makes this point twice in his letter to the Colossians. He says that 'God was pleased to have all his fullness dwell in him' (1:19). He also says that 'in Christ all the fullness of the Deity lives in bodily form' (2:9). The way he makes this point undoubtedly owes something to the particular errors he is combating in this letter.[49] But what he is saying can be found throughout his letters: namely, that Jesus Christ is truly and fully God. Everything that makes God 'God' – all of his 'Godness' – lives in the Lord Jesus. There is no one who could surpass him in Deity; no one who could be more fully God.

Paul draws two important conclusions about our growth as Christians from this fact. The first is that we should continue as we began (as we discovered in Chapter 2). We grow not by moving on to someone else, but by continuing in and with the Lord Jesus: 'just as you received Christ Jesus as Lord, continue to live your lives in him' (2:6). The second is something we learned in Chapter 3: namely, that we start from a position of completeness: 'in Christ you have been brought to fullness' (2:10). Our completeness is not a distant goal but our starting-point. This means that we grow not so much by moving on to what we do not have yet, but by moving further into what we have and where we are – we grow by 'possessing our possessions'.

> God would have nothing full but Christ, that our souls might rest in nothing else, and have him our centre... Let us therefore love him, and serve him, and make him our end, and think ourselves

---

49   See especially Colossians 2:4, 8, 16-23.

complete in him.[50]

Both of these basic principles of Christian growth reflect the uniqueness of the Lord Jesus as 'our great God and Saviour'.[51]

12.3.2. *The highest name*

The second of our four superlatives is that Jesus Christ has the highest possible name.[52] This refers to the fact that he is 'the Lord'.[53] At one level, this title tells us that he is the master and teacher of all who are his disciples.[54] But it also tells us much more than this, for 'Lord' is God's own name, to be shared with no one else.[55] Yet Paul tells us here[56] that it is God himself who gave this name to the risen and exalted Jesus.[57] That is why Paul applies Scripture passages referring to the Lord God to the Lord Jesus.[58] He is convinced that Jesus is Lord and God just as the Father is.[59] So he is head not only of the church, but over every actual or conceivable power in the entire cosmos.[60] There is no one who is greater or higher than him – and no one who could be.

It is important that we do not go astray here. We must be clear that the Lord Jesus' supremacy over all does not make him a rival to God the Father. On the contrary, it was the Father who gave him this supremacy by exalting him to his right hand.[61] So the world's acclamation of Jesus Christ as Lord is to the glory of God the Father.[62] In the Son, the Father is revealed:[63]

---

[50]   Goodwin, *Works*, 4: pp 567, 569.

[51]   Titus 2:13.

[52]   Philippians 2:9.

[53]   Philippians 2:11.

[54]   John 13:13-14.

[55]   Isaiah 42:8.

[56]   Philippians 2:9.

[57]   See also Acts 2:32-33, 36; Romans 1:4; 10:9.

[58]   Romans 10:12-13 [Joel 2:32]; 1 Corinthians 1:31/2 Corinthians 10:17 [Jeremiah 9:24]; 1 Corinthians 2:16 [Isaiah 40:31]; 1 Corinthians 8:5-6 [Deuteronomy 6:4]; Philippians 2:9-11 [Isaiah 45:23]; Philippians 4:5 [Psalm 145:18].

[59]   See especially Romans 9:5; 1 Corinthians 8:5-6; 12:5-6; Ephesians 4:5-6; Titus 1:3-4; 2:13; 3:4, 6 Cf. John 1:1; 20:28; 2 Peter 1:1.

[60]   Ephesians 1:20-23; 4:15; Colossians 1:15-18; 2:10; 1 Peter 3:22.

[61]   Acts 2:32-33; 5:31; Romans 8:34; Philippians 2:9; Colossians 1:18; 3:1; 1 Peter 3:21-22.

[62]   Philippians 2:11; cf. Daniel 7:14.

[63]   Matthew 11:27; John 1:1, 14, 18; 14:7-9; 2 Corinthians 4:4-6; Colossians 1:15, 19; Hebrews 1:1-3; 1 John 2:22-24; 5:20.

Christ is a certificate wherein the world may read how excellent, wise, bountiful, just, faithful, holy, God is.[64]

Through the Son, we are redeemed and adopted as sons of God.[65] His death is intended to bring us to God.[66] And by turning to the raised and glorified Jesus we come to place our faith and hope in God the Father.[67] Thus, while an authentically biblical piety will be centred upon Jesus Christ, it will not be confined to Jesus Christ – our faith is in the Father and the Son; our fellowship is with the Father and the Son; we are united with the Father and the Son; we know the Father and the Son.[68]

12.3.3. The 'indescribable gift'

This brings us to our third superlative: that Jesus Christ is God's 'indescribable gift'.[69] By 'indescribable' Paul means that no narrative is capable of giving a complete account of all that Jesus is and has. He is a gift that surpasses description. In fact, so supreme is he, that by giving him the Father has effectively pledged to give us everything else as well.[70] And nothing that God has to give bears any comparison with him, no matter how glorious it might be. So great is this gift that it should leave us 'lost in wonder, love, and praise'. But that is not all, for behind such a magnificent gift stands an amazing Giver:

Faith rests upon Christ as a gift, upon God as the donor.[71]

So our wonder, love, and praise should not be directed only at the Lord Jesus, but also at the Father who gave him up for us. In this respect too, Jesus Christ leads us to the Father. But nor are we to respond to the Father alone, for in this giving Jesus Christ was no passive object but a willing subject. Yes, the Father gave him – but he also gave himself for us.[72] So while Paul ends his discussion of the collection-project[73] with 'Thanks be to God for his indescribable gift!', he begins it by reminding the Corinthians:

---

[64]   Charnock, *Works*, 4: p 138.
[65]   Galatians 4:4-5.
[66]   1 Peter 3:18.
[67]   1 Peter 1:21.
[68]   See especially John 8:19; 14:1, 7, 23; 17:3; 2 Peter 1:2; 1 John 1:3; 2:24; 2 John 9.
[69]   2 Corinthians 9:15.
[70]   Romans 8:32.
[71]   Charnock, *Works*, 5: p 165.
[72]   Galatians 1:4; 2:20; Ephesians 5:2, 25.
[73]   2 Corinthians 8-9.

you know the grace of our Lord Jesus Christ, that though he was rich, yet for your sake he became poor, so that you through his poverty might become rich.[74]

They knew the grace of Christ because he was both gift and giver – and this giving thus displays both his grace and the grace of God.[75] God's indescribable gift tells us of the astounding love of the Father and also of the Son. There is none greater – and none that ever could be.

12.3.4. The 'boundless riches'

And so to our fourth and last superlative: that the riches of Jesus Christ are 'boundless'.[76] By this Paul means that no amount of searching through them would enable us to trace them fully. They surpass our comprehension. It is not that they cannot be understood at all, for when Paul brings the gospel to the Gentiles, this is what he proclaims. There would be nothing he could say if these riches were incomprehensible. What he means is that they cannot be grasped completely – they are simply too great for us to get our minds around them. And what are these riches? By the 'riches of Christ' Paul could mean either the riches that Jesus Christ has or the riches that he is. But perhaps we do not need to decide between these meanings. Paul's reason for making the riches of Christ the centre of his gospel is that they impact upon us. So whether they are what Jesus Christ has or what he is, he does not keep them to himself – we benefit from his riches. It seems that here too we meet him as both the giver and the gift.

When we think of him as the giver, we are dealing with 'the riches of God's grace'[77] – all the riches that come to us as a result of God's free, full love, given to us in his Son. And how does he enrich us? In a word, with the gift of 'salvation' – by grace, we are 'saved'.[78] This is a huge word, for it refers to everything God does to rescue and restore us. This begins in eternity past, when God set his love upon us.[79] And it stretches all the way ahead of us into eternity to come, when God will go on pouring out 'the incomparable riches of his grace, expressed in his

---

[74] 2 Corinthians 8:9.
[75] Galatians 2:20-21.
[76] Ephesians 3:8.
[77] Ephesians 1:7.
[78] Ephesians 2:5, 8.
[79] Ephesians 1:4-5.

kindness to us in Christ Jesus'.[80] In the present, it means that we are adopted,[81] redeemed,[82] raised to life,[83] reconciled,[84] made new,[85] forgiven,[86] cleansed[87] – and so much more besides. These riches are truly 'boundless', for they proceed from a love that surpasses knowledge.[88]

When we think of the Lord Jesus as the gift, his 'boundless riches' are the many aspects of his fullness. Ephesians gives us some idea of how great this is: he is our Lord,[89] the Son of God,[90] the head of the church and the whole cosmos,[91] our Saviour.[92] In him we find grace and peace,[93] life,[94] love,[95] truth,[96] light,[97] power[98] – indeed, every spiritual blessing.[99] By having him, we have everything we need – and much more than we need. Such riches call forth a many-sided response. So to him we direct our hope,[100] faith,[101] praise,[102] reverence,[103] obedience,[104] service,[105] love.[106]

Whether we think of the fullness of the person of the Saviour or the hugeness of his work of salvation, the riches we have because of him are

---

[80]   Ephesians 2:7.
[81]   Ephesians 1:5.
[82]   Ephesians 1:7.
[83]   Ephesians 2:4-6.
[84]   Ephesians 2:16.
[85]   Ephesians 4:23-24.
[86]   Ephesians 4:32.
[87]   Ephesians 5:25-26.
[88]   Ephesians 3:18-19.
[89]   Ephesians 1:2, 3; 3:11; 6:24.
[90]   Ephesians 1:3; 4:13.
[91]   Ephesians 1:22-23; 4:15-16; 5:23.
[92]   Ephesians 5:23.
[93]   Ephesians 1:2; 2:14; 4:7; 6:23-24.
[94]   Ephesians 2:5.
[95]   Ephesians 3:18-19; 4:16; 5:2, 25; 6:23.
[96]   Ephesians 4:21.
[97]   Ephesians 5:8-14.
[98]   Ephesians 6:10.
[99]   Ephesians 1:3.
[100] Ephesians 1:12.
[101] Ephesians 1:15; 3:12.
[102] Ephesians 5:19.
[103] Ephesians 5:21.
[104] Ephesians 6:5.
[105] Ephesians 6:6-7.
[106] Ephesians 6:24.

boundless. We will never exhaust them, no matter how long and deep our exploration of them. This is true not only of this age, but of all the ages to come. As the poet George Herbert recognized, addressing him as the 'King of glory, King of peace', 'even eternity's too short to extol thee.'

We must draw our discussion to a close. This is easier said than done, however, as there is so much more about the Lord Jesus that could be considered. Yet we have done enough to show that he is at the heart of everything that true devotion means. Whatever else we do, it is clear that we must continue to 'grow in the grace and knowledge of our Lord and Saviour Jesus Christ'.[107] This will mean continuing to explore

> the excellency of his person, the fullness of his satisfaction, the worth of his graces, the mystery of his will in the gospel, the sweetness of ... communion with him, the dimensions of his love, the riches of his righteousness ... that you may partake more of his riches, taste more of his sweetness; that you may adore, admire him more, and be more in his praises; that you may be engaged and enabled to honour him more, and serve him better, to do and suffer more for him ...[108]

And as we discover more of the surpassing worth of knowing Jesus Christ as our Lord,[109] our deepest desire, like Paul's, will be ... to know him![110] To know him at all is to want to know him more. So this will be our resolve:

> let us keep up continual communion with the person of the Lord Jesus! Let us abide in Him daily, feed on Him daily, look to Him daily, lean on Him daily, live upon Him daily, draw from His fullness daily...[111]

Day by day, he must be at the centre of our lives. Through all our days, he must have our heart and soul.

---

[107] 2 Peter 3:18.
[108] Clarkson, *Works*, 1: pp 262, 265.
[109] Philippians 3:8.
[110] Philippians 3:10.
[111] J.C. Ryle, *Warnings to the Churches* (Edinburgh: Banner of Truth, 1967), pp 169f.

13.   The End of the Beginning

We began this study by noting what John Calvin has to say about our piety:

> Who has promised them that God will accept their devotion and all that they offer him? ... all our prayers and supplications will never be worth anything, but prove utterly unprofitable and vain, if they are not conformable to God's Word. From that Word we must take our rule.[1]

In line with this approach, we have been seeking to determine the character of a devotion that is 'conformable to God's Word.' Our attempt to define biblical spirituality has meant taking the Bible as an entirely sufficient guide to life with God. It also involved learning from the Reformers, Puritans, and Evangelical leaders how to grasp what the Bible teaches us in this area. So where has our investigation taken us?

We have shown how the chief mark of true devotion is that it is a spirituality of the gospel (Chapter 2). This is responsive (Chapter 3), paradoxical (Chapter 4), and relational (Chapter 5) – a direct consequence, respectively, of the gospel of grace, of the shape of God's saving work, and of the nature of the Triune God. This is a spirituality of grace and faith; a spirituality of the Son of God, the Spirit of God, and the word of God. It is a spirituality of faith, hope, and love; a spirituality of the heart; and a spirituality shaped by the in-between time in which we live.

We have then contrasted this with a mystical approach to spirituality – one which looks for direct, unmediated experience of God (Chapter 6), which sees prayer as a conversational dialogue and thus relies upon the Spirit's 'whispers' (Chapter 7), which regards wordless contemplation as the highest form of prayer (Chapter 8), and which finds God by turning inwards to the soul (Chapter 9). In each case, we have argued that this approach cannot be endorsed, for it is not what the Bible teaches us. In view of claims that we will be enriched by adopting it, we then examined why the Reformers rejected the Catholic piety on which they had been reared (Chapter 10).

---

[1]   Calvin, *Ephesians*, p 286.

Our investigation concludes by calling for a re-discovery of the practice of biblical meditation (Chapter 11), and by spelling out the radically Christ-centred character of true devotion (Chapter 12).

If you have worked your way through the previous chapters, several things will have become clear to you. Perhaps the most obvious is that it was not false modesty when I began by saying that you would be reading the words of a spiritual pygmy! The process of writing this book has made that clearer to me than ever. But along the way, you have stood with me on the shoulders of some giants, who, seeing further and more clearly than most of us, have pointed out the path of true devotion. I hope you have found their words as encouraging and helpful as I do. That is why I have quoted them so frequently. But in case these quotations have given you the wrong impression, let me say what I have not been trying to do.

I am not suggesting that we should attempt to model ourselves on the Reformers and the Puritans. I think we should honour their legacy, but not by trying to copy them – something that is not really possible anyway, given all the ways in which our context is not like theirs. Instead, we should aim to do in our very different world what they were aiming to do in theirs: namely, to honour the Lord by holding fast to the gospel and being faithful to the Bible.

I am not encouraging you to give the views of the Reformers, Puritans, and Evangelical leaders the same authority as the Bible. Nothing would have horrified them more! They were seeking to live under the authority of God's word—and that is the standard by which we must test what they say.

It will also be clear to you that I have concerns about where some contemporary authors are turning to find true devotion. I have done my best to engage with their writings in the spirit of critical openness I outlined in the Introduction. So I hope it is obvious that the reason for my concerns is not that these writers have challenged some traditions that matter to me, but that they have not done justice to the Bible. But since that is the standard I have applied to them, it should also apply to what I have written. That is what I have been trying to do, and that is the test by which this book must be measured – have I been faithful to what the Bible teaches? That is what determines whether our devotion is true or not.

I expect that it has also become obvious that there are many other things which should be said about true devotion. A careful study of the nature and necessity of prayer is a prime example – but this is by no means the only matter to which we should give our attention. In fact it is not really an exaggeration to say that a thorough study of our subject would involve all of the Bible and all of Christian theology! What this book has done is to examine those issues where I think there is the greatest need for clarity and faithfulness today. But I am well aware that what I have done can be challenged in two ways. You might disagree with the choices I have made about what to include and what to exclude. You might also think that what I have said is not as clear or faithful as it needs to be. This would not surprise me, for writing this book has been a reminder that my grasp of the Bible is both limited and fallible. I still have much to learn about God and his ways.

If you can see gaps and flaws in the book, can I urge you not to leave it there? That would be to make reading the book the end of the story. Instead, I hope that reading it will encourage you to go further and deeper than I have been able to take you. One way you can make such progress along the path of true devotion is to fill in the gaps and correct the flaws you find in what I have written. And as you work away at this, it would be good to share what you are learning with others. In the quest for true devotion, we ought to help and encourage each other more than we usually do. Despite its faults and limitations, that is what I want this book to do for you. So now that you have finished reading it, I hope this won't be the end of the journey. Instead, may it be only the end of the beginning, as you 'press on to know the LORD'.[2]

If you have enjoyed this book, you might like to consider

- *supporting the work of the Latimer Trust*
- *reading more of our publications*
- *recommending them to others*

See www.latimertrust.org for more information.

---

[2]   Hosea 6:3.

Latimer Publications

Anglican Foundations Series

Latimer Publications

Latimer Briefings